Irish Shame

Irish Shame

A Literary Reckoning

Edited by Seán Kennedy and
Joseph Valente

EDINBURGH
University Press

Edinburgh University Press is one of the leading university presses in the UK. We publish academic books and journals in our selected subject areas across the humanities and social sciences, combining cutting-edge scholarship with high editorial and production values to produce academic works of lasting importance. For more information visit our website: edinburghuniversitypress.com

Edinburgh University Press Ltd
13 Infirmary Street
Edinburgh EH1 1LT

First published in hardback by Edinburgh University Press 2025

Typeset in 11/13 Adobe Sabon by
IDSUK (DataConnection) Ltd, and
printed and bound by CPI Group (UK) Ltd, Croydon, CR0 4YY

A CIP record for this book is available from the British Library

ISBN 978 1 3995 4691 1 (hardback)
ISBN 978 1 3995 4692 8 (paperback)
ISBN 978 1 3995 4693 5 (webready PDF)
ISBN 978 1 3995 4694 2 (epub)

MIX
Paper | Supporting responsible forestry
FSC www.fsc.org FSC® C013604

This book is printed using paper from well-managed forests, recycling and other controlled sources

Contents

Figures

Acknowledgments

This book took time to produce and there was pain along the way. The editors would like to thank everyone who attended the conference at SUNY Buffalo, from which this book emerged, for their patience. We thank Grace Dyas, Erin Layton, Mark Davis and Paulo Nunes dos Santos for permission to cite their work in Claire Bracken's essay. Thanks also to *Éire-Ireland* for permission to reprint the essay by Abby Bender, 'Shame and the Breastfeeding Mother in Ireland', *Éire-Ireland* 56:3/4 (Fall/Winter 2021): 104–29. 10.1353/eir.2021.0017

Notes on Contributors

Abby Bender is Associate Teaching Professor in the Languages and Literatures department at Sacred Heart University, where she directs the Irish Studies programme and teaches at Sacred Heart's campus in Dingle. She is the author of *Israelites in Erin: Exodus, Revolution, and the Irish Revival* (2015). Her recently published articles include 'Nursing the Revival: Patrick Pearse, Breastfeeding, and Sacrifice', in *The Irish Revival: A Complex Vision* (2023), and 'Irish Jewish Studies at the Border: Precarious Solidarity from Ulysses to Nine Folds Make a Paper Swan', in *American Journal of Irish Studies* (2021). She is Literature Representative for the American Conference of Irish Studies.

Claire Bracken is Professor of English at Union College, Schenectady. She is co-editor of *Anne Enright* (with Susan Cahill, spring 2011) and *Viewpoints: Theoretical Perspectives on Irish Visual Texts* (with Emma Radley, 2013). Her book *Irish Feminist Futures* was published in 2016. In 2017, she co-edited with Tara Harney-Mahajan a double special issue of the journal *LIT* entitled *Recessionary Imaginings: Post-Celtic Tiger Ireland and Contemporary Women's Writing.* A special issue with Cara Delay, on reproductive justice and women's health, for *Éire-Ireland*, appeared in the Fall 2021 edition of *Éire-Ireland.* She also contributed an essay on 'Gender and Irish Studies, 2008–Present' to the recent *Routledge International Handbook of Irish Studies* (2021).

Kathleen Costello-Sullivan is Professor of Modern Irish literature at Le Moyne College in Syracuse, NY and a past President of the American Conference for Irish Studies. She has published widely on nineteenth–twenty-first-century Irish fiction; her monographs are *Mother/Country: Politics of the Personal in the Fiction of Colm Tóibín* and *Trauma and Recovery in the Twenty-first-Century Irish Novel.* She has also edited critical editions of Sheridan Le Fanu's *Carmilla* and Norah Hoult's *Poor Women!* Most recently, with Cian

McMahon, she co-edited *Routledge's History of Irish America*. She is the current Editor of Syracuse University Press's Irish series.

Alison Garden is a Senior Lecturer and UKRI Future Leaders Fellow at Queen's University Belfast. She is the author of *The Literary Afterlives of Roger Casement, 1899–2016* (2020) and is currently completing *Love Across the Divide: Desire and Colonial Culture in Northern Ireland, 1970–present*.

Marjorie Howes is Associate Professor of English at Boston College, where she specialises in nineteenth- and twentieth-century Irish literature, late Victorian literature, Anglo-American modernism, feminist studies and postcolonial studies. She has numerous publications, including *Yeats's Nations: Gender, Class, and Irishness* (1996) and *Colonial Crossings: Figures in Irish Literary History* (2006), has edited Bram Stoker's *Dracula* (1993), is co-editor of *Semicolonial Joyce* (2000), *The Cambridge Companion to W. B. Yeats* (2006), *Yeats and Afterwords* (2014), and is a contributing editor to *The Field Day Anthology of Irish Women* (2002).

Seán Kennedy is Professor of English and Coordinator of Irish Studies at Saint Mary's University, Halifax. They are also a scavenger artist. Recent academic works, as editor, include *Beckett Beyond the Normal* (2019) and *Samuel Beckett and Biopolitics* (2019). A history of neoliberalism in *America, Send in the Clowns: Popular Politics After Neoliberalism*, written with James McNaughton, was published by O/R books in 2024.

Sarah E. McKibben is Associate Professor of Irish language and literature, concurrent faculty in Gender Studies, and Fellow of the Keough-Naughton Institute for Irish Studies at the University of Notre Dame. She is author of *Endangered Masculinities in Irish Poetry, 1540–1780* (2010) and various articles on early modern and contemporary Irish literature. She is working on a new book to be called *Tradition Transformed: Bardic Poetry and Patronage in Early Modern Ireland*, c.*1560–1660*, for which she received fellowships from the American Council of Learned Societies and the National Endowment for the Humanities.

Alexandra Poulain is Professor of Postcolonial Literature and Theatre at the University of the New Sorbonne (France). She has published widely on modern and contemporary Irish drama and performance, in particular Yeats and Beckett. Her latest book, *Irish Drama, Modernity and the Passion Play* (2016), looks at rewritings of the Passion narrative as a modality of political resistance in Irish plays from Synge to the present day. Her current research focuses on decolonial projects in contemporary theatre and art, with a special focus on the dynamics and creative potential of shame. She is also interested in the intersection between political and environmental activism, theatre and the visual arts in South Africa. She is a former President of the International Yeats Society and of the SAES (the French Association of English Professors in Higher Education).

Moynagh Sullivan is Professor of English at Maynooth University, with specialties in Gender, Intersectionality, Motherhood, and Irish Studies. She has numerous publications and edited collections and is an activist researcher.

Joseph Valente is UB Distinguished Professor of English and Disability Studies at the University at Buffalo. He is Past President of the Northeastern Modern Language Association and the former Treasurer of the International Yeats Society. He has authored *The Myth of Manliness in Irish Nationalist Culture, 1880–1922* (2011), *Dracula's Crypt: Bram Stoker, Irishness and the Question of Blood* (2002, 2012), and *James Joyce and the Problem of Justice: Negotiating Sexual and Colonial Difference* (1995, 2009). Most recently, he co-authored *The Child Sex Scandal and Modern Irish Literature: Writing the Unspeakable* (with Margot Gayle Backus, 2020). His edited collections include *Quare Joyce* (1997), *Disciplinarity at the Fin-de Siecle* (with Amanda Anderson, 2002), *Yeats and Afterwords* (with Marjorie Howes, 2014), *Joycean Possibilities: A Margot Norris Legacy* (with Vicki Mahaffey and Kezia Whiting, 2023), *The Irish Revival: A Complex Vision* (with Marjorie Howes, 2023), *Ireland in Psychoanalysis* (with Seán Kennedy and Macy Todd, a special issue of *Breac*), *Urban Ireland* (a special issue of *Eire-Ireland*), *Joyce and Homosexuality* (a special issue of the *James Joyce Quarterly*). In addition, he has published over seventy-five journal articles and book chapters in such venues as *Critical Inquiry*, *Diacritics*, *Novel*, *ELH*, *Narrative*, *Modern Fiction Studies*, *Journal of Modern Literature*, *Style*, *Contemporary Literature*, *Éire-Ireland*, *Irish University Review*, *James Joyce Quarterly*, *Joyce Studies Annual*, *Studies in Romanticism*, *The Journal of Literary and Cultural Disability* and *The Journal of Critical and Religious Theory*.

Eve Watson is a psychoanalyst and is involved in psychoanalytic training, education and research in Dublin, Ireland. She has published over forty essays on psychoanalysis, sexuality, film, culture and literature. Her co-edited books are *Critical Essays on the Drive: Lacanian Theory and Practice* (with Dan Collins, 2024) and *Clinical Encounters in Sexuality: Psychoanalytic Practice and Queer Theory* (with Noreen Giffney, 2017). She is the academic director of the Freud Lacan institute (FLi), Dublin, and the Editor of *Lacunae*, the International Journal for Lacanian Psychoanalysis. In 2022, she was the Erik Erikson Scholar-in-Residence at the Austen Riggs Centre in Stockbridge, Massachusetts.

Kezia Whiting is an independent scholar with a doctoral degree from the State University of Buffalo. Their article 'Free Indirect Palaver' appeared in *Joycean Possibilities: A Margot Norris Legacy*, a volume they co-edited with Joseph Valente and Vicki Mahaffey (2023).

Introduction: Writing Irish Shame

Seán Kennedy and Joseph Valente

If we can infer anything from the myth of our expulsion from Paradise, it is that humans are, ought to be, or feel they ought to be, ashamed of themselves. A sense of shame seems inherent to our very existence as a species, and forms one intractable legacy of our accession to self-awareness. Shame is, in short, a fundamental element of subjectivity. As self-conscious animals, we 'see ourselves as others see us', as Leopold Bloom puts it in *Ulysses*. Our self-experience and self-conception emerge from the beginning in the imaginary mirror of other people's evaluations, of what we believe other people will or do think of us. Shame is thus a burden of our constitutively social being, or, to be more precise, of the peculiar constitution of our social being. We tend to live, as thinkers from Hegel to Sartre to Lacan have variously theorised, in the theatre of the other's gaze, where we enact a dialectical internalisation and projection of its views on our merit.

Upon the death of his last sibling, Kurt Vonnegut bemoaned that he had no one left to show off for, and then proceeded to show off for a less narrowly defined public for years thereafter. In a sense, he, and we, cannot do otherwise. To say we are social beings is also to say that we are inevitably performative beings. We are perpetually in an arena devised by others, playing to an audience that is, belatedly and involuntarily, of our own device. It is in this compounding of internalisation and projection – the internalising of others' symbolic authority and the projection of how others actually judge us – that our inveterate vulnerability to shame resides. In this regard, shame may be nicely differentiated from guilt as a social effect. It reflects upon the always precarious moral worth of who we are, which shadows in turn the moral worth of what we've done.

Because the phenomenology of shame outlined here involves our innermost sense of self, it affixes itself quite readily, on a collective basis, to the prevailing categories of statutory identity: to gender and sexuality, to ethnicity and national origin, to class trajectories and to race. But because the phenomenology of shame involves our selfhood on a socially interactive (which is to say dialectical) basis, shame does not attach to these several identity forms, individually or intersectionally, in the same fashion. To generalise most grossly (all that the space of an introduction allows), the more dominant the social identity, the more likely shame is incurred by a perceived failure to be a proper specimen thereof, to possess or maintain the idealised properties – physical, intellectual, moral or ideological – mythically identified with its entitlement. Conversely, the more subdominant the social identity, the more likely shame weighs upon the subject-position itself, on whatever disfavoured properties are stereotypically identified with its perceived inferiority.

Shame has haunted the people of Ireland since the inception of Irishness itself and, as such, has come to seem an ineluctable modality of Irish life. But in fact, and quite remarkably, the contours of Irish shame have evolved over time, shifting with alterations in their colonial predicament and in their own response, complicit or resistant, to their attendant economic, political and cultural dispossession. To take one signpost, Andrew Marvell famously deemed shame the appropriate Irish response to their military humiliation by Oliver Cromwell,[1] and his poeticised observation can stand, it seems to us, for a far larger canvas of Irish mortification at the continuing insults and depredations of British colonial rule: from the Flight of the Earls, to repeated campaigns of early modern plantation, to the battles of the Boyne, Aughrim and Limerick, to the dissolution of the patriot Parliament and to the Famine, with its mass deracination of the Irish peasantry.

But if the long run of Irish colonial history induced shame of the subdominant in surplus, its more recent stages conduce to the obverse affective condition. Enfolded into the United Kingdom by the Act of Union, Irish men, in particular, were galvanised implicitly or explicitly by the post-Darwinian acceleration of pseudo-scientifically endorsed white supremacism, the latest warrant for the Euro-imperial project. Some Irish identified with the British on this basis and clamoured for a share in the fruits of Empire. Others arrayed themselves, as presumptively European subjects, in campaigns of physical or moral force against British suzerainty. Both courses of action

[1] Andrew Marvell, 'An Horatian Ode Upon Cromwell's Return from Ireland', in Elizabeth Story Donno, ed., *The Complete Poems* (Harmondsworth: Penguin, 1985), 55–8.

assumed significant liability to the shame of (relative) entitlement, of the failure to display the needed power, tenacity, resourcefulness or resilience to successfully press the claims that their racialised dignity seemed to demand. To take a signpost at the other end of Ireland's colonial history, the graveside oratory and rabble-rousing essays of Patrick Pearse regularly looked to shame his audience into exhibiting the virtue and *virtu* ostensibly native to the Irish race. In an especially acute irony, any failure to rise to Pearse's standard of stalwart racial fitness would not only trigger the recently potentiated shame of feckless entitlement but would also reinforce the stereotype of perennial Irish inefficacy (Arnold's 'they went forth to battle but they always fell'), precipitating the original shame of subdominant deficiency.

This double-barrelled species of shame was institutionalised in post-independence Ireland first in the Irish family and then in the various social organisations that supported it, but all under the now theocratic sway of the Roman Catholic Church. Having established itself over the long centuries of Anglo-Protestant Ascendancy as the sectarian insignia of native Irish identity, the church wielded authority across all aspects of Irish life, personal and professional, by instilling the experience of shame as a corollary of spiritual aspiration and somatic abjection simultaneously. To be a proper exponent of Irish Catholicism was to have internalised shame in the very espousal of its Jansenist creed, which deemed all the libidinal stirrings that animate and sustain our material existence to be base, blameworthy, ignominious. Along the way, sexuality and shame were rendered all but synonymous, and this during the same cultural era wherein sexuality, broadly conceived, was installed as a keystone of social identity. Accordingly, the Irish were not just abashed as Catholics; rather as Catholics they understood themselves to be shameful as human animals and were both elevated and debased in that understanding. The Irish cogito would run: 'I am a good Catholic and therefore I think I am shameful; I am ashamed and therefore I am a good Catholic'. Shame thus haunted the labour of virtue no less surely than the luxury of vice.

As **Sarah McKibben** documents here, however, the root of Ireland's shame problem might be humiliation. In early modern Ireland, shame served a regulative function. It was an aspect of manliness, of social prestige (and social posturing). But with the Flight of the Earls, the defeat at Kinsale, Irishnesss was emasculated, structurally. And this unbearable sense of humiliation was quickly displaced onto available scapegoats: women and their children. Metaphorically, betrayal was sexualised. Literally, sexuality became treacherous. It was the beginning of Ireland's split national fantasy of itself as a woman both wronged but also, at the same time, inherently given to wrongdoing. This humiliation was both displaced and sublimated into song: 'Unspeakable humiliation was transposed into the all-too-speakable shame of a safely detached, feminised Ireland, national symbol and scapegoat. This admitted the problem of humiliation by displacing it, enabling a fragile, provisional recuperation of male standing.' From then on, Irish shame was an always-already-overdetermined assessment of moral fitness and/as tribal belonging. Colonial appropriation of sovereignty – the body politic – would be countered in fantasy by an overweening obsession with the appropriateness of the Irish (woman's) political body.

For **Marjorie Howes**, the Young Ireland movement understood the shame of enslavement and used it to frame that 'new subject of history' – the nation – as a recovery project.[2] Slavery in America, these writers saw, was no shame: an involuntary abduction. But the Irish condition was something otherwise. Howes elaborates on the paradoxes attending the importation of abolitionist tropes and perspectives into the discourse of Young Ireland. By framing the oppression of the Irish as a form of slavery, the nationalist tracts of a Thomas Davis risked confessing a weakness in Irish resistance that could all too readily, in the circumatlantic slavery debates of the time, signify emasculation, feminisation and hence degradation. By the twentieth century, Howes denotes, the Irish nationalist experience of imposed shame had mutated in the stirring screeds of Patrick Pearse into rhetorical self-flagellation as an instrument of recruitment to the cause and incitement to violent action. Instead of risking the shame of deficient masculinity in the eyes of the metropole, Irish nationalists began shaming themselves, or one another, on the same grounds. What Howes's careful discursive analysis ultimately expounds is how the unquestioned prevalence of patriarchal gender assumptions greatly complicated, not to say abrogated, the oppositional invocation of slavery to describe Ireland's aggrieved colonial circumstance.

Abby Bender shows how Irish shame underlies erotophobic discourses of maternal care. Breastfeeding became a conflicted site of female domination: at once pronatalist and pathological, urgent and unacceptable. Bender argues that the public attitudes on breastfeeding have been shadowed by the long history of institutional abuse of young mothers, who were alternately forced and forbidden to breastfeed their

[2] Michel Foucault, *Society Must be Defended: Lectures at the College de France, 1975–1976*, translated by David Macey (London: Picador, 2002), 134.

babies as punishment for having them in the first place. Breastfeeding's associations with the exposure of the sexualised and therefore shameful female body warred in the popular, mainly Catholic imagination with breastfeeding's reputed nutritional benefits. Women were accordingly faced with the choice of being shamed as (overly) sexual in their very embodiment or maternally deficient in their unnatural practice. At the same time, a feminist counter-discourse celebrating that same embodiment and the constructive power it bears met feminist resistance to the way breastfeeding seemed to consign women to an all too familiar biological determinism. A full-blown double bind of the Irish breast has emerged and, in Bender's view, shows no sign of resolution anytime soon.

In a magnificently intuitive reading of *Dubliners* and *Ulysses*, **Kezia Whiting** discusses how Joyce's renovation of free and direct style stages the extra-territoriality of thought, both its constitutive importation of other people's discourse and its ongoing performance for an imagined audience, an internalised other of judgement. What ensues from Joyce's intervention is a general economy of colonialism, a production of subjectivity not just by particular material and spiritual forces, but by way of a social dependency so profound it blurs the line between the most properties and stirrings most interior and most exterior to the self, a narrative rendering of the Lacanian concept of extimacy. Whiting proceeds to elucidate this deep self-ambivalence as perpetually opening upon the experience of shame as its condition of possibility. It is, in her psycho-stylistic analysis of Bloom and Gertie, our affective and evaluative otherness to ourselves – our emergence as subjects in the estranging mirror of the other's gaze – that ties our necessary, sustaining self-approval, our primary narcissism, to our continuing, reflexive liability to shame.

In 'Let Us Prey', **Joseph Valente** shows us how moral terror suffuses Catholic *bildung* as a precondition of the Catholic child's quest for love. To be recognised as lovable, one must also recognise damnation – eternal Hell – as the necessary fate of all those who fall away from the faith. The role of Irish clerics in effecting this species of moral and theological indoctrination positions them, with respect to their young charges and to their own self-conception, to wield virtually unlimited sway in a simultaneously arbitrary and self-congratulatory manner, the recipe for the sort of runaway narcissism at work in the Church child sex abuse scandals. The summary burden of Valente's essay is that such abuse scandals are as unsurprising as they are shocking, consisting as they do with the foundational framework of Catholic *bildung*. **Seán Kennedy**'s paper takes the problem of internalisation in Joyce and shows how art – aesthesis – provides a means of recovery from inculcation to the moral terror of Catholicism. Joyce's is an art of discovery, of self-making, of *poiesis* as *autopoiesis*, by which internalised shame is transmuted into the dignity of self-possession and resistant writing. Joyce is well known for his elevation of the office of the artist to a priestly or prophetic status, a mind-set he communicates, with self-aware irony, to his alter ego, Stephen Dedalus. Far from simple cultural elitism, however, Joyce's enthronement of artistry speaks to its vital function in encouraging and enabling a certain detachment from inherited scripts for thought and conduct. Another of Joyce's alter egos, Richard Rowan, of the play *Exiles*, boldly states, 'I don't take my ideas from other people', an aspirational claim to intellectual independence grounded in his own aesthetic sensibility but available, through aesthetic experience taken seriously, to everyone.

For **Alexandra Poulain**, Samuel Beckett's *Not I* is an unsettling performance of the defacing experience of (Irish) shame. Mouth's predicament is less a product of transcendental homelessness than a culturally inflected experience of repudiation from within her society. Mouth is an orphan who is abandoned and then incarcerated by the state, recalling Ireland's now-infamous architecture of containment. However, Beckett does not limit himself to Ireland. More generally, Mouth on stage enacts shame on show, embodying (just about) the theatrical aspect of shame, as theorised by Jean-Paul Sartre and Jacques Lacan. For Lacan, after Sartre, shame always occurs under the gaze of the Other. In Poulain's reading, Beckett uses the space of theatre to enact that dynamic, enmeshing his audience in a sense of dread – shame's contagion – that defines their experience of the play.

Eve Watson uses Lacan to show how the Irish national project appealed to shameful ontologies (hontologies) that rendered 'being ashamed' synonymous with Being. Shaming is distinct from shame in psychoanalytic theory, and Watson carefully traces the parameters of 'a toxic shamescape of individual scapegoating' in Ireland, past and present. Watson's case study is Ireland's Mother and Baby Homes. The effort to rid Ireland's social body of sexuality required certain subjects to embody the obscene. This, then, justified their incarceration as fallen: their containment as contaminants. They were framed as pathological elements of a social body always-already suffused with the pathogen it sought to expel. For Watson, the failures of the recent government report on these institutions betray resistance to any final reckoning with Ireland's history of shaming. In the case of the Magdalene Laundries, **Claire Bracken** suggests, Ireland's attempts to confront history have, themselves, been shameful and somewhat theatrical. She reads the official state narratives of apology as attempts to exonerate the neoliberal present in designation of the problem of shaming to an abject past. Successive governments – whether of Fianna Fáil or Fine Gael, or both – have sought to distance the state from complicity in the trauma of Ireland's fallen women. Contemporary Irish theatre by women like Grace Dyas and Erin Layton, by contrast, seeks accountability in confrontation with Ireland's all-too-present past.

If there is a shame inherent to Irish nationalism, it suffuses Irish republicanism too. **Alison Garden** spotlights how the formal experimentalism of Susannah Dickey's novel *Tennis Lessons* experiments with second person narration as a response, both revelatory and defensive, the cooperation of those supposedly inimical Catholic and Protestant nationalisms in maintaining a brutally misogynistic patriarchy through the infliction of sexual violence and the shaming of its victims. The effect of this gender-based, collectively instilled trauma in *Tennis Lessons* is precipitation of a shame that is all but existential: the humiliation of womanhood is so profoundly naturalised that it attaches to the simple fact of being a woman. When the Irish decolonisation project indexed itself to fantasies of national fitness, ablenationalism was inevitable: what bodies were fit enough to represent the national body?[3] Who was representative/representable? These questions would bear down with particular weight on Irish women. **Moynagh Sullivan** reads Emilie Pine's *Ruth & Pen* against the many ways the pro-natalist and neurotypical norms of the Irish state operate to shame women. *Ruth & Pen* 'unpicks how re/productive shame is carried by the bodies of those whose value as citizens was not assured in the 1937 constitution', since Pen, who is autistic, would have been forbidden from reproducing in law in Ireland as recently as 2015. Ablenationalism promulgates the notion that the disabled cannot also be productive, or reproductive. **Kathleen Costello-Sullivan** reads Caitríona Lally's *Eggshells* as challenging the normative dichotomy of autistic percipience and imaginative panache, whereby the neurodivergent are denied the possibility of being both disabled and richly creative, vulnerable and impressive, at the same time. The shaming persistence of this dichotomy manifests, on Costello-Sullivan's reading, not only in the regularity with

[3] David T. Mitchell and Sharon Snyder, *The Biopolitics of Disability: Neoliberalism, Ablenationalism, and Peripheral Embodiment* (Ann Arbor: University of Michigan Press, 2015).

which the protagonist, Vivian, encounters it on the streets of Dublin, but in the near unanimity with which the reviewers of the novel, its public readers, have reproduced the either/or approach to Vivian. In sequestering their quirky, whimsical profile of Vivian from the disability attendant to her autism, the reviewers reinforce the shaming of neurodivergence that the novel critiques.

The essays in this volume demonstrate the rare combination of scope and particularity that the experience of shame entails. Shame arises from various institutional sources – religious, colonial, ethno-national, cultural. Each site of shame canvassed herein bears contours specific, if not unique, to Ireland and yet resonates with predicaments generative and exploitative of toxic humiliation across cultures throughout the world. By the same token, shame comes in various shapes as defined by its purchase on the subject: moral, sexual, biological, mental. But all are socially engendered and politically reinforced; all are individually suffered and collectively enjoined. Each type of shame canvassed herein bears its own distinctive properties, possesses a distinctive structure or, if you like, issues in a distinctively aversive experience. At the same time, it is central to the phenomenology of shame that it is transmissible, hence generative, self-reproducing, from one circumstance, one modality, one subject to another. Shame is famously the most infectious of affective states. We are all prone to feel some form of shame in the presence, however mediated, of a shame experience. A truly extraordinary implication follows from this affective contagion. Shame, properly understood as indignity somaticised, especially demeaning to our sense of human worth turns out to be, in its communicability, closely akin to that foundation of human worth, our capacity for empathy. We nourish the hope that the inflictions and afflictions of shame described, discussed and analysed in this volume will, among other things, arouse an intellectualised empathy in its readers.

Part I

Ethnic Shame

Chapter 1

Colonial Emasculation in Early Modern Irish Poetry: From Shame to Humiliation

Sarah E. McKibben

As English authority was imposed upon Ireland over the sixteenth and into the early seventeenth century, there was a crucial shift from shame to humiliation in the understanding of, response to and internalisation of that conflict by the native Irish literati. As I detail in my first book, *Endangered Masculinities in Irish Poetry*, gendered incitements to shame adapted the regulatory role of early modern Irish poetry to the realities of an aggrandising Tudor-Stuart state.[1] From around 1540, poetic satire began to mock cultural anglicisation and deride submission to English authority as profoundly unmanly, while marshalling fighting spirit and religious outrage amongst rebels. It did this while simultaneously positioning the speaker – and choice patron(s) – as set *apart* from the problem: a foundational dynamic of satire, but ultimately an untenable one under the circumstances. The poet condemns colonial accommodation as a shame, but finesses the question of native – his own, his patron's – complicity, even as it becomes ever more unavoidable with the brutal suppression of insurgency and the ultimate success of the renewed conquest.

This rhetorical sleight of hand prolonged the bardic expression of the socio-symbolic order into the early seventeenth century but did not – *could not* – answer the relentless incursion of the colonial state. As the confederated Irish forces suffered abject defeat at Kinsale in 1601, and with the end of the Nine Years' War in 1603, followed by the departure into exile of key northern leaders in the Flight of the Earls in 1607, enabling the plantation and full subjection of Ireland, poets were professionally obligated to catalogue Ireland's sufferings, which they had to acknowledge amounted to nothing less than abject

[1] Sarah E. McKibben, *Endangered Masculinities in Irish Poetry, 1540–1780* (Dublin: University College Dublin Press, 2010).

collective dishonour. Worse, the poets had to admit to being humiliated by the very ideals of masculinity they themselves long promulgated. In response to this conundrum, bardic poets fashioned tropes of unspeakable humiliation to capture the unprecedented collective experience of defeat, subordination and dispossession, placing that horror at the limits of expression or language itself. Then, in turn, they came to express the unspeakable by way of a displacement of object. Having first spoken, haltingly, of a humiliated collectivity (consisting of the *men* or *people* of Ireland, or various noble lineages), they increasingly projected Ireland's humiliation onto an abstraction: the personification of Ireland as a woman. By making the female Ireland bear the burden of emasculation – recoded first as feminine vulnerability and suffering, and later as a harlot's willing submission to conquest – humiliation (and Irish manhood) could recover its voice. Unspeakable humiliation was transposed into the all-too-speakable shame of a safely detached, feminised Ireland: a national symbol and scapegoat. This admitted the problem of humiliation by displacing it, enabling a fragile, provisional recuperation of male standing.

In this cultural moment, we discern a new subject of history – the nation – emerging out of the subordinated (indeed, *subjected*) collectivity in relation to the retrospective dream of an originating faith and fatherland, pursued the more intensely because the father's mandate to the son can no longer be fulfilled.[2] As Cynthia Enloe observes, nationalism typically springs from a combination of 'masculinised memory, masculinised humiliation and masculinised hope'.[3] Thus, Ireland, long the culturally and geographically distinctive target of native political ambition, became retrospectively consolidated and intensified by way of its constitution as the patrimony ('athartha', from 'athar', father – or even, duplicatively, 'atharrdha a n-aithreadh', patrimony of their fathers – as well as the more overtly political, less explicitly gendered 'ceannas', sovereignty) so shamefully lost to the English.

Having shunted that shared masculine dishonour onto the personified female figure of the nation, Irish poets further develop the modern political *aisling* poetic genre in the eighteenth century.

[2] Hiram Morgan, 'Faith and Fatherland in Sixteenth-Century Ireland', *History Ireland* 3:2 (Summer, 1995): 13–20; and Mícheál Mac Craith, 'Creideamh agus athartha: idé-eolaíocht pholaitíochta agus aos léinn na Gaeilge i dtús an seachtú haois déag', in Máirín Ní Dhonnchadha, ed., *Nua-Léamha: Gnéithe de Chultúr, Stair agus Polaitíocht na hÉireann c.1600–c.1900* (Baile Átha Cliath: An Clóchomhar, 1996), 7–19.

[3] Cynthia Enloe, *Bananas, Beaches and Bases: Making Feminist Sense of International Politics* (Berkeley: University of California Press, 1989), 44.

The lamenting female Ireland becomes for the most part a victimised wife or widow mourning her suffering and losses, in so doing demanding pity, grief and, ultimately, rescue from Irish *men* recast (once more, normatively) as her heroic saviours. She is consequently 'less a metaphorical representation of Ireland' than 'a metonym for the oppressed Catholic population familiar to the poets'.[4] This shift elided, but could not erase, the gendered humiliation it encoded: it was a resistant historiography that nonetheless wanted to erase itself.

To retrace this narrative, we must turn to bardic poetry, one of the few verbal records reflecting the political and dynastic concerns of the Irish elite. For around 450 years, a highly trained, hereditary, male professional class of literati produced this formulaic, metrically and lexically complex encomiastic, religious, didactic, genealogical, historical or narrative verse. Bardic poets crafted the most common subgenre, praise poetry, in prolonged effusions of chiselled, end-stopped stanzas, as an 'expensive prestige purchase' for elite Gaelic and gaelicised noblemen in a mutually beneficial, androcentric, homosocial exchange.[5] Though occasionally mentioned as poets in early medieval materials, women were kept out of the formal profession as a matter of course, their supposed inferiority and exclusion naturalised by widely circulating misogynistic aphorisms.[6] Instead, women were sometime objects of a genre overwhelmingly dedicated to men (in occasional poems to the lord's wife, mother, widow or child, or incidental references to her in verses addressing to him). Thus, male control over the symbolic order was naturalised along with the male authority it subtended. Bardic professional poets sought to eternalise existing hierarchies by publicly affirming the lords of the day in time-honoured, deeply conservative phrases, images and stories.[7] The professional poet famously proclaimed that, in exchange for 'fleeting

[4] Máirín Nic Eoin, 'Sovereignty and Politics, *c.*1300–1900', in Angela Bourke et al., ed., *The Field Day Anthology of Irish Writing* (New York: New York University Press, 2002), 273–92, 274.

[5] Katharine Simms, 'Poems to the Medieval O'Donnell Chiefs and their Historical Context', *North American Journal of Celtic Studies* 1:1 (May, 2017): 45. On the homosocial, Sarah McKibben, 'Queering Early Modern Ireland', *Irish University Review* 43:1 (2013): 169–83.

[6] Máirín Nic Eoin, *B'ait Leo Bean: Gnéithe den Idé-eolaíocht Inscne i dTraidisiún Liteartha na Gaeilge* (Baile Átha Cliath: An Clóchomhar, 1998). On female poets, see Máirín Ní Dhonnchadha, 'Women in the Medieval Poetry Business', in Ailbhe Darcy and David Wheatley, eds, *Cambridge History of Irish Women's Poetry* (Cambridge: Cambridge University Press: 2021), 40–56.

[7] On naturalising gendered domination, Pierre Bourdieu, *Masculine Domination*, translated by Richard Nice (Cambridge: Polity Press, 2001), 8, 9.

wealth' (handsome patronage in tax-free land, livestock and gear), he offered his patrons 'immortal fame' in the form of precise, ornate verse inscribed in manuscript anthologies that would long outlive poet and patron alike.[8] Indeed, his praise poetry offered not just *future* fame but *present* legitimation in the competitive system of succession – but only as long as the nobles adhered to societal norms.

Those who failed to uphold societal norms risked severe, public sanction. Formal satire was originally understood as a kind of curse, causing actual physical mutilation or death, but continued to provoke dread even when understood to merely redden the cheek. It was most feared for its profound reputational damage – the exact opposite of praise. In a society that understood honour to reside in one's good name, satire was 'the formidable weapon with which members of the poetic orders . . . enforced the claims on their own behalf or on behalf of others': a prerogative they sought to monopolise against those of lower status.[9] Within this genre, shame had a productive, because regulative, function. Bardic poetry voiced the symbolic mandate of the nobility by tirelessly rehearsing the obligations of elite men to make war, enforce peace, proffer lavish hospitality and patronise men of learning. If lords faltered in their duty, bardic poems mobilised shame (or, often, just the threat of it) to recall the lords to their rightful selves: legitimate concerns understood to be of public import.[10] Unjustified satiric attacks were punished by fines, unless expiated by praise poems conferring the immortal fame poets usually promised.[11] It was the other side of the praise bardic poets typically produced,

[8] Damian McManus, 'The Bardic Poet as Teacher, Student and Critic: A Context for the Grammatical Tracts', in Cathal G. Ó hÁinle and Donald E. Meek, eds, *Unity in Diversity: Studies in Irish and Scottish Gaelic Language, Literature and History* (Dublin: School of Irish, Trinity College Dublin, 2004), 105–6.

[9] Daniel Binchy, quoting Liam Breatnach, 'On Satire and the Poet's Circuit', in Cathal G. Ó hÁinle and Donald E. Meek, eds, *Unity in Diversity: Studies in Irish and Scottish Gaelic Language, Literature and History* (Dublin: School of Irish, Trinity College Dublin, 2004): 25–35, 25; Robin Chapman Stacey, *Dark Speech: The Performance of Law in Early Ireland* (Philadelphia: University of Pennsylvania Press, 2007), 138.

[10] A poet gave a tripartite preliminary warning of impending satire identifying the grievance, naming the offender and then offering praise that presumably encouraged him to reform; see Katharine Simms, 'Bardic Poems of Apology and Reconciliation', in Liam Mac Amhlaigh and Brian Ó Curnáin, eds, *Ilteangach, Ilseiftiúil: féilscríbhinn in ómós do Nicholas Williams = A Festschrift in Honour of Nicholas Williams* (Dublin: Arlen House, 2012), 175–6.

[11] Fergus Kelly, *A Guide to Early Irish Law* (Dublin: Dublin Institute for Advanced Studies [1988] 2005), 49–51.

and no less central than praise to the poet's power and prestige in the symbolic economy he oversaw, and as enduring.[12] Thus when we discuss shame (or indeed masculinity) in a medieval and early modern Irish context, we are, therefore, talking about a powerful, long-lived and particularly public, rather than mainly interior, phenomenon.[13]

Yet the public nature of Irish shame in this period was not unique. Their English counterparts felt a similar drive to protect their good name. English court life, Stephanie Trigg reminds us, was similarly 'fraught . . . with the constant possibility of shame, which was often ritualised and performative', and similarly 'embedded in anxieties about social and political hierarchy and public reputation'.[14] Despite obvious parallels, however, the English emphasised the barbaric, primitive difference of Irish people and their customs, blaming poets for stoking false pride and 'insolence'. Bardic poets' longstanding role – their function as guardians of the *doxa* of native Irish society – placed them in direct conflict with Tudor authority, which targeted them at least as early as the 1530s. A parade of hostile witnesses relentlessly denounced poets and their craft.[15] Irish manuscripts were deliberately destroyed and the bearers of the literary tradition targeted for assassination.[16] Such attacks were part of the larger attempt to undermine Irish cultural integrity, to denigrate Irish people and to disrupt, replace or destroy traditional homosocial bonds. In English works of the period, Ireland and the Irish are made to appear – once more – *archaic* vis-à-vis the fetishised modernity of a self, the 'civilised subject' said to emerge on adjacent shores by early moderns and early modernists alike.

[12] The fear of satire was so great that it continued to be a penalty written into political treaties well into the early modern period and to serve as quasi-legal mode of protest and redress. See Róisín McLaughlin, 'A Threat of Satire by Tadhg (Mac Dáire) Mac Bruaideadha', *Ériu* 55 (2005): 39.

[13] Cf. Regina Schwartz and Valeria Finucci's insight in *Desire in the Renaissance: Psychoanalysis and Literature* (Princeton: Princeton University Press, 1994) that many (English) Renaissance writers are preoccupied with interiority, and their reference to 'that psychoanalytic discourse known as "Renaissance literature"', 3.

[14] Stephanie Trigg, '"Shamed be . . .": Historicizing Shame in Medieval and Early Modern Courtly Ritual', *Exemplaria* 19:1 (2007): 76, 84.

[15] Alan J. Fletcher, *Drama and the Performing Arts in Pre-Cromwellian Ireland: Sources and Documents from the Earliest Times Until c.1642* (Cambridge: Brewer, 2001), 169–95.

[16] Donnchadh Ó Corráin, 'Cad d'imigh ar lámhscríbhinní na hÉireann?', in Ruairi Ó hUiginn, ed., *Oidhreacht na Lámhscríbhinní*, Léachtaí Cholm Chille, 34 (Maynooth: An Sagart, 2004) 7–27; and 'What happened Ireland's medieval manuscripts?', *Peritia* 22:3 (2011): 191–223.

Such archaism was (and is) inseparable from the colonial knowledge structures it legitimates: another iteration of the ubiquitous trope of native backwardness. The Irish were the non-modern object by which the modern English subject of civilisation would be defined and delimited. Indeed, even in recent criticism, exact Irish contemporaries of those emblematic English figures of Renaissance transformation continue to be framed as that kind of 'medieval' – premodern, archaic, trapped in the past, unable fully to discern, much less cope with, change figured as an inexorable and ultimately necessary imposition from without and above.[17] Of course, such claims of backwardness themselves produce shame, and are central to the justification of colonial domination, which is also understood as inherently shameful. Whereas English modernity might be said to incite shame, modernity for Ireland could only mean humiliation, in *both* colonial *and* anticolonial rhetoric. It was both unspeakable and inescapable, even in the view of its object. And we should understand how enraging and emasculating all those forms of symbolic castration were intended, and no doubt felt, to be.

In addition to rampant physical and cultural violence, early modern bardic poets also faced an existential threat.[18] In the anglicised Ireland envisaged by Henry VIII and his successors, the nobility would neither need nor desire bardic poetry for entertainment, much less legitimation, nor would native bonds need reinforcement once they, like native culture and language, were ruptured and replaced in keeping with Irish lords' pledges to shun Gaelic ways. Confronting all these threats, some bardic poets turned to gendered satiric shaming to defend the manly habitus by catalysing powerful individual and collective bodily responses (blushing, trembling, rage, disdain) to deride anglicisation and urge resistance, even as Tudor rule eroded existing Irish gender norms.[19] At the same time, these same poets continued to perpetuate the conventions of elite manhood through encomia for an

[17] See Lee Patterson, 'On the Margin: Postmodernism, Ironic History, and Medieval Studies', *Speculum* 65:1 (January 1990): 87–108; David Aers, 'A Whisper in the Ear of Early Modernists; or, Reflections on Literary Critics Writing the History of the Subject', in David Aers, ed., *Culture and History, 1350–1600: Essays on English Communities, Identities, and Writings* (New York: Harvester Wheatsheaf, 1992), 177–202; and Dipesh Chakrabarty, *Habitations of Modernity: Essays in the Wake of Subaltern Studies* (Chicago: University of Chicago Press, 2002).

[18] Marc Caball, *Poets and Politics: Reaction and Continuity in Irish Poetry, 1558–1625* (Cork: Cork University Press, 1998), 94–5.

[19] Bourdieu, *Masculine Domination*, 38.

ever-shrinking pool of patrons.[20] This accords with satire's function 'as a literary mechanism for the production of differences in the face of anxiety about . . . identity, sameness, and undifferentiation', for poets faced the same challenges as the lords they served.[21] By shaming others, poets diverted attention from their own pragmatic accommodations to English authority, and positioned themselves as nobly apart from the compromises they disdained. That said, symbolic compensation could not defend securely against an emasculation felt to be inherent in the colonial relation, which became ever more pressing – hence the vehemence with which it is maintained.

As early as the early 1540s, one of the many Irish words for shame starts and ends the astonishing anonymous bardic poem, 'Fúbún fúibh, a shluagh Gaoidheal' (Shame on you, O Gaelic host), which bitterly castigates Irish lords, both collectively and individually, for acceding the English policy of surrender and regrant – giving up their native titles and legal claims while promising to anglicise themselves and their families – in formal recognition of English sovereignty.[22] The poet weaponises English definitions of masculine nobility, portraying them as a betrayal of native norms. This incitement to shame occurs in direct response to the realities of submission to Henry VIII, just as he makes *all* Irish his subjects and *these* Irish noble subjects. Styling this as a choice, rather than an emasculating imperative in response to Tudor military might, the poet derides them, saying 'is trua an aithis' (pitiful is the disgrace; 7) of their failure to follow Gaelic ways, and 'is trua an toirbheart' (pitiful is the surrender; 11) of their turning their 'druim re hoighreacht a n-athar' (backs on their ancestral inheritance; 12). He names and shames them each in turn before tepidly praising one seemingly resistant patron. He seizes upon the luxurious gold chain of royal favour as a shameful sign of subordination like the noblemen's failure to defend their faith before the apostate king. The poet concludes, venomously, 'ná habraidh feasta acht "faobún"' (henceforth say nothing but 'shame'; 40). Pronouncing the verdict they are condemned to reiterate in perpetuity, he neatly recurs, in traditional bardic fashion, to the poem's opening

20 Sarah E. McKibben, 'Guaranteeing What Cannot Be Guaranteed: Defending and Adapting Bardic Patronage in *Ag so an chomairce, a Chormaic* (*c.*1585) by Tadhg Dall Ó hUiginn', *North American Journal of Celtic Studies* 2:1 (2018): 1–36.

21 Fredric V. Bogel, *The Difference Satire Makes: Rhetoric and Reading from Jonson to Byron* (Ithaca: Cornell University Press, 2001), 21.

22 Text and translation, Brian Ó Cuív, 'A Sixteenth-Century Political Poem', *Éigse* 15 (1974): 261–76.

word in a caustically dismissive formal *dúnadh*, or poetic 'closing'. In attacking the compromise of surrender and regrant, satire reframes it as a shameful, ignoble submission that will echo down the ages.

Numerous works dating from the last third of the sixteenth century attack anglicisation with increasing intensity just as various insurgencies broke out in the two and a half decades leading up to the Nine Years' War. By suggesting noblemen have shown stupidity as well as disloyalty, poets from across the island marshalled the power of the symbolic mandate in defense of their own position as the guardians of noble masculinity. By doing so, however, they also made collective dishonour – understood as humiliation – undeniable after the final defeat.

Hence, the warning in one poem to a patron not to 'go haimhglic' (foolishly) allow himself to be 'meallta' (tricked or lured) to trade genuine honour and nobility – and Ireland itself – for false English promises and trinkets, thereby violating his 'dúthchas' (heritage; inherited right; native land).[23] In another poem, north Connacht master poet Tadhg Dall Ó hUiginn uses a familiar metaphor to exhort Riocard Óg Búrc (Burke) not to violate his primary obligation to his family honour – 'ná tabhair cúl red chéadmhóid' (do not turn your back on your first pledge; 2).[24] Acceptance of an English title would dishonour the lord's patrimony and threaten his inheritance; he should desist 'finnleargtha an ghruaidh suil ghríostair' (lest the fair curves of [his] cheek be scorched; 232) with the poet's satire. Here, the traditional evocation of blushing signals the seriousness of the danger to the patron's honour. Similarly, Wexford poet Doighri Ó Dálaigh attacks the noble betrayal of 'uaisle' (nobility) and 'eineach' (honour) in abandoning the literati, making all but his own patron 'anuasal' (ignoble [543]).[25] In turn, some years later, the same poet's son, Aonghus Ó Dálaigh, stirs

[23] 'Gaoidhil meallta nó mac Néill' (Gaels deceived like the son of Néill) by Uilliam Óg Mac an Bhaird addresses Turlough Luineach Ó Néill in warning', in Damian McManus and Eoghan Ó Raghallaigh, eds, *A Bardic Miscellany: Five Hundred Bardic Poems from Manuscripts in Irish and British Libraries* (Department of Irish: Trinity College Dublin, 2010), 361–3.

[24] 'T'aire riot, a Riocaird Óig' (Take heed, Riocard Óg), which dates to sometime between 1571 and 1586, addresses Riocard Óg Búrc, who was executed in 1586 by order of Sir Richard Bingham, President of Connacht. Text and translation from Eleanor Knott, *The Bardic Poems of Tadhg Dall Ó hUiginn (1550–1591)*, 2 vols (London: Irish Texts Society, 1926), i: 160–8; ii: 106–11.

[25] 'Cia as uaisle do Laighneachuibh?' (Who is noblest of the Leinstermen?), written sometime between 1557 and 1579, may be found in Seán Mac Airt, ed., *Leabhar Branach: The Book of the O'Byrnes* (Dublin: Dublin Institute for Advanced Studies, 1933, reprint 2022), 20–3.

up the forces of the Baltinglass rebellion of 1580 in south Leinster by marshalling the threat of shame – warning the insurgents, 'ná cluintior claoiteacht oraibh' (let not submission/cowardice be claimed against you; 3,738) in defending your 'dúthchas' (heritage, that keyword that recurs again and again).[26] The Irish 'laochruidh' (heroes) have been strangely 'mall' (slow) to fight, acting unaccountably 'urramach umhal / do mhearshluagh gusmhar ghallda' (respectful and submissive to an aggressive, pushing band of foreigners; 3,763–4) – despite the fact that 'nách goirthior dhíobh 'na ndúthchus / acht ceithearn chúthail choill-eadh' (they are called, in their own native land, nothing but sneaking woodland bandits 3,771–2). That is, dismissed as uncivil, outlawed in their own land by a violent and predatory regime, the Gaels must fight back or risk dishonour, as acknowledged by a contemporaneous text describing the near-universal defeat of the Gaels as 'scél náir ré thuir-oimh is truaighe' (a tale of shame it is sad to relate; 3,867).[27] Though Ó Dálaigh doesn't use the word 'náir', he hardly has to: shame permeates his exhortatory text, as it does the collective bardic response.

Still more potent is the doubly gendered attack (both *on* and *by means of* gender) mounted by Monaghan poet Laoiseach Mac an Bhaird around 1590 on an anglicised young man, targeting his noble manhood in withering fashion. This satire names the man who has adopted English clothing, hairstyle and gear only as no 'deagh-mhac Donnchadha' (good son of Donnchadh), implicitly disinheriting him, dramatically ratcheting up the stakes.[28] The target has unmanned himself – becoming desexed, ridiculous, unready for battle – unlike Eóghan Bán (fair Eóghan), his suitably rebellious, virile counterpart, who displaces the nameless son from his own poem. Worse, the man who follows English ways allows himself to be sodomised by his own puny English weapon: a devastating sign of sociopolitical subordination. Satire (like praise) both claims authority and reasserts cultural norms so as to try to make them live on. But symbolic mandates cannot fulfill themselves, however viciously they are asserted. Here, a mandarin class at once deploys and reinscribes tradition in defense of

[26] Text of 'Dia libh, a laochruidh Gaoidhiol' (God be with you, O heroes of the Gaels), in Mac Airt, *Leabhar Branach*, 142–4. Translated by Standish H. O'Grady, *Cat. Irish MSS in the British Museum* (London: Longman, 1926): 504–6.

[27] Tuileagna Ruadh Ó Maolchonaire, 'Fuath gach fir fuidheall a thuaighe' (Every man hates the remnant of his axe), in Mac Airt, ed., *Leabhar Branach*, 147–8.

[28] Text and translation, 'A fhir ghlacas a ghalldacht' (O man who follows English ways), occasionally modified, from Osborn Bergin, *Irish Bardic Poetry*, edited by David Greene and Fergus Kelly. (Dublin: Dublin Institute for Advanced Studies, 1984), 49–50, 231–2.

the status quo. They persist in imposing censure and contesting new systems of value, desperate to both confront and de-scribe an ongoing process of accommodation. In this fashion, they sought both to repudiate and recast the shame encoded in colonial encounter and its sociopolitical structures.

None of this could deny the pervasive sense of trauma, alienation and communal dispossession that would be occasioned by the Flight of the Earls in 1607 and the large-scale plantation it enabled: an unprecedented rupture that unleashed a full-voiced, comprehensive lament for the unspeakable humiliation of colonial conquest.[29] Bardic poets could no longer deny their own precipitous loss of status – the final collapse of their symbolic mandate – any more than they could finesse the realities of colonial defeat.[30] This is the point where *shame* becomes *humiliation*: decisive and devastating because undeniable in accordance with the poet's own internalised ideals.[31] Having trumpeted the shame of colonial defeat, Ireland's poets were obliged to confront it on their own ground. Now, Ireland's humiliation would have to be spoken, even as poets claimed to quail at having to speak it and struggled to find adequate terms to do so. There is no one term for the humiliation of conquest. Instead, a series of attempts to speak the unspeakable registers the obligation and limit-point of linguistic and poetic expression, seen also in their multiplicity and hyperbolic, intensifying prefixes and superlatives. The bardic poet as guardian of Irish manliness is refigured as the reluctant witness to emasculation. This generated a new rhetoric in which recurrent tropes of unspeakability – employing preterition and exclamation – try to speak the unspeakable. Time and again, the speaker says he cannot bear to (or dares not) articulate the Irish condition – even as he does so. The centre of poetic gravity shifts as individual poets try to express a loss they figure as both collective and emasculating – though they avoid specifying the soul-stealing acts of pragmatism defeat surely necessitated. The poet who voices this trope is newly foregrounded as lone witness, functioning as a sort of public intellectual who attempts to make sense of the devastation, despite being sadly diminished in contrast to his former social position. While patronage (and even conventional

[29] Marc Caball, 'Dispossession and Reaction: the Gaelic Literati and the Plantation of Ulster', *History Ireland* 17:6 (November/December 2009): 24–7, 25.

[30] On that historical sense of humiliation, see David Edwards, 'Political Change and Social Transformation, 1603–1641', in Jane Ohlmeyer, ed., *The Cambridge History of Ireland*, vol. 2 (Cambridge: Cambridge University Press, 2017), 48–71.

[31] Adam Phillips, 'Just Rage', in *The Beast in the Nursery: On Curiosity and Other Appetites* (New York: Vintage, 1998), 119–40.

praise poetry) persists well into the seventeenth century, in *these* powerful poems the poet becomes an isolated figure in his own text as his patrons recede from view. Yet in these works, the distressed poet speaks for his community. An anonymous poem found in the Book of O'Conor Don (1631), 'Mo-chean don loing-se tar lear' (Good fortune to the ship over the sea), mourns the departure of the earls as resulting in collective disgrace as Caball remarks, the poet lamenting that 'na Gaoidhil aniú sa neart / go fiú an aoinfhir ar n-imtheacht' (the Gaels and their power today / have vanished to the last man; 23–4), which has brought 'Tár . . . oruinn' (shame/disgrace on us all; 28).[32]

Similarly, northern poet Fear Flátha Ó Gnímh's 'Beannacht ar anmhain Éireann' (A Blessing upon the soul of Ireland), composed in the years following the Flight of the Earls, confirms the communal humiliation by focusing on the emblematic figure of the suffering female Ireland, a figure who would become crucial in the poetic response to the traumas of colonisation.[33] The poem opens and closes with an anguished prayer for Ireland 'na gcéimeanna gcorrach' (of the faltering steps; 2), said to be dying through the degradation of her people and the concomitant suppression of religion, law and culture, although the poet claims that 'eagla an ghallsmaicht' (fear of foreign law [or oppression]; 13) prevents him from relating the horror that he in fact attempts to capture. The departure and death of Ireland's nobility further humiliates this unfortunate but distanced female figure, such that both practices and people do not live or live no more ('ní mhaireann'). Of this, the poet intones 'd'fhearaibh Éireann is iomnár' (to the men of Ireland it is a disgrace; 32), and, in the penultimate stanza, declares that 'gan toidheacht aice ón oilbhéim, / dá lamhadh sinn a mhaoidheamh' (she cannot recover from the stigma, if we dared to proclaim it; 62–3), and still more powerfully, 'd'fhine Gaoidheal is oilchéim' (it is an infamy to the race of the Gael; 62), rhyming 'oilbhéim' (stigma) with 'oilchéim' (infamy) to drive home the message.

Writing slightly later, Munster poet Lochlainn Ó Dálaigh, in 'Cáit ar ghabhadar Gaoidhil?' (Where have the Gaels gone?), describes a land emptied of its rightful people, the poet abandoned and appalled at their replacement by 'dírim uaibhreach eisiodhan' (an arrogant,

[32] In Marc Caball's words, the lords take the literal and actual supremacy of the Gaels with them; see 'Dispossession and Reaction', 25. Text and translation, edited by Paul Walsh, *Beatha Aodha Ruaidh Uí Dhomhnaill*, 2 vols. (Dublin: Irish Texts Society, 1948–57), vol. 2, 118–23.

[33] Text and translation, occasionally modified, from Bergin, *Irish Bardic Poetry*, 115–17, 264–5.

impure crowd; 30), who are dividing the Gaels' land amongst themselves, leaving native seats of government desolate, places of worship violated, masses held outdoors, land wasted and misused.[34] Ó Dálaigh exclaims 'trom an pudhar' (heavy the shame; 45) , and refers to his horror at being obligated to record this travesty: 'uch! a n-áirmhim dá n-aitheis' (Och! the extent of their humiliation I [have to] relate!; 64). The Gaels' oppression 'gadaidh asda a n-anmanna' (steals away their souls; 70), transforming them into 'cuirp bheó-mharbha' (half-dead corpses; 72) before his eyes.

Such images evince shameful subjugation, historical rupture and social death: at once articulating and deflecting colonial humiliation. They voice the predicament of those Eochaidh Ó hEodhasa termed 'daoine ar n-éag gan oighidh' (people who have died though unslain; 8).[35] Irish men are weak, lifeless and forgetful of their martial ways, while Irish people are universally persecuted and thus collectively humiliated. From this period, a ramifying Counter-Reformation providentialism blames Irish sinfulness for God's punitive anger and offers repentance as a remedy for past sins and present disempowerment. Providentialism both provides an explanation and proffers hope for change, when Irish men might rise as belated rescuers of the Ireland they had not managed to defend.[36] The story is never over: the much-lamented end is not the end. Yet the problem remained of how to express what was properly inexpressible: a manhood undone. If this self-defeating mandate (speaking the unspeakable) were to be maintained, a scapegoat would have to be found.

For this reason and at this time, the gendered landscape of Irish poetry alters decisively. Over subsequent decades, the collective humiliation of Irish *men* recedes from view, displaced onto the female figure of Ireland, a sexually victimised yet relentlessly culpable figure.[37] National allegory is born. Ireland personified as woman (a reflex of the traditional sovereignty goddess) is said to be dead or dying, her own and her people's souls lost or stolen: in bondage like the Israelites. Éire, 'for long the passive partner in the symbolic union of sovereign

[34] Text and translation, William Gillies, 'A Poem on the Downfall of the Gaoidhil', *Éigse* 13:3 (1970): 203–10.

[35] 'Beag mhaireas do mhacraidh Ghaoidheal' (Few live of the sons of the Gael), in Damian McManus and Eoghan Ó Raghallaigh, eds, *A Bardic Miscellany* (Dublin: Department of Irish, School of Languages, Literatures and Cultural Studies, 2010), 65–7.

[36] See, generally, Breandán Ó Buachalla, *Aisling Ghear: Na Stiobhartaigh agus an tAos Léinn, 1603–1788* (Baile Átha Cliath: An Clochomhar, 1996).

[37] On this trope, see Revathi Krishnaswamy, *Effeminism: The Economy of Colonial Desire* (Ann Arbor: University of Michigan Press, 1988).

and territory, comes to be presented as morally reprehensible—as a shameless whore or an adulteress, or as a bad mother who rejects her own offspring and suckles the foreign horde'.[38] The insistent nastiness of these texts betrays the stakes of the ideological agenda they are enacting. As Adam Phillips suggests, there is 'no rage without the betrayal of an ideal'.[39] Men emasculated by fantasies of themselves insist ever more hysterically on the blameworthy nature of their chosen scapegoat.[40] As Kaja Silverman puts it, 'historical trauma' interrupts the logic of patriarchy's 'dominant fiction' because 'a large group of male subjects . . . are . . . unable to sustain an imaginary relation with the phallus'.[41] Trauma necessitates *de-scription* of blame to protect those responsible for occasioning it, here all the more powerfully because the effect of the historical trauma is, among other things, to radically displace those who were previously responsible for producing the dominant fiction.

So it is that, when lamenting the state of the female Ireland, northern poet Eoghan Ruadh Mac an Bhaird writes suggestively, 'iomdha a huilc 'sa héigcinnte' (many are her evils and her uncertainties; 6), and refers to her 'neamghlóir' (unglory; 7) and 'saobh' (perversion; 7), terms registering the system of representation as, in fact, one of prior negation – before describing foreigners having 'a n-algas don eing' (their wicked will [or lasciviousness] of the land; 19).[42] He thus evokes shameful sexual violations visited upon the country, thereby demonising early modern English colonialism as sinful debauchery. (Intriguingly, in his later appeal to Moses-figure Hugh O'Neill, the poet invokes early modern feminist icon Judith's triumph over Holofernes as a model for a contrastingly triumphant, vengeful female heroine!)

Most of the period's poems on the national question, however, continue in the same vein – prompting us to recall that repetition is evidence of trauma. The insistence of the trope betrays the inefficacy of the displacement. Tipperary priest-scholar Seathrún Céitinn (Geoffrey Keating) opens 'Mo thruaighe mar táid Éire' (My sorrow

[38] Máirín Nic Eoin, 'Sovereignty and Politics, *c.*1300–1900', 273.

[39] Phillips, 'Just Rage', 122.

[40] See Jean Laplanche and Jean-Bernard Pontalis, 'Projection', in *The Language of Psychoanalysis*, translated by Donald Nicholson-Smith, introduction by Daniel Lagache (New York: W. W. Norton, 1974), 349–56.

[41] See Kaja Silverman, *Male Subjectivity at the Margins* (New York: Routledge, 1992), 54.

[42] Text and translation, occasionally modified, from Tomás Ó Raghallaigh, ed., *Duanta Eoghain Ruaidh Mhic an Bhaird* (Gaillimh: O Gormain, 1930), 206–21, 371–6, 429–30.

at the state of Ireland) with Ireland as vulnerable, abandoned, victimised nurse or spouse, but concludes by terming her 'Meirdreach gan iocht gan onóir' (A whore without mercy or honour; 65).[43] A second poem attributed to Céitinn, 'Óm sceól ar ardmhagh Fáil ní chodlaim oíche' (At the news from Fál's high plain I cannot sleep), remonstrates with an Ireland he addresses as 'A Fhódla phráis' (O brazen Fódla; 5), who does not recognise her shame in not nourishing the native Irish instead of the foreigners.[44] Another poem, attributed to many different poets in token of its broad cultural currency, refers to Ireland suffering a rape she is too stupefied to sense, with every single man violating her, but then blames her for being loose and whorelike, refusing no man (when, within the traditional sovereignty motif, Ireland should reject wrongful leadership by becoming unfruitful).[45] She is debased, 'do thréig a náire' (she has abandoned shame; 29), he pronounces, neatly shifting the blame for conquest (for evidently, blame there must be) away from men and onto the personified country who bears 'bastardadh' (bastards; 32).

All these elements are brought together in a short, bitter poem by Munster poet and priest Brian Mac Giolla Phádraig. The titular first line insists on the humiliation Ireland should feel, signified by the blush that *men* were said to feel in earlier works: 'Ábhar deargtha leacan do mhnaoi Chuinn é' (The wife of Conn's cheek should blush red).[46] It is a cause of shame for Ireland 'táir is tarcaisne a thabhairt dá saorchlainn féin' (to bring insult and contempt onto her own noble family; 2), depriving them of her own love and giving sustenance instead 'ar bhastard nach feadair cé díobh puinn é' (to a bastard who doesn't know from whom he springs; 4). She permits her own violation and willingly succours foreigners, underscoring Irish humiliation as at once self-declared and projected away by means of the gendered sleight of hand. The poet next addresses her as 'A Éire, a chailleach is malartach bréagach foinn' (O Ireland, O hag of the fickle deceitful desire; 5) and 'a mheirdreach bhradach le sealad nár éim' ach sinn' (O thieving whore who lately has naught refused but us; 6). Then he again accuses

[43] Text, Brian Ó Cuív, 'Mo thruaighe mar tá Éire', *Éigse* 8:4 (1957): 302–8. Translation is my own.

[44] Text from and translation by Seán Ó Tuama and Thomas Kinsella, *An Duanaire 1600–1900: Poems of the Dispossessed* (Portlaoise: Dolmen Press, 1981), 84–7.

[45] 'Iomdha éagnach ag Éirinn' (Many causes of lament has Ireland), text and translation, Lambert McKenna, ed., *Dánta do chum Aonghus Fionn Ó Dálaigh* (Dublin: Maunsel, 1919), 73–5.

[46] Text from Pádraig de Brún, Breandán Ó Buachalla and Tomás Ó Concheanainn, eds, *Nua-Dhuanaire*, vol. i (Baile Átha Cliath: Institiúid Ardléinn Bhaile Átha Cliath, 1986), 12. Translation is my own.

her of consenting to her own ongoing domination: 'do léigis farat na Galla-sa i réim id eing' (you have allowed the foreigners to reign in your valley; 7); by allowing the taking of her land/groove/gap (a simultaneously geographical/military and sexual image), Ireland destroys each of her own children 'mar bhastard' (like a bastard; 8), having already suckled foreign offspring.

Next, in a conventional religious turn, the anguished Mac Giolla Phádraig asks whether such plundering and destroying of the Gaels 'ag cách' (by all; 10) can be acceptable to a beloved Lord. He describes the Gaels as 'gan bú ná brí' (without kindness or strength; 13), instead passively 'súil gach lá / le cúrsa gaoithe' (hoping every day / for a change of wind; 13–14), the description acknowledging the social death and impotence of the Irish men it makes victims. The poet must ultimately testify to male humiliation, however, concluding by exclaiming in vividly embodied grief, 'Ailiú lem chroí!' (Alas my heart!; 15), and asking plaintively, ''mbiam choíche ag umhlacht dáibh / nó an dtiubhra an bríste díol don triús go brách?' (Will we be ever yielding to them / or will the trews [trousers, worn by Irishmen] give satisfaction to the breeches [worn by Englishmen] forever?; 15–16). In these lines, Mac Giolla Phádraig expresses his fear that the Gaels will face perpetual submission or bowing down ('umhlacht') in economic and political subordination to their new overlords by giving them 'díol' (pay; compensation; rent; requital and hence revenge or payback). The translation of 'díol' as satisfaction evokes not only this dual sense of payment and retaliation but also the fraught power dynamics and sexualised humiliation encoded in the metonymic reference to garments for men's lower bodies, where *trousers* bend or bow in submission before vengeful and dominant *breeches*. The recurrence of the charged sodomitical representation of English political dominance in this last, resonant image encodes the particularly masculine humiliation from which all these post-Kinsale poets cannot quite escape – except in dreams of heroic resistance by resurgent Irish men.

I wish to thank the editors, Tanya Gressley, Jeannette Jones, Margot Gayle Backus, Hildegund Müller, Mariann Jelinek, the Hesburgh Library staff and the scientists at Pfizer and Moderna. All mistakes my own.

Chapter 2

Young Ireland, Slavery and the Gender of Shame

Marjorie Howes

This essay examines the ideological, rhetorical and historical complexities of Young Ireland by focusing on the shifting, varied and messy uses of the term 'slavery', and their relation to shame, in the Atlantic world of the 1840s. The most prominent Young Irelanders included subsequently canonised patriots such as Thomas Davis, Charles Gavan Duffy, John Dillon and John Mitchel. The journal associated with them, the *Nation*, began publication in 1842. It immediately became a huge success with an unprecedented circulation, and in 1843 the editors began publishing the *Spirit of the Nation* volumes, which collected poetry from the journal. These books proved massively popular, were reprinted in Great Britain and the United States and, according to the editors in 1845, were 'to be found everywhere, from the English Admiral's cabin to the Irish peasant's – from Dublin to Boston, to Sydney, to Calcutta'.[1] Historically speaking, it was these books of poetry that had the most enduring influence on later generations of Irish and Irish-American readers. Given that influence, surprisingly little work has been done to analyse the specific poetic, iconographic and ideological features of their literary production. As a group, they were far from monolithic, and there is much to be said about the differences and debates among them. But here I focus on patterns of representation that characterised the movement as a whole and help place it in the larger international context of its time. I argue that the particular shape of Young Ireland's complexities owes a great deal to their previously neglected

[1] John Kelly, ed., *The Spirit of the Nation* (Poole and Washington DC: Woodstock Books, 1998 [facsimile of *The Spirit of the Nation* (Dublin: James Duffy, 1845)]), v. Subsequent references will be cited parenthetically.

engagement – a partial, reluctant and contradictory engagement – with American chattel slavery and with the abolitionist discourses circulating around the Atlantic world during the period.

The Slipperiness of Slavery

The complexities of this engagement were illustrated in September 1847, during the height of the Great Famine, when the *Nation* printed two items whose titles announced they concerned the subject of slavery.[2] The first was a brief item called 'Slavery in America'. The *Nation* reported that 'James Haughton has sent, for publication in the *Nation*, a rather lengthened argument not only against Slavery and Slaveholders, but against Irishmen receiving aid from Slaveholders, speaking kindly of Slaveholders, or omitting, whenever they speak of America and the American War of Independence, to denounce and execrate the 'criminals' who have Slaves in that country'. The editors continued, 'We have long since expressed our opinions on these points, and shall not enter into controversy about them again; but inasmuch as we do not undertake to defend the institution of Slavery, and hold all kinds of cruelty and oppression in quite as deep abhorrence as Mr. Haughton does, we willingly give the extract he sends us from the advertising columns of American papers; let these advertisements tell their own story and produce their own natural impression. We do not believe any comments of Mr. Haughton could add to the effect in the least:

> Ran away, my negro man Richard. A reward of twenty-five dollars will be paid for his apprehension, dead or alive. Satisfactory proof will only be required of his being killed.
>
> D. A. Rhodes, Alabama.
>
> About the 1st of March last, the negro man Ramsom left me, without the least provocation whatever. I will give a reward of twenty dollars for said negro, if taken dead or alive; and if killed in any attempt, an advance of five dollars will be paid. B. Johnson, Crawford Co., Geo.
>
> Was committed to jail, a negro boy named Jim – had a large lock chain round his neck. Wm. Toler, Sheriff, Simpson Co., Miss.
>
> Ran away, a negro man named David, with some iron hobbles around each ankle. H. Loflana, Staunton, Va.'[3]

[2] I am greatly indebted to Rose Novak for calling my attention to these articles.

[3] *Nation*, 27 September 1847.

A few pages later, a longer article appeared, this one entitled 'Irish Slaves'. Reprinted from the *Times* of London, the article described the harrowing conditions on the coffin ships, and the appalling situation in Grosse Isle, Canada, where thousands of Irish migrants had died – in transit, in quarantine or shortly after arrival – in the preceding months. Grosse Isle became one of the most notorious and horrific episodes of the Famine.[4] While the editors had declined to interpret the reprinted material in 'Slavery in America', or to include Haughton's interpretation, claiming that the advertisements would speak for themselves, they pointedly described the reprinted material in 'Irish Slaves', which was already highly interpreted, as a picture to make men 'mad, or stern as death in their hatred of the system that makes them slaves'. The *Times* writer compared the plight of the Irish to the sufferings of other peoples in history, and claimed that the Famine Irish endured a level of suffering that was unique:

> There is one horrible feature of the recent, not to say the present visitation, which is entirely new. The fact of more than a hundred thousand souls flying from the very midst of the calamity across a great ocean to a new world, crowding into insufficient vessels, scrambling for a footing on a deck and a berth in a hold, committing themselves to these worse than prisons, while their frames were wasted with ill fare and their blood infected with disease, fighting for months of unutterable wretchedness against the elements without and pestilence within, giving almost hourly victims to the deep, landing at length on shores already terrified and diseased, consigned to encampments of the dying and of the dead, spreading death wherever they roam, and having no other prospect before them than a long continuance of these horrors in a still farther flight across forests and lakes under a Canadian sun and a Canadian forest – all these are circumstances beyond the experience of the Greek historian or the Latin poet, and such as an Irish pestilence alone could produce. The writer concludes: The worst horrors of the slave trade which it is the boast or the ambition of this empire to suppress, at any cost, have been re-enacted in the flight of British subjects from their native shores.[5]

The juxtaposition of these two articles embodies a complex set of interlocking circumatlantic discourses involving the term 'slavery' in different ways and including various acts of shaming or attempted shaming. First, and most obviously, the editors of the *Nation* apparently saw no contradiction in using slavery to denote both American chattel

[4] Michael Quigley, 'Grosse Ile: Canada's Famine Memorial', in Arthur Gribben, ed., *The Great Famine and the Irish Diaspora* (Amherst: University of Massachusetts Press, 1999), 133–54.

[5] *Nation*, 25 September 1847.

slavery and the plight of the Famine Irish. This was not uncommon; during the nineteenth century, the term was used by various observers to describe a wide range of oppressive situations. As Murray Pittock has shown, 'slavery had . . . long been used to describe the nature and condition of the politically disaffected'.[6] During the 1840s, when powerful circumatlantic voices argued for abolition, such linguistic promiscuity, while widespread, did not pass uncontested. During his nearly two-year speaking tour of England, Scotland and Ireland, which had ended in April 1847, Frederick Douglass regularly went out of his way to repudiate uses of the term 'slavery' to describe the oppression of the Irish. He insisted over and over again that the Irish were poor, but they were not property.[7] In December 1845 in Belfast, for example, he reported that, 'since he had come to Ireland, he had been thus accosted: "We are slaves here as well as your countrymen in America"'. He replied that such statements 'did not sufficiently distinguish between certain forms of oppression and slavery. Slavery was not what took away any one right or property in man: it took man himself and made him the property of his fellow. It was what unmans man, takes him from himself, dooms him as a degraded thing'.[8] I will return to Douglass's gendered sense of slavery as 'unmanning' and degrading later in this essay.

Pittock's analysis of how, during the eighteenth and nineteenth centuries, 'the language used to describe slavery as a condition remained slippery and problematic' focuses specifically on a 'damaging metaphorical confusion between the voluntary and involuntary status of slavery', the former being 'inherited from an earlier language unconcerned with black slavery, but seeing the condition as one brought about by tyranny and voluntary subjection to it'.[9] This older discourse of slavery involved the idea that 'to be a freeman and not a slave was in some sense a *moral* choice'.[10] In other words, the slipperiness Pittock describes involved the issue of culpability, and therefore of shame – in particular, the question of who should be shamed: the tyrant/slaveholder or the slave? Here I am less concerned with shame as an actual affect that is felt by individual subjects, or is to be distinguished from guilt, than I am with how

[6] Murray Pittock, 'Slavery as a Political Metaphor in Scotland and Ireland in the Age of Burns', in Leith Davis, Holly Faith Nelson and Sharon Alker, eds, *Robert Burns and Transatlantic Culture* (Farnham, Surrey; Burlington, VT: Ashgate, 2012), 20.

[7] John Blassingame, ed., *The Frederick Douglass Papers Series One: Speeches, Debates, and Interviews Volume 1: 1841–46* (New Haven and London: Yale University Press, 1979), 78, 93, 134–5, 183, 273, 365–6, 399.

[8] Blassingame, *Frederick Douglass Papers*, 93.

[9] Pittock, 'Slavery', 19.

[10] Pittock, 'Slavery', 19–20.

political discourses seek to appeal to, mobilise and direct shame. In this sense, I am interested in 'shame' as a verb, an action, successful or not, rather than as a noun or a subjective state.

Both *Nation* items engaged in complex acts of shaming. James Haughton was a well-known and uncompromising Irish abolitionist; along with Richard Webb (who published *The Narrative of Frederick Douglass* in Dublin) and Richard Allen, he was at the centre of the Dublin anti-slavery scene. Haughton sought to shame the Young Irelanders into taking a decisive stance against American chattel slavery; he did so by transferring a well-known abolitionist tactic for shaming American slaveholders to an Irish context. The *Times* writer, on the other hand, sought to shame the British for their hypocrisy in congratulating themselves on their commitment to abolition while ignoring the plight of the Famine Irish. Intentionally or not, the writer also seems to borrow from abolitionist discourses by offering a version of the 'middle passage' associated with slave ships. The editors of the *Nation* resisted Haughton's effort to shame them. They reprinted the material Haughton sent them, but they did so grudgingly and partially, suppressing Haughton's letter and declining to comment on the material presented. In contrast, they enthusiastically embraced the *Times* writer's shaming of the British, delivering a forceful political comment on the *Times* article that placed it in the broader context of ongoing nationalist calls to action.

Young Ireland's cautious, arm's-length treatment of Haughton reflected a significant tactical and rhetorical dilemma. With the (later) notorious exception of John Mitchel, who eventually settled in the United States in 1854 and did become overtly pro-slavery, Young Irelanders did not want to defend American chattel slavery. But they had also watched Daniel O'Connell's failed efforts to win Irish Americans over to the abolitionist cause and were reluctant to risk alienating Irish Americans by criticising slavery overtly. As the evident exasperation of the editor of the *Nation* in the 'Slavery in America' article indicates, they had indeed been expressing themselves on the issue of slavery for some time, despite their desire to avoid the subject, and their views had evolved noticeably. As early as 1839, when Davis and Duffy wrote for a different publication, they felt compelled to state their positions on slavery. Early in 1841, two editorials on the 'Abomination of slavery' appeared in the *Morning Register* a week apart, written by either Davis or John Dillon.[11]

[11] John Neylon Molony, *A Soul Came Into Ireland: Thomas Davis, 1814–1845: A Biography* (Dublin: Geography Publications, 1995), 62.

A few weeks later, Davis accused the Tories of hypocrisy over their anti-slavery stance and stressed his own condemnation of slavery.[12] A few years later, in 1845, editorials written by Davis condemned slavery, but stressed gratitude for American support for Repeal, and urged Irish Repealers not to damage the cause by provoking debates on other subjects.[13] Another editorial borrowed a rhetorical sleight of hand from the British that was commonly used to argue in favour of colonial rule for Ireland by claiming that the ignorance and degradation of the oppressed, which had been produced by their very oppression, rendered them unfit for freedom. It opined that 'The wickedness of slavery has made emancipation perilous; for the negro has all the vices, ignorance, and wild impulses of a slave. Yet the system is doomed to perish . . .'.[14] In February 1847, the *Nation*, now edited by Duffy, featured an editorial that claimed 'we have really so very urgent affairs at home – so much abolition of white slavery to effect if we can . . . that all our exertions will be needed in Ireland. Carolina planters never devoured our substance, nor drove away our sheep and oxen for a spoil'. By September 1847, then, Young Ireland had arrived at a stance towards abolitionists like Haughton that verged on hostility.[15]

Weapons and Wounds

However, during these same years the poetry Young Ireland was producing was profoundly influenced by abolitionist discourses in general and by the kind of imagery evident in Haughton's submission to the *Nation* in particular. In sending American newspaper advertisements concerning runaway slaves to the *Nation*, Haughton was employing a well-established abolitionist tactic. Some such advertisements in the American press were placed by slaveholders and described runaway slaves in the hope of securing their return; others were placed by local officials. Reprinting them shamed slaveholders by turning their own words against them; they recorded their brutal inscriptions of identifying marks on the bodies of their slaves and highlighted the

[12] Molony, *A Soul Came*, 69.
[13] *Nation*, 5, 19 April, 9 August 1845. See also Moloney, 285, and Helen F. Mulvey, *Thomas Davis and Ireland: A Biographical Study* (Washington: The Catholic University of America Press, 2003), 187.
[14] *Nation*, 9 August 1845.
[15] For a strong version of this claim, see Ian Delahanty, 'A Noble Empire in the West': Young Ireland, the United States, and Slavery', *Britain and the World* 6:2 (2013): 171.

instruments of captivity and torture used to perpetuate the system. The rhetorical strategy of reprinting them helped counter pro-slavery claims that abuses were rare under slavery, that slaves did not want to run away and that abolitionists often made up their accounts of brutality. Reprinted advertisements cast slaveholders as hypocritical and self-defeating, and abolitionists as truthful and their claims as independently verifiable. They were particularly effective in conveying the horrors of slavery to people outside the American South. As texts, most of them emphasised two things: the slave's body, marked and wounded, and the physical weapons slaveholders employed – whips, brands, collars and chains. Their laconic, unemotional descriptions were initially created for use in a legal and economic context. When transferred to a moral and political context, however, they could become sensational spectacles of violence that both shamed the people who found the initial context appropriate – slaveholders – and solicited sympathy for the enslaved.

On the other hand, as scholars have been noting for decades, such representations are deeply problematic in several respects. Elaine Scarry has proposed that any effort to craft 'verbal strategies for overcoming' physical suffering's assault on language through representations of wounds and weapons threatens to obscure pain further, to give a voice to the torturer rather than the victim.[16] And scholars like Marcus Wood have analysed the unique problems raised by depictions of the suffering of slaves. In particular, Wood observes that, in visual artists' representations of slave torture, the reliance on objects tends to render slaves themselves as objects: 'The slave emerges predominantly as an object afflicted, not as a subject capable of describing his or her affliction. The pain of slaves, then translated into imagery and visual narrative, is related to, imparted through, a series of objects. These objects are not unique to slavery, but familiar to Western experience: shackles, chains, collars, stocks, brands, gallows, cages, bits, bridles, thumbscrews, fires and whips.'[17] Meredith McGill notes a related danger inherent in reprinting the newspaper advertisements, specifically in the act of taking them out of their original contexts and transferring them to new ones. As a result, she suggests, they can threaten to 'float free of reference, slipping from moral condemnation into voyeurism'.[18] In reprinting Haughton's

[16] Elaine Scarry, *The Body in Pain* (New York: Oxford University Press, 1985), 13, 17.

[17] Marcus Wood, *Blind Memory: Visual Representations of Slavery in England and America* (New York: Routledge, 2000), 216.

[18] Meredith McGill, *American Literature and the Culture of Reprinting, 1834–1853* (Philadelphia: University of Pennsylvania Press, 2003), 129.

ads, and in incorporating into their writings imagery and vocabulary derived, in part, from them, Young Ireland introduced still other potentially problematic representational issues.

The iconography of wounds and weapons evident in the advertisements constitutes one abolitionist discourse among many, of course, but it was a discourse that circulated very widely across the Atlantic world during the 1840s. Theodore Weld's best-selling 1839 abolitionist pamphlet *American Slavery As It Is: Testimony of a Thousand Witnesses*, which reprinted large numbers of them, was perhaps the most influential and pervasive instance. When it was published, it ranked as the best-selling anti-slavery tract in American history, selling 100,000 copies in the first year.[19] It also provided a wealth of material for other writers. In 1842, Charles Dickens took some advertisements from Weld's book, choosing examples from chapters entitled 'Tortures, By Iron Collars, Chains, Fetters, Handcuffs, &c' and 'Brandings, Maimings, Gun-Shot Wounds, &c'.[20] and reprinted them in *American Notes for General Circulation*. The book recounts his travels in the United States and indicts an America built, in part, on slavery. The chapter of *American Notes* entitled 'Slavery' recounts and refutes pro-slavery arguments, reprints related newspaper articles, and includes advertisements very similar to Haughton's: 'Run away, Negress Caroline, Had on a collar with one prong turned down. . . Was committed to jail, a negro man. Says his name is Josiah. His back very much scarred by the whip; and branded on the thigh and hips in three or four places, thus (JM). The rim of his right ear has been bit or cut off.'[21] Ten years later, Harriet Beecher Stowe would also draw on Weld's book in *A Key to Uncle Tom's Cabin*, which she published to refute accusations that the portrait of slavery in her famous novel was inaccurate.

Haughton, Weld, Dickens and Stowe were not the only contemporary observers from whom Irish audiences learned about reprinted advertisements for runaway slaves and the shocking imagery they contained. Abolitionist orators often read advertisements during their speeches and, further, sometimes displayed physical objects as well. Douglass's tour had begun in Dublin, and Haughton introduced him there on 1 October at the Dublin Music Hall, where Douglass told audiences 'I have felt the lash myself; my back is

[19] Stephen Browne, '"Like Gory Spectres": Representing Evil in Theodore Weld's *American Slavey As It Is*', *Quarterly Journal of Speech* 80 (August 1994): 277.
[20] McGill, *American Literature*, 128.
[21] Charles Dickens, *American Notes for General Circulation* (London: Penguin, 2000 [1842]), 255, 256.

scarred with it.'[22] He spoke all over England, Scotland and Ireland, and he employed a cluster of related rhetorical strategies designed to highlight the suffering bodies of slaves and the violent brutality of slaveholders. (This cluster represents just one element in Douglass's abolitionist discourse; he was a mesmerising performer and was well-known for the skill and variety of his oratorical techniques.) He read advertisements for runaway slaves from American newspapers[23] and invoked Weld's book.[24] He referred to the scars on his own back, and described his own abuse, and the abuse of others, at the hands of slaveholders.[25] He argued that, since slaves were never contented with their lot, slavery could only be maintained through constant violence, and he repeatedly gave his listeners gruesome lists of what he called the 'bloody paraphernalia' of slavery: whips, chains, brands, thumb-screws and other weapons.[26] Sometimes he held up actual objects. During a speech in Limerick in 1845 he exhibited, to spectacular effect, a collar, leg irons, handcuffs and a bloody whip.[27] Finally, even in his more abstract discussions of slavery, Douglass constantly used a metonymic vocabulary that kept the physical brutalities of slavery before his listeners. His speeches are filled with references to chains, fetters and the lash as terms that embodied the general condition of slavery.

Douglass was not the only African-American abolitionist to take his message, and this iconography of slavery, to the British Isles. In fact, beginning in the 1830s, substantial numbers of African Americans left the United States and embarked on such speaking tours. Their numbers peaked during the 1840s and early 1850s, and the

[22] Blassingame, *Frederick Douglass Papers*, 34, 36. On Douglass in Ireland, see Fionnghuala Sweeney, *Frederick Douglass and the Atlantic World* (Liverpool: Liverpool University Press, 2007), Alan Rice and Martin Crawford, eds, *Liberating Sojourn: Frederick Douglass and Transatlantic Reform* (Athens: University of Georgia Press, 1999), Laurence Fenton, *Frederick Douglass in Ireland: The Black O'Connell* (Cork: Collins Press, 2014), Christine Kinealy, ed., *Frederick Douglass and Ireland: In His Own Words* (New York: Routledge, 2018) and Fionnghuala Sweeney, Fionnuala Dillon and Maria Stuart, eds, *Ireland, Slavery, Anti-Slavery, and Empire* (New York: Routledge, 2018).

[23] Blassingame, *Frederick Douglass Papers*, 51–2, 155, 164, 190, 275–6, 367, 377–8, 401.

[24] Blassingame, *Frederick Douglass Papers*, 275, 279.

[25] Blassingame, *Frederick Douglass Papers*, 37, 41, 323, 357, 375, 418, 461, 467.

[26] Blassingame, *Frederick Douglass Papers*, 17, 37, 43, 94–5, 136–7, 160, 190, 238, 274–5, 276, 282, 322, 327, 343, 349, 373, 380, 404, 409, 418, 465, 470, 476–7, 479.

[27] Nini Rodgers, *Ireland, Slavery and Anti-Slavery: 1612–1865* (London: Palgrave Macmillan, 2007), 283. See also Blassingame, *Frederick Douglass Papers*, 35, 85.

group included Charles Lenox Remond, Henry Highland Garnet, Josiah Henson, Sarah Remond, William Allen, William Wells Brown, Edmund Kelly and Henry 'Box' Brown. A number of them were particularly well received in Ireland; Peter Ripley observes that several of these Black lecturers 'discovered that an Irish tour could rejuvenate a flagging British anti-slavery mission'.[28] Their performances varied, of course, in a number of respects, but many of them shared, at least to some extent, the verbal and visual language of wounded bodies and instruments of violence. The *Nation* studiously avoided reporting on their speeches, but the Young Irelanders were surely aware of them.

Douglass, in turn, was acutely aware that he was participating in a circumatlantic discourse, and that the iconography of wounds and weapons had a significant public impact. Speaking in Scotland in 1846, he claimed that 'the notice of Dickens had more effect in calling attention to' slavery in the British Isles than 'all the books published in America for ten years'.[29] He later invoked Dickens's slavery chapter as evidence that physical abuse must be used to keep slaves in slavery.[30] Similarly, Daniel O'Connell read *American Notes*, was impressed by it, and was particularly struck by the newspaper advertisements. He commented, 'his chapter containing the advertisements respecting negro slavery, is more calculated to augment the fixed detestation of slavery than the most brilliant declamation, or the most splendid eloquence'.[31] Dickens, meanwhile, in his conclusion to that chapter, had wrapped up his anti-slavery argument by introducing the example of the Irish, though not necessarily in a way that the Irish were likely to appreciate. He compared the violence of slavery to agrarian crime in Ireland, asking: 'shall we declaim against the ignorant peasantry of Ireland, and mince the matter when these American taskmasters are in question? Shall we cry shame on the brutality of those who hamstring cattle and spare the lights of Freedom upon earth who notch the ears of men and women, cut pleasant posies in the shrinking flesh, learn to write with pens of red-hot iron on the human face, rack their poetic fancies for liveries of mutilation which their slaves shall wear for life and carry to the grave, break living limbs as did the soldiery

[28] C. Peter Ripley, ed., *The Black Abolitionist Papers Volume I the British Isles, 1830–1865* (Chapel Hill and London: University of North Carolina Press, 1985), 332.

[29] Blassingame, *Frederick Douglass Papers*, 220.

[30] Blassingame, *Frederick Douglass Papers*, 275.

[31] From a letter quoted in the *Foreign Quarterly Review* (American edition), XXXI, 152:2 (April 1843). Quoted in Louise H. Johnson, 'The Source of the Chapter on Slavery in Dickens's *American Notes*', *American Literature* 14:4 (January 1943): 430.

who mocked and slew the Saviour of the world, and set defenseless creatures up for targets!'[32]

Dickens's language emphasises the *legibility* of slaves' wounded bodies and the implements that mutilated them: they were texts or liveries, created by pens and poetic fancies that demand to be read and interpreted. And his question highlights the act of shaming rather than shame itself; he does not ask – who should be ashamed? Rather, he asks: who should we shame? Who should we cry shame on? This question, and the imperative to interpret that it presupposes (an imperative the editors of the *Nation* had refused in relation to Haughton's ads), lay at the heart of Young Ireland's uncomfortable engagement with the term 'slavery' in general. Their writings, especially their poetry, display a profound hesitation about where the true shame of slavery lay: was it an involuntary and blameless state or a voluntary and therefore shameful one? This confusion was amplified by their partial absorption of the iconography of wounds and weapons that was circulating so prominently at the time. Pittock suggests that, beginning in the early nineteenth century, 'the increasing use of chains as an iconographic symbol of enslavement may have had something to do with the importance of depicting slavery as an externally imposed, not inwardly accepted state'.[33] This was certainly true of abolitionist discourse generally and of O'Connell, whose public displays sometimes featured or imitated Josiah Wedgewood's famous image of a kneeling African in chains. But Young Ireland's literary production combined those patterns with an older vocabulary, one that was based in classical republicanism. This definition of slavery suggested it was a voluntary or semi-voluntary state, and that the marks of physical violence indicated degradation, passivity and shame rather than simply signifying suffering. Thus, Young Ireland appropriated the imagery of wounded bodies and the instruments of violence and captivity but, by combining them with claims that to be a slave was to be culpable, degraded, helpless and/or feminised, they reinforced precisely the ambiguity that Pittock argues such imagery was designed to counter in other contexts.

There are a number of issues and themes that recur in Young Ireland's literary production, such as the importance of knowledge and education, the imperative to overcome sectarian division, and the need to foster and embrace self-reliance, courage and militarism. Underlying, and complicating, all these ideological tenets and rhetorical

[32] Dickens, *American Notes*, 265.
[33] Pittock, 'Slavery', 25–6.

gestures was Young Ireland's contradictory discourse around slavery and shame, wounds and weapons. Young Ireland's poetry embraced the *Times* writer's use of 'slavery' to describe the general plight of the Irish under British rule. But they also invoked the kind of weapons and instruments of captivity that characterised slavery the way Haughton's advertisements did. No constellation of words and images appears so often in the poetry of the *Nation* as a cluster including slavery, chains, fetters, the lash and branding. In the 1845 version of the *Spirit of the Nation*, which contains 147 poems, there are roughly eighty such references. Rather than producing homogeneity or repetition, however, this iconography embodies a series of complex and incomplete negotiations around how to define the term 'slavery', how to interpret bodily marks of abuse or suffering, and exactly who nationalist literary culture should shame, and why.

The Gender of Shame

Some Young Ireland verse emphasised that the Irish were 'poor fetter'd slaves' bound with 'the captive's chain' (10), helpless victims of shameful British brutality who were waiting to be rescued by some external force. Sliabh Cuilinn's 'The Thirtieth of May' describes Ireland as 'Down-stricken, gagged, and chained' (205), Duffy's 'Innis-Eoghain' predicts 'not long shall the nation in slavery groan' (111) and Davis's 'Song of the Volunteers of 1782' asserts 'The chain is broke – the Saxon yoke / From off our neck is taken' (36). John O'Connell's 'What's my Thought Like?' wishes for a time when Ireland will be 'no longer marked and cursed with slav'ry's withering brand' and 'No longer Slave to England!' (42). D. F. M'Carthy's 'The Voice and the Pen' testifies to the liberatory power of words, asking 'What burst the chain far o'er the main, / And brightens the captive's den?' (211). The poem continues: 'Let a word be flung from the orator's tongue, / Or a drop from the fearless pen, / And the chains accursed asunder burst, / That fettered the minds of men!' (212). In these instances, Irish slavery is an involuntary, and therefore blameless, captivity, a state that the slave has no power to resist or change on his or her own, and all the shame belongs to the British tyrant.

Such a model lent itself particularly to poems representing Ireland as a helpless woman in need of rescue. John O'Connell's 'Was it a Dream?' (95–6) imagines Ireland and England as two female figures, the former held physically captive by the latter. Ireland is a figure 'in woe and chains' and is a 'hapless slave' while England boasts, 'I hold thy chain thou busy fool, mine ire thou mayest provoke, / And bring destruction on thine head, but never shake my yoke'. In this poem, Ireland's inability to resist her oppression is coded as an appealing form of femininity; she is 'beauteous', 'mild and calm', and meekly prays to God for deliverance. England's domination of her is merely physical and is embodied in implements of violence and captivity: 'Again the proud one scornful laughed, and waved again her brand, / The other mutely rais'd to Heaven her chain'd and fetter'd hand'. The end of the poem imagines some external force – God or 'a storm' that 'passed o'er the scene' – sweeping in to lay England low and rescue helpless Ireland.

Such 'feminine' passivity was more problematic in Young Ireland's poems about Irish men, given their penchant for urging the Irish to adopt manly virtues like self-reliance, bravery and military valour. Most often, Young Ireland employed the iconography of wounds and weapons to characterise Irish slavery as a voluntary or semi-voluntary state, one that registered the political weakness and abjection of the Irish and urged the need for rebellion. Much of their writing used 'slave' as an epithet, an insult – it signified a degraded and shameful state in which the oppressed fail to resist their subjugation. Ironically, the poetry appealing to this definition of slavery also returns obsessively to the suffering bodies and implements of captivity that abolitionist discourses associated with chattel slavery – chains, fetters, branding and the lash. For example, William Drennan's 'The Irish Arms' Bill' laments 'My country, alas! we may blush for thee now, / The brand of the slave broadly stamp'd on thy brow!' (24). Sliabh Cuilinn's 'The Union' laments that 'ruined trade and wealth decayed are slavery's surest brand' (148). In these and other similar poems, bodily wounding, the brand, demands to be read and interpreted – and is found to shame the Irish for their voluntary enslavement.

Another poem of Drennan's, 'The Slaves' Bill' (135–6), revolves almost entirely around the imagery of branding. The opening stanza shames the Irish through multiple images of the brand: 'Aye, brand our arms, nor them alone, / But brand our brows; degraded race'. Such branding is explicitly allied with a loss of masculinity: 'Men! Are we men? We talk as such, / Heav'ns, how we talk! but – vain alarms – / Nought masculine endures so much, / Then brand our brows, as well as arms!' The brand represents the Irish as shamefully, even willfully, complicit in their oppression: 'This brand is not an ugly thing – / May seem an ornament, indeed; / The shame to some would be the sting, / But not to slaves who dare not bleed!' The Irish are slaves because they accept their condition, and because they are not ashamed of this; they are degraded but do not feel their degradation; they cannot feel disgrace. The task of nationalist literature lies in the act of shaming them. Each stanza returns to the image of the brand, which has a complex function. It shames the Irish for their weakness, coded simultaneously as feminisation and slavery, and for their inability or unwillingness to resist British rule effectively. It begins as a physical mark and expands into a metaphor for the shaming of the entire nation: 'Yes, brand our language, faith, and name!' The final stanza predicts that eventually the Irish will be driven to resist, at a time when 'rage finds weapons, ev'rywhere, / For Nature's two unbranded arms!'

Scores of other poems produced by Young Ireland writers during the 1840s employ similar terminology and imagery. 'Tyrol and Ireland', attributed to Theta, asks, 'Oh, idiots! Feel you not the lash?' (17). 'Aid Yourselves and God Will Aid You', by Sliabh Cuilinn, threatens the Irish that if they remain 'Drugged with slavery's cup like Circe's' then 'Slave of slaves' shall be engraven / On your foreheads evermore' (281). The same author's 'England's Ultimatum' expresses this ultimatum as 'Slaves lie down and kiss your chains' (199). The poem contains a version of the wounds and weapons, the 'bloody paraphernalia' of slavery, including 'English gyve on Irish sinew' and 'Leaded thongs for rebel hides, / Flaming thatch, and burthen'd gibbet' (200). A number of such poems emphasise the slaves' responsibility for perpetuating their own oppression. 'Cymric Rule and Cymric Rulers' proposes that 'Coward hearts are self-subduing; / Fetters last by slaves' renewing'.[34] And 'Our Own Again' proposes that 'By the slave his chain is wrought'.[35] Other invocations of slavery as voluntary, and therefore shameful, in *The Spirit of the Nation* include 'slavish yoke', 'coward-slave', 'slumbering slaves', 'slaves and starvelings', 'recreant slave', 'willing slave', 'brawling slave', 'slavish fear', 'slavish knee' and 'tranquil slave'.[36] It is difficult to over-estimate just how pervasive these terms, and the iconography of slavery attached to them, are in Young Ireland's poetry. They associate slave status with servility, cowardice, complacency, ignorance and emasculation.

A number of poems illustrate how this iconography of slavery as shameful was particular to men. D. F. M'Carthy's 'A New Year's Song'

[34] Thomas Davis, *The Poems of Thomas Davis* (Dublin: James Duffy; London: Simpkin, Marshall and Co., 1846), 54.
[35] Davis, *The Poems of Thomas Davis*, 61.
[36] Davis, *The Poems of Thomas Davis*, 50, 56, 72, 58, 198, 285, 310, 152, 55, 183.

(190–1), which describes Ireland's captivity as 'base ignoble chains', scolds: 'Too long we've borne the servile yoke – / Too long the slavish chain', and concludes, 'The coward slave is never freed'. Standing up to the English involves reclaiming Irish masculinity: 'But, oh! Let not our foes forget / we're *men*'. Or, as 'The Thirtieth of May' puts it, 'Better to live man's life one day / Than sleep a hundred years away / A brute, or stone, or slave' (207). The famous ballad 'The Memory of the Dead' begins, 'Who fears to speak of Ninety-Eight?' (46–7), and the following lines paint a portrait of such a man, who is 'all a knave, or half a slave'. The poem's refrain repeatedly invokes, in contrast, 'true men, like you, men'. Davis's essays and poetry consistently advocate education, self-help, masculinity and military bravery as the Irish path to independence, and contrast these virtues with passivity, slavery and shame.[37] As he wrote in 'The History of Ireland', the Irish must 'try, by teaching and example, to lift up the souls of all our family and neighbours, to that pitch of industry, courage, information and wisdom necessary to enable an enslaved, dark and starving people to become free, rich and rational'.[38] Thus the involuntary or chattel slavery suggested by chains, brands and whips in other contexts became, in much of the *Nation*'s literary production, a shameful, willing, feminised helplessness that functioned as the opposite of nationalist self-reliance and self-assertion. Young Ireland's version of wounds and weapons, the grisly imagery offered by advertisements for runaway slaves and Douglass's litanies of the 'bloody paraphernalia' of slavery all circulated publicly throughout the Atlantic world during the 1840s, and the writers and thinkers who employed them were clearly aware of one another. Like most abolitionists, Douglass admired O'Connell immensely; Douglass met him during his tour, was terrifically impressed with him as an orator, praised him in his speeches, and was pleased when O'Connell referred to him as the 'Black O'Connell of America'. Douglass lamented that, by 1847, the year of O'Connell's death, Young Ireland had decisively refused to embrace his uncompromising abolitionist stance, remarking that O'Connell had been 'succeeded by the Duffys, Mitchells, Meaghers and others, men who loved liberty for themselves and their country

[37] See Davis, *The Poems of Thomas Davis*, 59, 86, 207, 216, 217, 326, 355, 381, 464–6. Patrick Maume connects Young Ireland with classical republicanism, which contrasts a corrupt central authority with the process of cultivating civic virtue through self-reliance, in 'Young Ireland, Arthur Griffith, and Republican Ideology: The Question of Continuity', *Éire-Ireland* 34:2 (Summer 1999): 157.

[38] Davis, *Poems of Thomas Davis*, 297.

but were utterly destitute of sympathy with the cause of liberty in countries other than their own'.[39]

The complexities of Young Ireland, slavery and shame extend beyond the fairly obvious facts that Douglass's opposition to Young Ireland here was just and that Young Ireland could be said to have misappropriated abolitionists' iconography of wounds and weapons. They also reveal deep, circumatlantic commonalities between Irish cultural nationalism and abolition, commonalities structured, above all, by gender. By 1847, Douglass had come to share, in different forms and for different reasons, Young Ireland's anxiety that the state of slavery might be feminised, degrading and shameful. As is well known, Douglass consistently equated freedom with manhood, not just in his famous *Narrative*, but in other contexts as well.[40] The remarks quoted earlier, in which Douglass rejected the notion of Irish slaves, did so by aligning slavery with emasculation and shameful degradation: slavery 'unmans man, takes him from himself, dooms him as a degraded thing'. Douglass, of course, insisted that slavery was an involuntary state and that the arsenal of weapons slaveholders employed proved this. However, his tendency to equate freedom with manhood and slavery with feminisation and degradation pointed towards slavery as a shameful state that indicated some lack or weakness in the slave. During his time in the British Isles this implication became increasingly uncomfortable for Douglass, and it did so because of the major transformation that scholars agree took place, or began to take place, during his tour there. The consensus is that he transformed himself from a runaway slave into a finished, 'bourgeois intellectual'[41] and American man of letters. He achieved greater confidence, and greater independence from William Lloyd Garrison and other white abolitionists who wanted to be his handlers. He came home ready to start his own newspaper, and he had earned enough money to buy his freedom. He wrote to Garrison from Belfast on New Year's Day 1846: 'I have spent some of the happiest moments of my life since landing in this country. I seem to have undergone a transformation. I live a new life.'[42]

[39] Quoted in Bill Rolston, 'Ireland of the Welcomes? Racism and Anti-Racism in Nineteenth Century Ireland', *Patterns of Prejudice* 38:4 (2004): 7.

[40] See Blassingame, *Fredrick Douglass Papers*, 94, 99, 136, 160.

[41] Rodgers, *Ireland, Slavery*, 284. See also Peter O'Neill, 'Frederick Douglass and the Irish', *Foilsiu* 5:1 (Spring 2006): 57–82, Fionnghuala Sweeney, *Frederick Douglass and the Atlantic World* and Alan Rice, *Liberating Sojourn: Frederick Douglass and Transatlantic Reform*.

[42] Peter O'Neill, 'Fredrick Douglass and Ireland', *Foilsiu* 5:1 (Spring 2006): 60.

This new life, and the dilemmas it posed for him, led to some subtle shifts in his rhetorical strategies. In his very early speeches, Douglass was often quite autobiographical and referred graphically to his own physical abuse while a slave. In an 1841 speech, for example, he said that 'while other abolitionists can describe the horrors of slavery, They cannot speak as I can from experience; they cannot refer you to a back covered with scars, as I can, for I have felt these wounds; I have suffered under the lash without the power of resisting.'[43] But, considering that Douglass thought of his journey to freedom as a reclaiming of his manhood, suffering without the power of resisting began to seem unmanly. Fairly early in his career he began to shift his emphasis, according to Cynthia Hamilton, to recounting cruelties he witnessed, like the whipping of his cousin Henny. This allowed him, Hamilton says, to 'protect his own masculinity from the depredations of acknowledged helplessness'.[44] During the British tour, he did mention both the scars on his own back and the weapons with which he had been assaulted. But he did so in a fairly brief and straightforward manner,[45] and over time he began to express reluctance to 'lift up the veil by giving you any experience of my own'.[46]

As time went on, he invoked Henny's abuse repeatedly and at greater length. The description of the violence done to her became a standard set-piece for Douglass and, as time went on, he couched that description in increasingly sensationalist terms. In Leeds, England, in 1846, for example, he introduced the Henny story this way: 'I am afraid you do not understand the awful character of these lashes. You must bring it before your mind. A human being in a perfect state of nudity, tied hand and foot to a stake, and a strong man standing behind with a heavy whip, knotted at the end, each blow cutting into the flesh, and leaving the warm blood dripping to the feet (sensation).'[47] As a number of scholars have noted, there is something voyeuristic, even pornographic about this kind of description, and this form of sensationalism was particular to Douglass's descriptions of women.

[43] Blassingame, *Fredrick Douglass Papers*, 77.
[44] Cynthia Hamilton, 'Frederick Douglass and the Gender Politics of Reform', in Alan J. Rice and Martin Crawford, eds, *Liberating Sojourn: Frederick Douglass and Transatlantic Reform* (Georgia: University of Georgia Press, 1999), 78.
[45] See Blassingame, *Fredrick Douglass Papers*, 16, 25, 36, 37, 41, 323, 357, 418, 461, 467.
[46] Blassingame, *Fredrick Douglass Papers*, 274. See also 375.
[47] Blassingame, *Fredrick Douglass Papers*, 485. See also 86, 188, 202, 279–80, 314, 357, 376, 401, 411–12, 418, 461, 482.

Young Ireland's references to slavery, wounds and weapons were less graphic and sensationalising, and were embedded in ballads rather than extended narratives. And their literary productions mostly lacked the rhetorical skill and imaginative richness and sophistication evident in Douglass's writings and speeches. But during the 1840s they inhabited a circumatlantic public sphere that brought them repeatedly into contact with the abolitionist discourses of thinkers like Douglass, Haughton and Dickens, and their work bears the marks of that contact. Young Ireland offers a specific example of how 'the language used to describe slavery as a condition remained slippery and problematic' at this time. The particular features of this example were rooted in the needs and dilemmas of an anti-colonial nationalism that sought to counter anti-Irish stereotypes and to encompass politics and culture, parliamentary agitation and physical force. How should the plight of the Irish be compared to chattel slavery, if at all? How should the visible signs of Irish suffering be interpreted? Did the oppression of Ireland bring shame upon the brutality of the British colonial power or upon the weakness of the Irish?

In conjunction with the 'metaphorical confusion' such examples of slipperiness indicate, it is also important to uncover the profoundly un-slippery, and indeed virtually immoveable, gender of shame: the assumption that to be shamed was to be feminised, and to be feminised was to be shamed. Joseph Valente has argued that late nineteenth-century Irish nationalisms embraced a 'myth of manliness' in which conventional masculine attributes such as aggression, passion and physical courage were combined with, and checked by, ethical/political principles such as self-discipline, duty and honour. For Irish nationalists, the purpose of this myth was to stand as an argument for their (masculine) fitness for self-governance while also preventing them from inhabiting an aggressive hypermasculinisation that would coincide with British stereotypes of the Irish as animalistic or uncivilised. As Valente shows, this formulation appears in numerous nationalist discourses, reaching its pinnacle in the works and thought of Patrick Pearse, especially in his characterisations of Cuchulain. The important role that ethical and moral principles played in it meant that shame, and the avoidance of shame, were crucial. Valente remarks that, for Pearse, 'Cuchulain rises to pre-eminence among the Irish heroes in adhering to and succeeding within a value system predicated upon the pursuit of fame and the avoidance of shame at any price'.[48]

[48] Joseph Valente, *The Myth of Manliness in Irish National Culture, 1880–1922* (Urbana; Springfield: University of Illinois Press, 2011), 160.

The opportunities and problems that slavery and abolitionism posed for Young Ireland were tactical, ideological, cultural and poetic all at once. And their responses to the circumatlantic prominence of the slavery question in the 1840s took multiple forms: willful avoidance, conscious engagement, unconscious borrowing and adaptation, and simultaneous participation in the same overarching structures of thought. During this period, the term 'slavery' was slippery in its own right and was employed by various commentators in various ways all over the Atlantic world. Young Ireland's uncertainty and discomfort over the issue, and its unstable imagery of weapons and wounds adapted from abolitionist discourse, added yet another layer of complexity. Through this imagery and other poetic strategies, their works display a profound hesitation over whether slavery was a voluntary or an involuntary state, and therefore over who should be shamed, the British or the Irish. Underlying all this complexity and hesitation was the foundation that Valente traces through various nationalist discourses, a foundation which, further, was shared by discourses surrounding slavery and abolition as well: the valorisation of manliness, and the association of shame with feminisation. Young Ireland and Frederick Douglass disagreed on whether or not the Irish could be called slaves, but they agreed on the gender of shame. Amid all their hesitations and uncertainties, Young Ireland's steady, unambiguous attachment to this deep ideological structure may go some way towards explaining why their poetry continued to be so influential as Irish nationalist discourses shaped and reshaped themselves in the following decades.

Part II

Religious Shame

Chapter 3

Recovering from Catholicism: The Internalisation Problem in Joyce

Seán Kennedy

In 'Belief and the Body', Pierre Bourdieu analyses how people internalise, and subsequently elaborate, a practical sense of the world. He challenges the pre-eminence of reason in philosophical accounts of human activity, including moral activity. Rather, practical sense is something we *do*. It is not always conscious or intentional. It is acquired and perfected in practice. Bourdieu distinguishes practical sense, from rational thought, as embodied feeling. It is an internalised capacity or disposition, not an innate ability, though it comes to seem like one, as experience is 'converted into motor schemes and body automatisms'. We become disposed to act and feel in certain unscripted ways. Driving is one obvious example: both spontaneous and habitual. Or riding a bike. What matters is not so much what we know or intend but those inculcated patterns of 'enacted belief' by which we react to things. At stake is less a state of knowledge than a 'state of the body'.[1] This lays the foundations for what we are calling the 'internalisation problem'. What if we no longer assent to our inculcated beliefs? What if we never had?

For recovering Catholics, the internalisation problem is one of unwitting complicity with a body of myth instituted in the body. Even as we no longer assent to Catholic orthodoxy with our minds, we continue to believe it with our bodies. How might we recover from this condition? The dictionary offers three definitions of 'recovery'.

Recover
Verb. Used with object.

1. to get back again or regain (something lost or taken away)
2. to make up for or make good (loss, damage, etc., to oneself)
3. to regain the strength, composure, balance, or the like, of oneself

[1] Pierre Bourdieu, 'Belief and the Body', in *The Logic of Practice* (Stanford: Stanford University Press, 1990), 68–9.

Of the three, the third is most pertinent to the recovering Catholic. There is no question of simply regaining something lost. Neither, since internalised beliefs endure – we become self-policing – can we simply make good our losses (of opportunity, of damage to oneself). Perhaps, then, recovery might mean the discovery of a new balance in oneself in the wake of inculcation. Having been constituted in submission to orthodoxy, we must recover ourselves from ourselves. But how can the site of the problem become the source of the solution? It is here that any 'recovering from Catholicism' project must situate itself. At stake is the possibility of integrity in the wake of inculcation to moral terror; required is a psychosexual and social anatomy of Roman Catholicism as embodied faith in an Irish context.

Joyce's Catholic Apostasy

The writings of James Joyce are an invaluable resource in this regard, since they offer just such an anatomy. They document the fate of one of Ireland's most famous recovering Catholics, James Joyce, in the guise of his fictional alter-ego, Stephen Dedalus. As is well known, Joyce's apostasy was not just the apostasy of an Irish Catholic but also an Irish Catholic apostasy. It was a rebellion against the Roman faith formulated in terms given to it – appropriated from within – the faith itself. Determined to escape the strictures of his faith through his art, Stephen can only transfigure himself into 'a priest of the eternal imagination, transmuting the daily bread of experience into the radiant body of everliving life'. His friend Cranly observes: 'It is a curious thing, do you know, how your mind is supersaturated with the religion in which you say you disbelieve'.[2] This is the internalisation problem. Even as he wishes to be free, Stephen must appeal to the very structures from which he desires to be liberated. Freedom is only conceivable within terms derived from his continuing domination. Even then, his body may not be biddable. He may resist his own recovery as a function of his inculcation. Much has already been written about the aesthetic aspects of this predicament: Stephen's 'applied Aquinas'.[3] The focus here is on the ethical aspect. Joyce was attuned to both.

[2] James Joyce, *Portrait of the Artist as a Young Man: A Norton Critical Edition*, edited by John Paul Riquelme (New York: Norton: 2007), 195; 212. Hereafter (P page).

[3] James Joyce, *Stephen Hero* (London: Paladin, 1991), 81. Hereafter (S page). Maurice Beebe, 'Joyce and Aquinas: The Theory of Aesthetics', *Philological Quarterly* 36 (1957): 20–35.

The ethical aspect of Joyce's internalisation problem is easily stated: internalisation precedes evaluation. As children of Catholicism, we internalise beliefs without the moral capacity to evaluate their content or implications. We accede to beliefs without the intellectual capacity to interrogate them. This is so, even as they become foundational aspects of our character. Kant's moral law was given *a priori*. Catholic law is an implant. This has momentous implications for the integrity of the Church, as well as for Catholic children. It is why Stephen can refer, famously, to the 'uncreated conscience of [his] race' (P 224). In effect, Catholic children are conscripted to an *ethos that is not one* – cannot be one – since any behaviour that is not a choice cannot be evaluated morally in the Kantian sense. Ethical conduct requires rational assent as its foundation.[4] If being raised Catholic is an early formation process, it is also an early deformation process, morally speaking. It precludes Catholics from obeying the law precisely by making them obedient to it. It is this short circuit which sets up the necessity for treachery that Joyce documents with such assiduity in *Stephen Hero*. Cranly asks:

> — You have left the Church?
> Stephen went over the interview phrase by phrase.
> — Then you do not believe any longer?
> — I cannot believe.
> — But you could at one time.
> — I cannot now.
> — You could now if you wanted to.
> — Well, I don't want to. (S 143)

As Stephen learns, however, it is not that simple. It is not enough to deny rational assent to faith. There is also the matter of internalised belief. Bourdieu describes a process of hidden persuasion: 'an implicit pedagogy which can instil a whole cosmology'. It is history that is forgotten as history and then experienced as second nature.[5]

'Give me the boy for seven years, and I will give you the man.' This famous Jesuit prescription gets to the heart of the matter. The 'docile life' that Jesuits eke out to their minions, no less than the 'marionette life' of their own vocation as dispensers of such 'illumination and rectitude', Stephen disdains as 'monstrous' (S 192). And yet, it is a

[4] Immanuel Kant, *Grounding for the Metaphysics of Morals* (Indiana: Hackett Publishing, 1993).
[5] See Pierre Bourdieu, 'Structures, Habitus, Practices', in *The Logic of Practice*, 52–65.

monster that lives within him. Hence his own 'stupor of powerlessness' (S 198). Cranly asks:

> — Why are you so impatient with the Jesuits?
> Stephen did not answer and, when they arrived in the next region of light Cranly exclaimed:
> — Your face is red!
> — I feel it, said Stephen
> — Most people think you are self-restrained, said Cranly after a pause.
> — So I am, said Stephen.
> — Not on this subject. Why do you get so excited: I can't understand that. It is a thing for you to think out. (S 147)

It is a thing to think out, but also to feel. Stephen's silence, this gap in his speech – his red face – articulates something. But what? For Bourdieu, it is a conflicted sense of domination by his own nature as it remains in thrall to orthodoxy. When we blush, or stutter, we betray 'insidious complicity' with our own oppression.[6] The many red faces in *Stephen Hero* – the flushes of anger and shame – anatomise this condition. Stephen spends a lot of time 'cursing' his own character (S 202). Cranly styles it as inconsistency, but Stephen retorts that it is a necessary lag: 'I am a product of Catholicism. I was sold to Rome before my birth. Now I have broken my slavery but I cannot in a moment destroy every feeling in my nature. That takes time' (S 144). Finally, Cranly admits that he, too, has 'considered leaving the Church in search of happiness, but that many considerations had restrained him' (S 148). He is enslaved, of his own volition, to an institution that has constituted him as its own.

Stephen's figure for the active passivity required of internalised complicity is the 'stationary march' (S 191). An ideal type of what Michel Foucault would later term 'disciplinary power', it connotes the energy required to maintain oneself in submission to orthodoxy. It is a perverse kind of Aristotelian physics: a world of moved unmovers. We witness it at work in *Stephen Hero* when Stephen encounters a poster announcing the Good Friday service at the Jesuit Church on Gardiner Street. He has already pronounced contempt for the Jesuits and their 'stale maxims' (S 42). He sees it as absurd that he should go 'crawling and cringing and praying and begging to mummers who are themselves no more than beggars' (S 238). All the same, 'and, without being keenly aware

[6] Pierre Bourdieu, *Masculine Domination*, translated by Richard Nice (Stanford: Stanford University Press, 2001), 38–9.

of it, he began to proceed in the direction of Gardiner St' (S 124). Stephen's Catholic *habitus* inclines him, more or less unconsciously, towards that which he would disdain. The lesson is subtle but demonstrable: as a Catholic apostate, he cannot expect to merely drift away from the Church. Left to his own devices, he is more likely to drift – irresistibly – back to it. The extent of his bodily capture is most viscerally expressed in *Portrait*, when he vomits after the hellfire sermon at his school retreat (P 120). If internalisation is the process by which something from the outside ends up on the inside, vomiting is the symptom that would reverse that dynamic. Stephen is trying to reject what he has already swallowed. But he is also sickened by himself in relation to it.

The Irish Catholic Family Romance

Alongside his critique of the Jesuits, Stephen's case against the Church is mounted in critique of the Catholic family: as a primal scene of indoctrination. In 'Family Romances' (1908), Freud provided a succinct account of the bourgeois family as the privileged site of psychosexual melodrama. Children desire their parents, but they are also frustrated by them. They want it all – love, recognition, possession – but they do not get it. And this feeling of being 'slighted' is a major source of the counterfactual fantasies that govern the family romance. In the child's megalomaniacal world, parents are found wanting, and so they invent preferable substitutes. Their real father is a prince, for example.[7] Joyce's Ireland offers a malign variant of the Freudian model: one in which the children, not the parents, are found wanting. Stephen makes particular reference to the fate of his sister, Isabel, who disappears from later works. Her spirit exemplifies the moral perversion of a Catholic upbringing: wasted by 'an abstention that it had not willed for itself' (S 170). Ireland's children are estranged from themselves and each other in service to submission to *doxa*:

> His sister had become almost a stranger to him on account of the way in which she had been brought up. He had hardly spoken a hundred words to her since the time when they had been children together. He could not speak to her now except as to a stranger. She had acquiesced in the

[7] Sigmund Freud, 'Family Romances', in *On Sexuality: Penguin Freud Library*, 7 (Harmondsworth: Penguin, 1977), 221–5.

> religion of her mother; she had accepted everything that had been proposed to her. [. . .] Her life had been and would always be a trembling walk before God. The slightest interchange of ideas between them must be either a condescension on his part or an attempt to corrupt. (S 131)

This problem of corruption had long shaped the moral cosmos of Christianity. From early on in the history of this radical sect, the idea of being buried next to heathens was anathema.[8] Later, when its theologians repurposed Greek philosophy to the promulgation of Christian doctrine, they appropriated the Platonic idea that corruption was inherent to all matter. Matter was degenerate relative to the ideals that animated it. Hence, the body was corruptible of the soul. When this logic was biologised, in the mid-nineteenth century, it consummated the birth of biopolitics, including the biopolitics of souls.[9] Individuals are like social cells. They are either fit to represent the group, or required to die – socially and otherwise – to keep it safe.[10] Irish Catholicism inherited this logic. It would provide the moral infrastructure of the institution.

Stephen is made aware of himself as a source of corruption throughout the novel and salutes Cranly for persisting in friendship with one known to be 'contaminated' (S 127). When Stephen's mother seeks to weaponise Isabel's illness against him – extorting him to Easter observances on her account – he reacts angrily, cracking the shell of his egg with a spoon (S 136). Stephen sees that he is to be given a choice: comply with social mores or risk excommunication – as moral pathogen – from Church and family. The cost of love is submission to *doxa*. The alternative is excommunication – social death – damnation:

> The Catholic husband and wife, the Catholic father and mother, are allowed to be natural at discretion but the same grace is not vouchsafed to Catholic children. They must preserve an unquestioning orderliness even at the risk of being upbraided as unnatural by the very preachers who assert that nature is the possession of Satan. (S 131–2)

[8] Richard Krautheimer, *The Pelican History of Art: Early Christian and Byzantine Architecture* (Harmondsworth: Penguin, 1965), 26.

[9] For biopolitics, see Michel Foucault, *Society Must Be Defended* (London: Picador, 1997). For the biopolitics of souls, see Simona Forti, 'The Biopolitics of Souls: Nazism, Racism and Plato', *Political Theory* 34:1 (2006): 9–32.

[10] Joseph Valente, 'Modernism and Cognitive Disability: A Genealogy', in Jean-Michel Rabaté, ed., *A Handbook of Modernism Studies* (New York: Wiley, 2016), 379–98; Orlando Patterson, *Slavery and Social Death* (Harvard: Harvard University Press, 2018).

This is a clear-eyed account of what is at stake: moral terrorism.[11] It is an assault on the integrity of the child at the level of their own nature. By inculcating obedience rather than accountability, and instrumentalising terror as the main instrument of instruction, the Catholic family denies its children the grace of sanctity as an ethical choice. They are either in thrall to the law or beyond it altogether. This is the perversion of ethics that Joyce rejects and that Stephen is trying to overcome within himself. He worries that Cranly will denounce him as an 'inhuman theorist' (S 131). But Stephen is not being inhuman, he is being ethical.

Joyce would have found support for this view in a resistant reading of Thomas Aquinas. For Aquinas, says Shawn Floyd, 'God ordains us to final happiness by implanting in us both a general knowledge of and inclination for goodness'. All substances seek their own perfection: a fully realised state of existence as an aspect of natural law. However, a substance cannot achieve perfection without the proper exercise of its species-defining powers, and the defining characteristic of human beings is reason. For Aquinas, human actions are those over which we have voluntary control. Reason is what distinguishes the ethical subject – the human subject – from their merely instinctual animal counterparts. Joyce saw that inculcation to moral terror pre-empted this process. His sister, Isabel, has been relegated to a realm beyond morality but also, Aquinas would say, humanity.[12] She has been made monstrous as a function of her inability to choose what is right. In this view, Isabel is not only corrupt, but irredeemable – a 'hopeless' case (S 131).

Art and Life

Joyce's ethical response to this – Stephen's too – is to become an artist. His exemplar was Henrik Ibsen, whose courage and integrity provide the foundation for a socially committed art. Stephen admires the 'excellence' of the art, but more that 'the very spirit of Ibsen himself' can be discerned moving behind it (S 45–6). He likewise determines to 'express his nature freely and fully for the benefit of a society he would enrich and also for his own benefit' (S 151). He will displace 'a system of mutual servile association' with the integrity of

[11] See Joseph Valente, 'Let Us Prey: Clerical Sex Abuse and Catholic *Bildung*', this volume.

[12] Shawn Floyd, 'Aquinas: Moral Philosophy', https://iep.utm.edu/thomasaquinas-moral-philosophy/

the 'aesthetic instinct in action' (S 191). But can he trust his instincts, given this problem of internalisation?

A main intertext of *Stephen Hero* in this regard is W. B. Yeats's short story 'The Tables of the Law', published in 1904. Stephen is enthralled by it, having found it by chance in a bookstore. He learns it by heart and would recount it, word for word, to Capuchin monks (S 182). Michael F. Hart reads it as staging the contradiction between aesthetic freedom and religious faith: one that Joyce reconciles in himself.[13] The story is divided formally into two encounters between the narrator, a recent convert to Catholicism, and Owen Aherne. In the first vignette, Aherne is high on the prospect of discovering the laws of his own being, by way of the heretical teachings of Joachim of Flora, which 'have swept away the teachings of the Father'.[14] Joachim divides the faithful into the biddable majority, who are children of the Father, and certain secret outlaws, children of the Holy Spirit, who dedicate themselves to an art of revelation, to art *as* revelation:

> Just as poets and painters and musicians labour at their works, building them with lawless and lawful things alike, so long as they embody the beauty that is beyond the grave, these children of the Holy Spirit labour at their moments with eyes upon the shining substance on which Time has heaped the refuse of creation [. . .]. (Y 12)

Aherne will then communicate his findings to his pupils: 'that they may discover their law in the study of my law, as poets and painters discover their own art of expression by the study of some Master'. Yeats melds an aesthetic apprenticeship to an ethics of *bildung* founded in artistic (as ethical) integrity. Two blank slates await inscription with these new laws – these new commandments – which are only discoverable in aesthetic revelation. Stephen's elation stems from identification with this prospect. He adopts Aherne's avowed intention as his own: 'I know nothing certain as yet but this – I am to become completely alive'. Aherne's 'fervour' is Stephen's 'fervour' as he contemplates becoming an artist in the true sense (Y 13; S 152).

In the second vignette, however, Aherne has returned to Dublin a chastened man. He realises he has become separated from God not in sin, which is redeemable, but precisely because he has discovered

13 Michael F. Hart, 'The Sign of Contradiction: Joyce, Yeats and The Tables of the Law', *Colby Quarterly* 30:4 (1994): 237–43.

14 W. B. Yeats, 'The Tables of the Law', retrieved at https://www.gutenberg.org/files/43611/43611-h/43611-h.html Hereafter (Y page).

the law of his own being. In his art, he had hoped to touch the Heart of God:

> in my misery it was revealed to me that man can only come to that Heart through the sense of separation from it which we call sin, and I understood that I could not sin, because I had discovered the law of my being. (Y 19)

Hart reads this as Yeats's cautionary tale of the dangers of an unwitting apostasy.[15] But it may be more correct to see it as staging the irreconcilability of aesthetic integrity with any continuing commitment to the mores of the faith. Hart builds his account on the ancient dichotomy of beauty and truth. The issue for Aherne, however, is not truth but law: 'I had discovered the law of my being, and could only express or fail to express my being, and I understood that God has made a simple and an arbitrary law that we may sin and repent!' (Y 19). Aherne's capitulation is symbolised by the 'elaborate casuistry' that comes to be inscribed in Latin on his blank tablets. These, we recall, were intended to document the laws of his being. Those, it turns out, are the laws of his adherence to the faith. They may be arbitrary, but they are not so for Aherne: 'we whose hearts perish every moment, and whose bodies melt away like a sigh, must bow and obey!' (Y 20). Aherne has internalised the logic of corruption at the heart of Catholic theology. For Yeats, it is internalisation that hampers Aherne's quest for artistic integrity. Bourdieu calls it eternalising the arbitrary. Historical forces of dehistoricisation make the contingent feel natural.[16] In this way, law is taken as truth.

Joyce admired Yeats's formulation of the problem. Aherne is trapped by his own faith (in himself). Stephen sees that Aherne might, in fact, achieve artistic integrity, but only at the expense of renouncing adherence to the faith altogether. Contra Hart, it is an *either/or* not a *both/and*, albeit an impossible one. Hence the split form of Yeats's story. Stephen determines to emulate Aherne up to a point not – as Hart would have it – by sublating beauty and truth into an art of reconciliation, but by conflating truth with the laws of his own being and artistic integrity with the expression of both. The problem being that – like Aherne – he has internalised the law and cannot merely shrug it off. As a 'vision seeking man', Yeats would say, Stephen must seek his anti-self: 'a Mask that delineates a being

[15] Hart, 'The Sign of Contradiction', 242.
[16] Bourdieu, *Masculine Domination*, vii–viii.

in all things the opposite of his natural state'.[17] But the internalisation problem obscures just what that natural state might be. Internalisation is a 'tyranny, external and internal' (S 214). The laws of Stephen's being are not (only) his own.

Hence the subtle qualification in Stephen's account of Ibsen's artistry: 'a human personality had been found united with an artistic manner which was itself almost a natural phenomenon' (S 46). *Almost*, but not inevitably. Stephen had always believed that being an artist was something that one *was*. It was an aspect of one's nature, at least for the elite few – the outlaws, of which he was one – in this avowedly aristocratic account (S 210). But he comes to realise that it is also something one must *do* – in art as in life – and often *against* one's own nature, given this problem of internalisation. Apostates like Aherne go only part of the way: 'They live beyond the region of morality, having chosen to fulfil the laws of their own being' (S 183). The next step is to contest those very laws as they have been implanted in the inculcation of a Catholic habitus. Otherwise, we continue to live like 'vapours' who 'lift their thuribles wearily' before 'deserted altars' (S 183). This is the true stake of the internalisation problem. Art and life must merge in any possible quest for integrity. Such was Ibsen's achievement. He had realised, in actuality, the potential of an artistic nature that might have found (false) expression otherwise. By his light, Stephen sees things clearly. He must live according to the 'voice of a new humanity, active, unafraid and unashamed' (S 199). But he must also betray himself.

Contemplating Stephen's essay 'Art and Life', Father Dillon accuses him of being a 'paradoxist' (S 101). Dillon is right, but he does not discern the true stakes of the tactic. The paradox being that treachery is the necessary precondition of any quest for artistic integrity on Stephen's part. He must betray himself in his own honour. He cannot trust his instincts, because they have been co-opted against him. In a restaging of the temptation of Christ, Stephen is attended in his apostasy by 'nimble pleaders' – the internalised voices of *doxa* – who mimic Cranly by preaching accommodation: 'Make one with us'. They cite his applied Aquinas, his disdain for Protestantism, his veneration for ritual. Just as the devil tempts Christ with material gain, Stephen is tempted (by himself) with the fruits of acquiescence: 'In temper and in mind, you are a Catholic still. Catholicism is in your blood' (S 211). This sounds like himself but is, in fact, himself rehearsing the views of his mother: 'None of your people, neither your father's nor mine, have a drop of anything but Catholic blood

[17] W. B. Yeats, *Autobiographies* (New York: Scribner, 1999), 201–2.

in their veins' (S 139). Stephen abhors this bloody logic. But he still believes it with his body.

The Law of the Mother

In Lacanian psychoanalysis, the father is the figure of law and the child separates out to them from blissful union with desire of/for the mother.[18] In Joyce's Ireland, says Joseph Valente, we must complicate this gendered division of labour.[19] It is not enough to distinguish between the body (of desire) and the word (of law), as the Catholic mother is a vehicle for both. From the outset of *Stephen Hero*, Stephen's battle for integrity is waged with his mother, May Dedalus, not his father, Simon. For his part, Simon offers little beyond occasional, half-hearted prognostications about respectability and getting on in the world. Like many Catholics of the time, his faith is indexed to the pursuit of other interests: to social and professional standing.[20] Stephen gently mocks his father's preoccupation, at one remove, with 'remunerative respectability' (S 53). Simon is too much of a hypocrite to bear the law: too Simony. This is why the great scenes of blasphemy in *Hero* are staged in confrontation with May (S 136–8). It is the law of the mother that signifies, not the Lacanian *nom-du-père*. This is one reason why Simon 'hates' May's maiden name (S 115).

Valente's paradigm is extrapolated from the work of Jean Laplanche, particularly his concept of the source-object of the sexual drive. Where Freud spoke of the drive as having a source and an object, Laplanche condenses the two. Where Freudian drives insist from within, Laplanche's source-object is an implant. It originates in primal seduction: the child's relationship to their primary caregivers, most often, in the first instance, their mother. Fatefully, says Laplanche, Freud gave up on his seduction hypothesis in 1897. He ought to have extended it to include the 'generality of seduction linked to maternal care'.[21] The adult feeds the infant and there is

[18] Jacques Lacan, *The Object Relation: The Seminar of Jacques Lacan, Volume IV* (New York: Polity, 2021).

[19] Joseph Valente, 'Mamafesta: Joyceance and the Law of the Mother', in Eve Watson, ed., *James Joyce's Writing and Psychoanalysis* (London: Routledge, forthcoming).

[20] Tom Inglis, 'Religion, Identity and Society', in Joe Cleary and Claire Connolly, eds, *The Cambridge Companion to Modern Irish Culture* (Cambridge: Cambridge University Press, 2005), 59–77.

[21] Jean Laplanche, 'The Drive and its Source-Object: its Fate in the Transference', in *The Unfinished Copernican Revolution, Selected Works 1967–1992*, translated by Luke Thurston (New York: Unconscious in Translation, 2020), 305.

always too much – an excess of need, the caregiver's unconscious need – which is implanted in the child in the form of inscrutable missives, or 'enigmatic signifiers'. From a position of abject helplessness, the child must try to make sense of adult desire: what does it want from me? The problem being that adult desire does not *itself* know what it wants, and so the child must interpret the uninterpretable. This institutes the frantic epistemology – the drive to make sense of things – that is infantile sexuality. Communication occurs at the level of signs and gestures, but also of feelings. The function of the child's theorisations is 'to bind the anxiety coming from the traumatic enigma'.[22]

In the classic Oedipal schema, then, the mother delights while the father terrifies. In Joyce's Ireland, it is Mother/Church that both delights and terrifies. It is not a question, as in the classical model, of a prohibited object of desire (the maternal body). Rather, the maternal source-object of desire is always-already constituted in prohibition of the very desire that it incites. May is the source *both* of the law that would proscribe desire *and* of the desire that would violate that law. As such, she does double duty in the ethical *bildung* of the child. She combines (into an exacting double-bind) the rival compulsions of *jouissance* and obligation to law. Her name cultivates the ambiguity of the condensed imperatives: 'you may, you may not'. It is a main source of the paralysis, the 'hemiplegia of the will', that Joyce diagnoses in *Stephen Hero* (S 199). By way of her Catholic upbringing, prohibition has been instituted in May's constitution and then implanted in her children – alongside desire – in the form of enigmatic signifiers that both demand and defy translation.

In Joyce's work, the aesthetic correlative of this enigmatic process is the epiphany. These vivid scenes of indeterminable purport allow for no final interpretation occasioning, instead, an ongoing drive to interpret – a more or less frantic epistemology – akin to Laplanchean translation. Each epiphanic scene is its own enigmatic signifier. *Stephen Hero* centres around one of Joyce's most haunting examples:

> A voice which he remembered as his mother's, a voice of a terrified human being, called his name. The form at the piano answered:
> — Yes?
> — Do you know anything about the body? . . .
> He heard his mother's voice addressing him excitedly like the voice of a messenger in a play:
> — What ought I do? There's some matter coming away from the hole in Isabel's . . . stomach . . . Did you ever hear of that happening? . . .

[22] Laplanche, 'The Drive and its Source-Object', 311.

— I don't know, he answered, trying to make sense of her words, trying to say them again to himself.
— Ought I send for the doctor. . . . Did you ever hear of that? . . . What ought I do?
— I don't know the hole. . . . What hole?
— The hole . . . the hole we all have . . . here. (S 168)

The hole in the narrative, the repressed signifier, is the navel. As the enigmatic index of Stephen's maternal origins – the signifier of an insidious complicity with the law and/as desire – it will haunt him throughout *Ulysses*. But it is unnamed – unnameable – here. Its absent presence signals the failure of symbolisation that is repression in Laplanche's model. For Laplanche, as for Freud, repression means failure of translation.[23] It is what happens when we cannot metabolise the enigmatic messages we receive: 'I don't know, he answered, trying to make sense of her words'. Freud famously suggested that every dream has its navel: a point beyond which it becomes uninterpretable.[24] The navel of the dream that is *Stephen Hero* is the navel itself. It marks the site of repression of maternal need – a mother's need of their child, but also a child's need of their mother – around which Stephen's quest for liberation is destined to falter.

We know this because the spectre of the mother does not dissipate for Stephen as a function of his apostasy. Rather, as Valente documents in his reading of *Ulysses*, *amor matris* continues to haunt him. It functions, Stephen surmises, as both subjective and objective genitive: both Stephen's love of his mother and his mother's love of him are in play. When May dies, those stakes are upped considerably. As Valente has it, owing to his split identification, Stephen swallows his mother in order to avoid swallowing his loss of her. Thus, May returns to taunt him as a 'Ghoul. Chewer of corpses'.[25] If corpse is in the plural here, the other corpse in question is the Eucharist. All faithful Catholics chew corpses by dint of transubstantiation. In *Stephen Hero*, Stephen's defiance of the body of maternal law overshadows his fretful veneration of the now (morally) indigestible body of Christ. He will avoid swallowing the Host in a vain attempt to avoid swallowing the law of his mother. In a neat condensation of the terms of the problem, Stephen dismisses any outward show of deference to Mother Church as 'mummery'. Ever the pragmatist,

[23] Laplanche, 'The Drive and its Source-Object', 307.
[24] Sigmund Freud, *The Interpretation of Dreams* (Harmondsworth: Penguin, 1991), 671.
[25] James Joyce, *Ulysses* (New York: Random House, 1986), 9. Hereafter (U page number); Valente, 'Mamafesta'.

Cranly would have him separate out his mum from his mumming, pointing out that he could: he could easily make a sacrilegious communion for her sake (S 142–3). But Stephen rejects this option, saying 'the outward show is nothing but it means a good deal' (S 144). As we have seen, however, the situation is even more exacting than that:

> — Do you fear then, Cranly asked, that the God of the Roman catholics would strike you dead and damn you if you made a sacrilegious communion?
> — [. . .] I fear more than that the chemical action which would be set up in my soul by a false homage to a symbol behind which are massed twenty centuries of authority and veneration. (P 215)

Here lies the problem. Having internalised the split imperatives of Mother/Church, Stephen's soul is always-already constituted in (false) homage to his mother. He is in homage in the sense that he remains in thrall to her as the source-object of his (prohibited) desire: and it is false in the sense that he is also constituted in violation of the very law that would enshrine that prohibition. Not surprisingly, Stephen struggles to articulate any practical solution to this intractable double-bind. Cranly is dubious:

> — How can you propose such a future to yourself and yet be afraid to trust yourself to perform even the simplest mumming in a Church?
> — That is my business, said Stephen, tapping at his forehead. (S 145)

This is hardly convincing. It is not enough – as Cranly would have it – to think these things out. Stephen is playing for time. Hence the 'enigma of a manner' that he cultivates in *Hero* (S 32). He understands that he is enmeshed in Mother Church at the level of his 'primal cells'. The trope of a chemical action in his soul acknowledges the insidious power of doctrine to infect and overwhelm its host (S 128). But, as yet, Stephen sees no final solution to the internalisation problem. This foreshadows the moment in the 'Circe' episode of *Ulysses* when he taps his forehead and says, 'in here it is I must kill the priest and the king' (U 481). But how?

The Art of Recovery

In *The Lucid Vigil*, Stella Gaon shows how Laplanche's theory of general seduction resolves one of Freud's defining aporia: that between narcissistic and melancholic accounts of the birth of the psychoanalytic subject. Freud could not decide: do we move out autonomously from primary narcissism or are we constituted from the outside by identifications?[26] In Gaon's account, primal repression first institutes an ego that then constitutes the subject retroactively in the translation of enigmatic messages from the parents (as in, 'be a good boy, Stephen'). The ego is conceived as both the 'I' that theorises and the 'I' that is theorised: as in 'am I good enough?' This is the ego-drive: the *telos* of our human being. In a neat short circuit of the Kantian model, Gaon calls it our desire for reason.[27] First, the ego is consolidated in relation to an ideal. Then, we are driven to make sense of ourselves in relation to that ideal.

Child abuse vitiates that ideal, and this includes the abuse of inculcation to moral terrorism. In Gaon's two-stage model, social mores regulate our self-ideal retroactively and we interpret ourselves in light of them. As many others have stressed, these mores tend to be both normalising and pathologising.[28] Gaon cites the example of compulsory heterosexuality.[29] But we can easily repurpose the model to Catholicism. The Catholic child can bind the anxiety of primal seduction, but only in the form of moral terror. First, they are made to internalise the laws of the Church. Then, they are made to feel structurally inadequate in light of them: not good enough (yet). Under the guise of love – of moral instruction – children are sold on their own humiliation: co-opted to the myth of a child's natural depravity. They come to be oppressed by their own preferences, humiliated by their own choices. Whatever else it might mean, to recover from Catholicism must mean to refuse this perversion of ethics that is the Catholic family romance.

Even so – and this is the final crux of the internalisation problem – it is never possible to wipe the slate clean: to simply recover what has been lost. The Jesuits were right. Seven years is a human eternity. There can be no going back. When Joyce told Frank Budgen he was losing interest in Stephen – his alter-ego – he explained: 'He has a shape that can't be changed'.[30] It is a bleak truth that finds even bleaker expression in the trajectory of Stephen's *bildung* across Joyce's *oeuvre*. He is stuck. Continued deference to Mother Church is impossible, and so is any final escape from her clutches. The best Stephen might hope for is some new balance within himself. It is the

[26] Stella Gaon, *The Lucid Vigil: Deconstruction, Desire and the Politics of Critique* (London: Routledge, 2019), 199–221.
[27] Gaon, *The Lucid Vigil*, 234.
[28] See, for example, Michael Warner, *The Trouble with Normal: Sex, Politics and the Ethics of Queer Life* (Cambridge, MA: Harvard University Press, 1999).
[29] Gaon, *The Lucid Vigil*, 218.
[30] Frank Budgen, *James Joyce and The Making of* Ulysses (New York: Harrison Smith and Robert Haas, 1934), 105.

governing metaphor of his apostasy in *Stephen Hero*. Yeats had also used it to describe Aherne's relapse into orthodoxy in 'The Tables of the Law':

> I noticed his black closely-buttoned coat, his short hair, and shaven head, which preserved a memory of his priestly ambition, and understood how Catholicism had seized him in the midst of the vertigo he called philosophy. (Y 19)

This is what Stephen must guard against in himself. Owing to the combative style of his writing, he comes to be regarded as a 'very disequilibriated [youth]' (S 32). But Stephen senses that, unlike Aherne, he must endure vertigo if he is to rediscover balance. 'Circe' is, perhaps, where this finally happens: 'My centre of gravity is displaced' (U 481). Morally speaking, this is precisely what is required. Stephen is grappling with a paradox. To be true to himself, he must commit acts that he believes (with his body) to be treasonous. Experiment, pleasure, permission, outrage: these are the necessary vehicles of his recovery. And the medium of his recovery will be his art. As Freud famously observed, before the creative artist psychoanalysis must 'lay down its arms'.[31]

Contrary to what Stephen claims, however, his art will never proceed 'from a free and noble source' (S 189). After abandoning *Hero* – in *Portrait* and in *Ulysses* – Joyce would give artistic expression to the intractable nature of his complicity with Catholicism. In Samuel Beckett's memorable formulation, he will fail, and fail again, and fail better to recover from Catholicism.[32] And he will recover from Catholicism only by admitting a final inability to do so. Recovery is interminable: the necessary quest for an impossible integrity in the wake of inculcation. This arduous process is the '*bonum arduum*' that Stephen desires (S 185). He will produce an unrelenting body of work that is also an unrelenting work of the body. It will be a mode of *aesthesis*. An outrageous regime of self-discovery in self-betrayal. *Poiesis* as *auto-poiesis*. Art as life. The prospect excites Stephen, he tells Cranly, but it also terrifies him (S 147). He is even afraid of himself (S 202). Finally, it is a choice between two terrors: terrorised diffidence to the Jesuit within and the vertiginous terrors of recovery.

[31] Sigmund Freud, 'Dostoevsky and Parricide', in *The Standard Edition of the Complete Psychological Works of Sigmund Freud: Volume XXI (1927–1931), The Future of an Illusion, Civilisation and its Discontents and Other Works* (London: Hogarth Press, 1961): 175–96, 177.

[32] Samuel Beckett, *Worstward Ho* (London: Calder, 1983).

Chapter 4

Let Us Prey: Clerical Sex Abuse and Catholic *Bildung*

Joseph Valente

Clerical sex abuse of children has been widely regarded within the Catholic community and beyond not only as an atrocity in its own right, but as an offense fundamentally inimical to the norms of education, mentorship and cultivation espoused by the Roman Church, within whose precincts it has been, and doubtless continues to be, perpetrated. Not only a sexual perversion, then, amounting to a crime in law and against nature, this species of violation, this form of rape, has been understood as a perversion of and a crime against the religious institution that housed it, an evil made all the more shocking by its godly context. At first glance, and even at a second or third, it is easy to see why this shocked estimation of the thing going on in various sacristies around the world still prevails. Orthodox Catholic instruction and discipline, particularly in the Jansenist mode endemic to modern Ireland, sought to defer and even pre-empt the sexual investments, not to say awareness, of its juvenile charges in order to preserve what passes in that symbolic order for their innocence. Shame, or, to be exact, the shaming of erotic desires, adherences and pleasures, has been the predominant instrument to this moral(istic) end. Sexual abuse, conversely, acts to pre-empt childhood innocence by prematurely and coercively exposing its unready victims to genitalised libidinal contact. Shame has been the predominant effect of this gross clerical violation of the same moral ends. But if the objectives of clerical predators are diametrically opposed at a certain level to the catechising protocols of the Catholic Church, the strategic logic whereby each proceeds is uncannily cognate, and this kinship in turn bespeaks a common, underlying aim, which the practices respectively occult: what claims to be about sexual excitement, pleasure and even affection or love is largely about power, about imposing control on an intimate personal basis; and what claims to be about salvation – the inculcation of spiritual values, virtues and even divine love – is largely about the generational reproduction of institutional power and control. At the heart of either case is the unseasonability and corresponding vulnerability of the youths being impressed (i.e. both affected and enlisted).

I would like to begin consideration of the continuity between sexual and devotional recruitment in modern Catholicism with a tenet recently articulated by Seán Kennedy: 'internalisation precedes evaluation', always and necessarily.[1] In the process of acculturation, certain sets of values, attitudes, principles, images and desiderata are instilled in our psychic makeup, in the phenomenological texture of our being-in-the-world, whether positively or negatively, before any consideration, let alone any judgement of them, can occur. On one hand, the effects of such prior internalisation can serve to contour in some fashion and degree any deliberative assessment, directing callow judgement as it wills and thus constituting our ethical nature on structurally compromised or heteronymous grounds (in the strict Kantian sense of the term). On the other hand, these effects can and do persist amid and in defiance of subsequent, contrary deliberative assessment, and precisely insofar as they affix to the sense of self prior to a proper capacity for considered judgement, they manifest in the subject not as guilt, but as moral shame, which might be defined as the visceral experience of this structurally compromised or heteronymous ethical condition. All this is to say – before we are rational agents, thinking for ourselves, we are desirous subjects, animated by unconscious triggers called signifiers that come to us from the Other as the vehicle and the voice of *our own* propensities. Whatever beliefs and values, attitudes and aspirations, principles and preferences we embrace are mediated in their very emergence by these tenders of our primary attachments and dependencies. The exogenous and endogenous roots of our motive forces are thus confounded.

The entanglement of self-generated and received prompts and intentions is of nothing less than existential consequence in the very young, in children, where it proves a necessary condition of their accession to the Symbolic Order, which is to say their graduation from human organism to human subject, from biogenetic to properly social being. Within the typical family romance, the formative scene of internalisation unfolds as an intense affectional bonding with parent or caregiver, in what amounts to a primal seduction, as theorised by Jean Laplanche. Informed by the unconscious, libidinous stirrings

[1] Seán Kennedy, 'Recovering from Catholicism: The Internalisation Problem in Joyce', this volume.

of those parental figures, this extended encounter activates the child's desire, understood specifically as the articulation (the splicing-cum-splitting) of bodily states or sensations with the demand, the prospect and the feeling of a love that is itself shadowed by the ever-present possibility of its withdrawal, which is felt on an ongoing basis as lack. The affective issue of this entry into the lists of adult sexuality and symbolic conduct is profoundly ambivalent, a traumatic *jouissance*. Because this compelling yet disquieting process is generative of the child's subjectivity in the first instance and its development or *bildung* in the aftermath, the compliance implicit in the child's internalisation of the other's disposition cannot even approach, let alone comprise, something like informed consent.

As elaborated in *The Child Sex Scandal and Modern Literature: Writing the Unspeakable*, paedophilic abuse draws upon and exploits this primal scenario, rehearsing its basic elements along more deliberate, predatory, explicitly genitalised and trauma-inducing lines.[2] The enactment of such abuse in a pastoral relationship – dedicated to redemptive instruction and mentorship in the ways of divine love, and undertaken by a figure designated 'Father' – rehearses the elements of primal seduction all the more precisely and traumatically. In tapping the child's already eroticised reflex of internalisation, such predatory conduct inflicts an injury even more serious than the assault on the child's body. It stimulates and thereby implicates the child's circuitry of desire against their will, effectively turning the child's libidinal energies against them and thus psychically incriminating the child in an action that the abuser alone commits and in a gratification that the abuser alone seeks.

More than simply counterfeit, this sort of extorted assent is positively toxic; it exacerbates, precisely in the attempt to mitigate or gloss over, the violence of the sexual assault. More than simply overriding or subjugating the will of the child, sexual interference, as the Irish call it, works to repossess that faculty, to appropriate not just the child's desires but their very command over them, to abrogate – and here the question of youth is most decisive – their as yet un- or underdeveloped powers to orchestrate their volitional impulses, conscious and unconscious. Particularly in clerical child molestation, traumatic infliction grows inseparable from traumatic conscription of the victim's internalised promptings and produces in the victim a sense of shame at their enforced complicity. Therein lies the most

[2] Joseph Valente and Margot Backus, *The Child Sex Scandal in Modern Irish Literature: Writing the Unspeakable* (Bloomington: Indiana University Press, 2020), 25–36.

devastating aspect of this species of violation and the source of its especially wide-ranging and protracted effects. At the same time, and for many of the same reasons, this entrapment of the victim's libidinal stirrings represents the consummation of the abuse as an expression of the predator's will to power (as opposed to mere sexual appetite). It is the pass through which coercion ascends to the sovereign heights of colonisation, defined as what the British called soul-making, the seizing control over a subject's internal promptings and investments.

The conscription described here is all the more readily accomplished given that the abuse occurs under a theocratic regime, wherein the role of the priest to mediate between deity and penitent serves as warrant for an ideology of clerical exceptionalism. This exalted pastoral standing harbours the evident danger that in relaying the always equivocal purposes of the deity, in channeling the already projected will of God, certain priests might admit a slippage between the inescapably phantasmatic aspect of religious faith and a religious, faith-based legitimation of personal fantasy. A clerical exceptionalism predicated upon a singularly intimate and empowering relationship to God and His canon of sanctity might plausibly, if illicitly, be translated into divine sanction for entertaining exceptions to those canons. By no premeditated design, then, but as a function of its hierarchical structure and theocratic sway, the Irish Catholic Church enabled its more malignant clerics to conflate their service to the Lord, with the lordship they asserted over their youthful charges in that service and with the servicing those youthful charges might render the cleric themselves.

The key to this aggrandised mode of conscription, however, is that the victim be given to understand the sexual overtures as in some respects licensed or at least provided for by the priest's holy office, that the desirousness implicated and the traumatic jouisaance produced in the sexual assault be somehow approved by the confessional authority the priest possesses, be sanctified by the piety he modelled, and be absolved by the godliness he embodied. However tacitly, the predator cleric effectively intimates to a necessarily susceptible mark the sketchy alignment of his own want and God's will, such that acquiescence in the former would seem in some rough conformity with the latter. The impressionability and credulity that the predator cleric relies upon in his sexual objects presuppose their supplementary internalisation of religious authority – no less than unconsciously eroticised parental affection – which precedes, resists and helps to shape the evaluation of that authority. I say relies upon rather than induces because in most cases the susceptibility consequent to the child's internalisation of Church and clerical rectitude would have been ingrained in their upbringing and juvenile education, as a kind of supplement to the internalised adherences binding them to their parental figures and inciting their desirousness in the first place. As the homely, concrete and more immediately cognisable analogue of the Holy Trinity, the widely circulated image of the Holy Family certainly had a role to play in this regard.

We can now turn to the parallelism mooted at the beginning of this talk, between the strategic logic informing clerical abuse on one hand and Catholic indoctrination on the other, only to discover that there is something beyond parallelism or analogy at work here. What we have called primal seduction, the unconscious, psychosexual messages that usher the child into the Symbolic Order, cannot but pass into the child internalising, before any possibility of evaluation, the parents' religious attitudes and beliefs as well, particularly in an ethnonational, theocratic arena where sectarian identification is a defining element of social identity. Under these circumstances, primal *seduction* comes trailing a corollary primal *induction* into the religious tribe. The predator clerics who populate the various reports on child sexual abuse (Murphy, Ferns, etc.) can be seen, on the psychoanalytic model floated here, to have weaponised the child's primal seduction, using their fatherly stature as ammunition. But this pernicious tactic is, if not facilitated by, certainly consistent with the enlistment procedures of the Church itself, which have been similarly dedicated to weaponising the child's primal induction into the faith.

Those ecclesiastical brain-carriers, the Jesuits, borrowed from Aristotle a motto that has become in turn a model for the catechising ethos and method of the Catholic Church, especially in contexts of sectarian difference and/or antagonism, as predominated in modern Ireland: Give me a child until he is seven and I will show you the man, or the more popular alternative, Give me a child until the age of seven and I have them for life. The age cited here is not accidental. It is the age designated by the Church itself as that at which a child acquires the use of reason, which is why it is also the age, traditionally, when children are appointed to receive their first Holy Communion. The age of reason, whether properly generalisable as age seven or, as I would argue, significantly later, with the maturation of the cerebral cortex, could take as its synonym the age of evaluation, the stage at which whatever strains of thought, feeling and desire have been internalised can potentially be addressed in an evaluative deliberation that they nevertheless continue to shape and so compromise. To target a child before that age – tendentiously and systemically – as the Jesuits have confessed, or professed, doing is precisely to exploit the comparative defenselessness of pre-critical/cortical internalisation. The Church's determination to pre-empt the child's capacity for such appraisal manifests itself glaringly in the area of so-called mixed marriages, where the insistence that all prospective offspring be raised exclusively Catholic serves to deprive the children themselves of any unbiased ground from which to weigh different religious traditions, observances and belief-value systems as they mature into properly rational subjects.

As we have seen, the predator cleric instrumentalises, implicitly or overtly, elements of the child's primal religious induction, their reverence for Church authority and sanctity, to assist in weaponising the child's primal seduction. By a similar, if not the same, token, the modern Church typically conducts the primal induction of its young charges by mining elements of their primal seduction, their traumatically eroticised accession to subjectivity within the family romance. To this end, Catholic indoctrination and training has traditionally

a) deployed outsized historical and metaphysical projections of parental figures – from the Holy Family triad to the Father and Son of the Holy Trinity, to the Fathers of the Church and their maternal counterparts in the convent; and
b) in their name divvied the internalised parental messages of profoundly ambivalent jouissance into a set of traumatising Manichean binaries: love or its withdrawal; abundant bliss or torturous deprivation; existential approval or reprisal; heaven or hell – replete with powerful images associated with each of these alternatives and likewise pegged to the child's intimate experience of love and lack. This plan of indoctrination amounts to nothing less than moral terrorism, with the aim of producing the moral equivalent of Stockholm syndrome.

The goal of having a child in this iconographic fashion is to take signifiers – images, tropes, profiles – that have been galvanised by their role in the eroticised family cell and submit them to the child's psychic reflex of internalisation, where they might operate with unconscious intensity. The raw affect thus released is not only immitigable at a certain limit by future conscious rumination, but works to inflect, or infect, that rumination in turn. Where the predator cleric moves the child to the suggestive by way of the submissive, Church teaching moves the child to the submissive by way of the suggestive. In this respect, the former, sexually abusive practice is a darkened reverse mirror of the latter, devotionally coercive practice. By way of reaction, the victimised child is disposed to resist recovery out of an ethical sense of shameful dread at their own involuntary complicity or out of an identification with the aggressor, while the indoctrinated child is disposed to shameful dread at any dawning resistance they might feel to continued identification with their preceptors, a resistance necessary to recovery.

The conflation of divine will and earthly want is less obvious in child indoctrination than in child molestation; it is also less personally venal and less immediately, consistently or obtrusively damaging to the child. In sum, it is far less abhorrent and therefore far more readily disavowed, especially as the colonisation of the child's pre-rational, pre-critical faculties is undertaken in the main by true believers, certain they are acting for the child's temporal and eternal good. But none of that means that the Church is without institutional self-interest (earthly want) in this mode of propagating the faith (divine will). At bottom, that selfish institutional interest, as I adumbrated at the start, is the securing of power, of a plenary kind that it wielded for centuries in Ireland. The Jesuit model, 'Give me a child until he is seven. . .', registers not just an insight but an intent, the managing of Catholic *bildung* so as to bring the unfledged under the permanent spiritual superintendence and control of a clerical hierarchy, or rather to bring a large mass of people under such control, one nascent subject at a time. The longer-term aim of such management involves *the* fundamental self-interest of any institution, its own reproduction, to which indoctrinated children will be required to contribute both ideologically and, on pain of grave sin and its traumatic consequences, in hard currency, as per the Fifth Precept of the Catholic Church. Lest we imagine that the reproduction of institutional standing and authority is not a decisive stake in the Church's attitude toward the treatment of children, we need only remind ourselves that it was precisely to protect that standing and authority, with all of the worldly goods they entail, that the Church prelates saw fit to shuttle predator clerics from parish to parish at the obvious risk of further sexual violation. Parallelism giving way to imbrication, we have come to a full, and rather vicious circle, the serpent swallowing its tail.

The Catholic Church's largely credited, if not creditable disavowal of material interest in the indoctrination of children – buttressed as it is by the presumptive sincerity of the beliefs being instilled – should not blind us to the existence these interests, to the Church's insistence on seeing them met, nor, most importantly, to just how badly the strategy of targeting the vulnerable, internalised adherences of childhood appears in the light such self-serving interests cast: at the least, a form of emotional hostage taking and at worst, as the Jesuit-trained James Joyce portrays in *A Portrait of the Artist as a Young Man*, a campaign of *moral assault*, which, not unlike sexual assault, has a long, sometimes lifelong, seemingly eternal, afterlife.[3]

'I wouldn't like any children of mine to have too much to say to a man like that'

Perhaps owing to his all but exclusively Jesuit training, combined with his experience of cultural dispossession under metrocolonial rule, James Joyce seems to have been especially attuned to the continuity between material and spiritual subjection, between the sexual assault on the premature body and psyche and the pre-emptive assault on the cognitive and critical faculty. The first story that Joyce published, 'The Sisters', his ur-fiction, if you will, represents in its final form a case study in this unholy alliance. For contemporary Irish novelists like Edna O'Brien, Patrick McCabe, Jamie O'Neill, Keith Ridgway and Anne Enright, Joyce's work marks the origin of the child sex abuse narrative in twentieth-century Ireland, and by the same token, the child sex abuse narrative, as exemplified in 'The Sisters', marks the origin of James Joyce as a major writer of twentieth-century fiction. It is, therefore, all the more significant that Joyce focuses at the start not only on clerical sexual assault, but on its commensal relationship to catechistic assault.

The critical heritage of 'The Sisters' comprises two main glosses on the boy narrator's association with the newly deceased Father Flynn. There is longstanding support for the official story of flawed doctrinal tutelage, which the boy's guardian and the priest's sororal caregivers seems to endorse, albeit equivocally. This line of thinking often carries forward a still older, allegorical treatment of the priest himself as an avatar of a broader and deeper social malaise, which Joyce famously denominated hemiplegia of the soul.[4] Equally well-established are suspicions of pederastic intimacy, provoked by a series of suggestive signifiers and gathered in the notorious ellipses that punctuate the various adult accounts of the priest's debility and decline. Strangely, however, little if any pressure has been placed on

[3] James Joyce, *A Portrait of the Artist as a Young Man* (New York: Norton, 2022).
[4] Richard Ellmann, *James Joyce* (New York: Oxford, 1959), 145–6.

the shared headwater of these interpretive currents in the assertion of personal and institutional power. This oversight conduces to the very assumption Joyce's tale disputes and the Church defends: that clerical sexual abuse is accidental and antithetical to, rather than cognate with, the course of Catholic indoctrination.

The scholars advancing these conflicting interpretations agree, for the most part, on the ominous air of corruption imbuing Flynn's instruction of the boy and on the boy's juvenile incapacity to process, let alone comprehend, the nature and extent of that corruption. In other words, both sides of the discussion acknowledge, at least implicitly, that it is the youth of the boy – his mental, emotional and physical immaturity – that determines the wrong of the priest, whether that wrong be viewed as tutelary and pastoral or sexual and pederastic.

Recent proponents of the former species of indictment have found it necessary to refute the latter take outright. Edward Brandabur dismissed any suggestion of a homoerotic bond between the priest and his young acolyte, even as he characterised their religious, ministerial relation as sadomasochistic.[5] James Pribels finds Father Flynn vaguely corrupt, while insisting that this amorphous miasma enveloping him bears no sexual overtones whatever.[6] Senator David Norris avers, 'There is clearly something ominous, perhaps unhealthy, in Flynn's tutorship of the boy, but judges the charge of pedophilia a very crude interpretation that does violence to the delicacy and subtlety of Joyce's message'.[7] Bonnie Roos concedes, 'We would be remiss to rule out the possibility [of] child molestation, particularly given its continued prevalence in the Church today', but she treats this prospective sexual abuse as a merely hypothetical allegory for colonial ethno-sectarian modes of exploitation.[8] Vicki Mahaffey, finally, holds that the charge of pederasty misreads social and theological indoctrination as *physical* abuse. She proceeds to declare flatly, 'There is no evidence that the priest has physically abused the boy in any way and, further, doctrinal abuse is not identical with

[5] Edward Brandabur, 'The Sisters', in R. Scholes and A. Walton, eds, *Dubliners: Text, Criticism and Notes* (New York: Norton, 1979), 340–3.

[6] James Pribek, 'Dubliner's Priests', in Oona Frawley, ed., *A New and Complex Sensation: New Essays on Joyce's Dubliners* (Dublin: Lilliput, 2000), 133.

[7] David Norris, 'The Unhappy Mania and Mr. Bloom's Cigar: Homosexuality in the Works of James Joyce', in Joseph Valente, ed., *Joyce and Homosexuality, James Joyce Quarterly* 31:3 (Spring 1994): 360.

[8] Bonnie Roos, 'Spies in Joyce's "The Sisters": Allegorical Histories, the Irish Rebellion, and *The Count of Monte Cristo*', *Joyce Studies Annual* (2018): 209.

sexual abuse'.[9] As we shall see, however, her own incisive analysis winds up showing that they are not entirely different either.

Proponents of the second, pederastic line of interpretation have tended to adopt a less eristic, more exegetical approach. Instead of rebutting the patristic reading, they have focused on mounting collateral evidence of sexual abuse as an alternative framework, a narrative double entendre. To take one example, Leonard Albert resignifies the title 'The Sisters' to refer not to Eliza and Nana alone, but to Flynn and the boy, as a pejorative epithet for the male effeminacy linked, by way of the inversion model, to homosexuality.[10] Still more influentially, Waisbren and Florence Walzl identify Father Flynn's paralysis, the chief symptom of his physical degeneration, with General Paralysis of the Insane or paresis, tertiary stage syphilis, the presumptive fallout of his moral failing.[11] They are followed in this view by such prominent Joyceans as Richard Ellmann, Brenda Maddox, Don Gifford and Terence Brown. Margot Norris, finally, offers a brief survey of the competing interpretive strains, plumping for the pederastic gloss in the end, while continuing to entertain both the more conventional account of pastoral errancy and the old allegorical standard of endemic sociocultural paralysis. Significantly, in accordance with the materials she reviews, Norris treats these strains as entirely discrete constructs, dividing them into innocent and guilty representations.[12]

But a genealogy of 'The Sisters' in its evolution from the initial appearance in the *Irish Homestead* (1904) to the final version at the opening of *Dubliners* tells a crucially different story than the critical heritage has allowed – a tale not of two narrative polarities or alternatives, but of a single narrative trajectory with interlocking thematic components.[13] Thus, in the original *Irish Homestead* rendition,

[9] Vicki Mahaffey, 'Silence and Fractals in "The Sisters"', in Vicki Mahaffey, ed., *Collaborative Dubliners: Joyce in Dialogue* (Syracuse: Syracuse University Press, 2012), 41.

[10] Leonard Albert, 'Gnomonology: Joyce's "The Sisters"', *James Joyce Quarterly* 27:2 (Winter 1990): 363.

[11] Burton A. Waisbren and Florence L. Walzl, 'Paresis and the Priest: James Joyce's Symbolic Use of Syphilis in "The Sisters"', *Annals of Internal Medicine* 80 (June 1974): 758–62. Richard Ellmann, *James Joyce II* (New York: Oxford, 1980), 163. Terence Brown, Introduction to *Dubliners* (New York: Penguin, 2000), xxxi. Brenda Maddox, Introduction to *Dubliners* (New York: Bantam, 1990), xv; Don Gifford. *Joyce Annotated* (Berkeley: University of California Press, 1982), viii. All cited in Michael Timins, '"The Sisters": Their Disease', *James Joyce Quarterly* 49:3–4 (Spring–Summer, 2012): 441.

[12] Margot Norris, *Suspicious Readings of Joyce's Dubliners* (Philadelphia: University of Pennsylvania Press, 2004), 19–28.

[13] For the evolution of 'The Sisters', see H. W. Gabler and W. Hettche, eds, James Joyce, *Dubliners* (New York: Garland, 1993), 124–74; Florence L. Walzl, 'Joyce's

there are no indications of either doctrinal abuse or sexual abuse on the part of Father Flynn. As Florence Walzl's landmark essay 'Joyce's "The Sisters": A Development' elaborates, the relationship of the boy and the cleric in the *Irish Homestead* rendition is merely circumstantial, without religious or ethical instruction or any suggestion of intimacy.[14] Both indications of abuse emerge in revision and at the same stage thereof. Still more importantly, many of the same textual additions and interpolations point to both forms of tort simultaneously. The reasonable inference to be drawn is that in revising 'The Sisters' Joyce decided that it was or should be a story about the catechetical foundation of clerical predation. A synoptic look at certain prominent elements of Joyce's revision corroborates what we might call the unified field theory of clerical sex abuse. Three distinct scenarios knitting together the indices of doctrinal violence and sexual misconduct – all decisive moments in the story – appear as later, synchronised emendations.

Scene 1: The Lighted Window

Long after the *Homestead* publication, Joyce famously introduced, in the establishing shot of the tale, in which the boy gazes at the dying priest's window, the key word 'paralysis' to describe the priest's fatal condition.[15] This state of muscular sclerosis and incontinence has been widely understood as symbolic of the proudly, but pathologically scrupulous rigidity of Flynn's approach to his office.[16]

> The duties of the priest towards the Eucharist and towards the secrecy of the confessional seem so grave to me that I wondered how anybody had ever found in himself the courage to undertake them. . . He told me that the fathers of the church had written books as thick as the Post Office Directory and as closely printed as the law notices in the newspaper, elucidating all these intricate questions. (*D* 5)

"The Sisters": A Development', *James Joyce Quarterly* (Fall 2012–Winter 2013): 73–118.

14 Walzl, 'Joyce's "The Sisters"', 80.

15 James Joyce, *Dubliners* (New York: Penguin, 1967): 1. Hereafter cited in text (*D*).

16 Edward Brandabur, *A Scrupulous Meanness* (Urbana: University of Illinois Press, 1971), 35–45; Fritz Senn, 'He Was Too Scrupulous Always: Joyce's "The Sisters"', *James Joyce Quarterly* 2 (Winter 1965): 192–5; Vicki Mahaffey, *Reauthorizing Joyce* (Cambridge: Cambridge University Press, 1988), 26–31; Hugh Kenner, *Dubliners* in Peter Garrett, ed., *Twentieth Century Interpretations of* Dubliners (Englewood Cliffs: Prentice-Hall, 1968), 41–3.

On Mahaffey's magisterial analysis, Father Flynn's doctrinal abuse consists in inflicting and infecting the boy with precisely this species of scrupulous adherence to authority as a supercilious badge of honour. He taught him obedience, in the form of deference to his superiors and contempt for those individuals he considers inferior. Flynn's indoctrination of the boy is thus a personal assertion of power in the name of the institution, the Church, that enables him. In activating this power dynamic, Flynn subjects the boy to a dialectics of shame. He wrongs the boy, as Mahaffey contends, by teaching him that he knows nothing, and silently derides him in the bargain for his ignorance.[17] 'Often when I thought of this I could make no answer or only a very foolish or halting one upon which he used to smile and nod his head once or twice' (*D* 5). By antithesis, the boy learns to silently shame those who appear to know nothing, like the priest's sisters, and he even remarks the parallel attitude at work by imagining the coffined priest is smiling with him at their lowliness.

However, no less importantly, the boy's characterisation of the word 'paralysis' – sounded like the name of 'some maleficent and sinful being' (*D* 1) – accords a moralised significance to the condition, more suited to its *other* point of reference, the General Paralysis of the Insane, or paresis. If Flynn's paralysis is to be construed as the effect of the third stroke he has suffered (*D* 1), the three strokes he has suffered need simultaneously, if antithetically, be construed as the effect of the tertiary stage syphilis he has contracted. Paralysis then simultaneously metaphorises the stiff, disdainful disposition the priest instills in the boy and metonymises, symptomatically, the sexual threat the priest is felt to pose.

Scene 2: Table Talk

This brings us to the second scene of Joyce's revision, the prandial post-mortem on Father Flynn by old Cotter and the boy's uncle. Before we turn to that pivotal scene, however, it should be observed that the second key word added to the story's opening, 'simony', has been taken to name Father Flynn's corrupt brand of indoctrination, his exploitation of the boy's trust and fidelity for his own selfish purposes.[18] Such a reading looks to obviate the need to identify the sinful complexion of the priest's paralysis with sexual errancy. But

17 Mahaffey, 'Silence and Fractals in "The Sisters"', 34, 35.

18 See Walzl, 'Joyce's "The Sisters"', 95, for a citation of others holding this view.

even here, the doubleness of Joyce's method obtains, to significant effect. The application of simony – the venal traffic in sacred items – to the priest's instrumentation of the boy for his own purposes is a bit of an interpretive stretch in any case. So too is the assumption that the boy is sufficiently conversant with the details of this rather obscure ecclesiastical ordinance to apprehend its metaphorical relevance to Father Flynn. It is therefore all the more salient that the boy's fascination with these key words centres more on their resonance than on their reference: 'It had always sounded strangely in my ears' (D 1). This sonic emphasis invites us to consider a certain homophonic play on Joyce's part and homophonic displacement on the boy's. As George Roberts, the initial publisher of *Dubliners*, was the first to intuit, the arcane 'simony' chimes with the more familiar 'sodomy',[19] a word the boy may well have gleaned in overhearing the adults in his household gossiping about Father Flynn. What is more, as a malaprop/substitute for sodomy, simony qua instrumentalisation serves to underline the power play at work in clerical paedophilia.

Gossiping about Father Flynn over dinner marks each version of 'The Sisters'. But whereas originally the elderly priest was said to have suffered some common form of invalidism and dementia ('the upper story . . . was gone'),[20] post-*Homestead* speculations are designed to cryptically impute entwined pedagogical and paedophiliac dangers to the cleric. Old Cotter, Flynn's nemesis, admonishes 'I wouldn't like children of mine to have too much to say to a man like that' (*D* 2), a sentiment which, given Flynn's sacerdotal role, goes directly to his suspect religious guidance and instruction. Cotter's rationale, however, seems to have something to do with the sexual bearing of Father Flynn. His initial designation of the priest is 'queer', a word with incipient homoerotic overtones, which Joyce elects to highlight by denominating the apparently pederastic loiterer in 'An Encounter' the 'queer old josser' (*D*, 18) The priest and the josser share more than an askance label or, rather, their shared label signals a correspondence in their conduct toward the boy narrator that is strictly germane to the questions we are exploring. Like Father Flynn, the josser offers himself as a preceptor to the boy, treating his education – in this case literary – as a vehicle of sexual initiation. His mode of inculcation/initiation is sadomasochistic, not unlike the priest's,

[19] Richard Ellmann, ed., *The Letters of James Joyce II* (New York: Viking, 1966), 305–6.

[20] H. W. Gabler and W. Hettche, eds, *Dubliners*, 126. See also Walzl, 'Joyce's "The Sisters"', 76–7, for the more innocent representations of Flynn's malady.

but more overtly so. Accordingly, as a secular analogue to Father Flynn, the josser serves to educe the exertion of force implicit in the latter's handling of his charge, a small-bore will to power over an undeveloped body and spirit. Here, unbeknownst to the author of the phrase, is the something queer about Father Flynn.

The suggestiveness of Old Cotter's use of the term 'queer' is not lost on the boy's uncle, to whom Cotter addresses his warning. The uncle embellishes his agreement in principle by praising his own 'daily habits, as a nipper, of a cold bath winter and summer, an old wives' antidote to youthful lust' (D 3). Nevertheless, the uncle's response, like Cotter's ongoing pontification, remains heavily coded, leaving deliberately unmentioned the very allegation they are raising – in the manner of an open secret. Pressed by the boy's aunt for clarification of their suspicions, both men punctuate their conjectures with strategic ellipses – elisions in the service of evasion. No one is prepared to denounce Flynn outright for what they believe he has been or has done. For he continues to command in his office as prelate, 'Father-figure' and confessor – all of the respect he fails to command in his person. But this reticence of judgement, on these specific grounds, is tantamount to conniving not at sexual abuse per se, but at the continuity, the cohesion, of clerical pederasty and Catholic pedagogy. The tutelary role of the priest insulates him, it would seem, from full-throated exposure and condemnation of his suspected sexual misbehaviour. Indeed, the more general, diffuse complicity of the Catholic Church in the clerical sex scandals of recent times may be regarded in this light, as a disavowal that turns *in its effect* into a defense of this continuity and cohesion.

Scene 3: The Inverted Confession

Although the boy-narrator professes anger at the course of the dinner table colloquy, his refusal to answer old Cotter's gaze, his awareness of being condescended to as a child, and his anxiety to 'extract meaning from [Cotter's] unfinished sentences' all bespeak an undercurrent of shame as well (*D* 5). Even as the adults carefully snipe at his counsellor, muffling and blunting their censure of Flynn's tutelage, they seem to enjoy carping *directly* at the boy's receipt thereof.

> My idea is to let a lad run about and play with young lads his own age.
> Let him learn to box his corner.
> That's what I am always saying to that Rosicrucian there: take exercise. (*D* 3)

Unwittingly, their deprecating mode of address to the boy merely duplicates the logic of his relationship with Flynn himself. Just as the Father signals his own feelings of being overwhelmed by the grave responsibilities towards the Eucharist and the secrecy of the confessional, only to shift that sense of inadequacy to the boy, so the adults chide the boy as the living surrogate for the priest's misbegotten ways.

It is Flynn, rather than his guardians, who preoccupies not to say haunts the boy in the aftermath of the dinner. Flynn alone comes to him in his dreams, the gateway to the unconscious and the staging ground of that formative psychic structure, the family romance. And indeed, by casting his juvenile protagonist as an orphan, whose closest intimate and great friend is a Father-figure (*D* 2), Joyce seems to be spotlighting how Catholic mentorship, of the type that regularly affiliates celebrants and their altar boys, poaches on the family romance, exploiting primary modes of oedipalised identification to enforce and, in certain cases, eroticise religious indoctrination.

The dream sequence later that evening is Joyce's amplest and most significant addition to the original tale, and it unfolds a drama of agonistic identification that fuses sacramental purpose and sexual possibility. The boy projects onto Flynn's image his own desire to assume the clerical power to which he has been subject, and to do so in the space of its greatest concentration, the confessional, where religious indoctrination unfolds under the promise of eternal bliss and the threat of eternal torment. In inverting the relation between Flynn and the boy, as confessor and penitent, the dream reveals the boy's sense of having been wronged in some fashion by his 'Father-figure', whom he wishes nevertheless to ally himself with or become – a textbook instance of oedipal identification/rivalry.

> I felt my soul receding into some pleasant and vicious region; and there again I found it waiting for me. It began to confess . . . and I wondered why it smiled continually and why the lips were moist with spittle. But then I remembered that it had died of paralysis and I felt that I too was smiling feebly, as if to absolve the simoniac of his sin. (*D* 5)

Notice that the inverted confessional grows out of an inversion *of* the confessional. By (verbal) definition, the pleasant and vicious region in which the two are met is a site of sinful (vice-ridden) enjoyment, immorality, even depravity. The irresistibly salacious association of said region finds further reinforcement in the libidinously salivating mouth of the priest, which renders his fixed smile a creepy appeal for the boy's affectionate sympathy – not unlike the queer old josser's affectionate plea that 'the boy' should understand him (*D* 20). In the dream, the boy wondered at these libidinal signs as a first step toward their disavowal; he explains them by reference to the paralysis linked, by unconscious metaphor, to Flynn's debilitating sacerdotal scrupulosity. The boy thus comes to apprehend the pedagogical nature of Flynn's wrongdoing, but mainly as a defence against its imbricated pederastic dimension. He obscures the sodomistic aura of that pleasant and vicious region behind the screen-concept of simony, which he pronounces Flynn's signature sin. In this respect, the boy-narrator proves the model exegete for a critical heritage that has largely failed to plumb the profound indissociability, antinomial as it is, of the spiritual-religious and the corporeal-sexual in Father Flynn's corrupt(ing) mentorship.

The boy's disavowal enables him to complete his movement of identification/rivalry with his Father-confessor: to absolve the simoniac of his sin by way of becoming/replacing him as the bearer of religious authority. In that moment, however, and as a clear reflexive sign of that surrogation, the boy mirrors in part the oral symptom of Flynn's erotic exercise of that authority, his feeble smile. The repressed returns in this facial gesture to evince the confluence of spiritual inculcation and sexual inveiglement in the acolyte's experience.

The repressed returns once more as a mnemonic fallout from the night's dream-encounter. Having walked past the house of mourning the next day, the boy suddenly recalls the furnishings of the dream-en-scene, 'velvet curtains and an antique lamp, reminiscent of a faraway land, Persia – I thought' (*D* 6). As Terrence Brown observes, the Orient of the nineteenth century was associated with sensuality and exoticism.[21] But, more than that, through works like Richard Burton's *The Book of a Thousand Nights and a Night*, the Orient was viewed in Europe as a pleasant and vicious region, a place of sexual ecstasy, excess and perversion. At the same time, the Orient was known for its bazaars, in which intense commercial bargaining occurred within velvet curtains and under antique lamps. Without remembering the sexual or the simoniac elements of the dream itself, the boy conjures forth, in accordance with the metonymic and metaphoric workings of unconscious thought, a set of motifs that rivet those elements together. Try as he might, the boy cannot sustain his disavowal of Father Flynn's blandishments or the attitudes they breed, as his stuffy alienation from Flynn's sisters, at his wake, bears out.

[21] Terence Brown, Notes to *Dubliners* (New York: Penguin, 2000), 243.

In sum, Flynn's perversely faith-destroying catechesis of the boy is a means, a distinctively Catholic means, of establishing mastery over an unripe mind and, as such, is of a piece with the will to dominance animating the pederastic sexual predation that he is intimated to enact and represent. In this regard, the sacramental and the doctrinal provide both an outward, visible paradigm – a wholly family romance – and a sanctified opportunity for the exertion of a power that implicates and so impairs the youthful desires it preys upon. It is a perverse dynamic that will be played out for over a century throughout the Catholic world (as the credits of the movie *Spotlight* proclaim) and with particular intensity in theocratic Ireland, where it became a national shame and the maiden object of narrative critique for the country's most celebrated writer.

Part III

Biopolitical Shame

Chapter 5

Laundering Complicity: Experimental Drama and the Temporalities of Irish Shame

Claire Bracken

Lisa McInerney's 2015 novel *The Glorious Heresies* is one of the few contemporary novels that engages the derelict afterlife of the Magdalene Laundry system, with a brief figuration of the Sunday's Well site, a former Good Shepherd Magdalene Laundry. As the object of an arson attack on three separate occasions between 2008 and 2020, the building stands as a foreboding and forbidding presence on the Cork city landscape. In McInerney's novel, Maureen, one of its central characters, walks up to the ruin:

> Ten minutes walk from her front door and she was at the entrance to the old Laundry [. . .] overgrown now, the city reclaiming its darker monuments.
>
> There were cracked stone steps leading up to the building, but the building itself was only a shell, the red bricks, the arches, the iron crosses on its towers, all stained and falling down [. . .]
>
> Statues everywhere. Some of them defaced. Here was a shepherd with a twirling black moustache, a lichened maiden with an alien name daubed on her robes. They stood in silent guard, oblivious to the unchecked march of the branches, grasses and fronds. Oblivious to Maureen. Relics of the past, swallowed by a world expanding.
>
> Christ it was silent.[1]

Maureen's encounter with the space, and its 'relics of the past', generates overwhelming emotion. Her own story – which saw her religious parents banish her to England and confiscate her newborn in the 1970s – connects her with the experiences of women in these Magdalene institutions, some of whom she has known and met in London. She is engulfed by communal memory: 'In the shadow of the landmark,

[1] Lisa McInerney, *The Glorious Heresies* (London: John Murray, 2015), 188.

Maureen Phelan picked her way through thickets and thorns, enduring memories, even the ones that were not hers'.[2] The abject space of the laundry becomes fused with the embodied memories of exiled women, as the site itself moves Maureen into a transpersonal realm where the boundaries between self and other co-mingle, even merge.

This is a difficult – indeed unbearable – place to be, and Maureen reacts with anger, first berating a homeless man who is sitting outside the laundry's 'shell', and then voicing a desire to get 'inside' the laundry 'to set another fire'. Her desire to 'cleanse' with fire chimes with the 'cleansing' of the laundry work and, as she walks away from the laundry site, she 'felt uneasy', 'like the heat of a pointed stare was burning up her shoulders, like the bitterness soldered to the past and to the ground the past was built on had touched her and marked her. There were places this city wanted no one to tread'. The past is figured as a structure here, 'built on a ground' and 'soldered' with 'bitterness', a bitterness that burns her with its 'pointed stare' of shame. So, on one level, the past is represented by the lineaments of the laundry itself and its panoptic forms of biopower. But by the same token, the images of her 'burning' connects the physical reality of the laundry's structure to Maureen herself, who stands as a representative of all the women who toiled within its walls and under its regime of shame.[3] The past and present are intertwined, as McInerney's novel enfolds Maureen – the contemporary subject/spectator/witness – into a state of being that attempts to affectively register (through intense empathetic affinity) both the horrors the incarcerated women endured, as well as the immediate sense of reticulated institutional complicity in their suffering. The past is everywhere, but so too is the present. The ruin is infused with life, as Maureen moves through a living, breathing space (with the 'unchecked march of the branches, grasses and fronds'). And it is embodied movement that is key here, as the visceral and affective charges of the body and its experiences are harnessed anamnesiacally: in refusal to forget the realities of the laundries' past.

In this essay, I claim that this same temporal and embodied strategy is at play in a number of key contemporary experimental theatre productions that take the Magdalene ruin as their mise-en-scène: Anu Production's performance *Laundry*, Erin Layton's play *Magdalen* and Grace Dyas's play *We Don't Know What's Buried Here*.[4] Each

[2] McInerney, *Glorious Heresies*, 189.

[3] McInerney, *Glorious Heresies*, 190.

[4] The site-specific production, *Laundry*, by Anu Productions, was staged at the Seán McDermott Street site in 2011, with over 200 performances. Erin Layton's *Magdalen*

in its own way engages the time of the ruin, infusing past and present as sites of what psychoanalyst Jean Laplanche, after Freud, terms *après-coup*, or afterwardsness.[5] Through their powerful evocations of place-in-body and body-in-place, these dramas stage confrontations with Ireland's history of systemic institutional abuse, as well as recent attempts to banish that abuse to the past. The visceral impact of theatre – the embodied potentials of performance – explain why it is this genre, above all others, that mounts such an affective critique of both. Like Maureen in *The Glorious Heresies*, the audience becomes identified with the victims. In these works, bodies on the stage, bodies in the audience, are forced to confront the past, confront the present, bearing both witness and experience to an ever-living trauma, complicity and shame.

Repurposing Shame

Ireland's public reckoning with the Magdalene Laundries and their traumatic histories begins in the early 1990s, even as one Magdalene Laundry – Seán McDermott Street – is still in operation. Maria Luddy notes that the laundries appear to have entered Irish public consciousness 'suddenly' in September 1993, after media reports of exhumations taking place at the High Park Laundry in Drumcondra.[6] At this time, Our Lady of Charity of the Refuge was overseeing a number of development deals: selling off sections of its land to housing and commercial developers. Part of the land was a graveyard called St Mary's that held the remains of the so-called 'consecrated Magdalenes' of High Park: women and girls who, in exchange for a vow to spend the rest of their lives in the laundry, were given 'quasi-religious status' and a guaranteed burial on the convent grounds. The graveyard was 'thoroughly neglected': both vandalised and overgrown.[7] To sell the land, the nuns had to seek an exhumation license. During this process, it became clear that many of the dead (133 in total in the application) had no registered

debuted at the New York International Fringe Festival in 2012. Grace Dyas's *We Don't Know What's Buried Here* was produced at Dublin's Civic Theatre in 2018.

[5] Jean Laplanche, *Après-Coup* (New York: The Unconscious in Translation, 2017).

[6] Maria Luddy, *Prostitution and Irish Society, 1800–1940* (Cambridge: Cambridge University Press, 2007), 76.

[7] For a history of this process, see Claire McGettrick, et. al., *Ireland and the Magdalene Laundries: A Campaign for Justice* (Dublin: Justice for Magdalenes Research, 2017), 166–7.

death certificates (with some not even listed with a full name). The exhumation process itself revealed at least twenty-two other remains not listed on the license application. All were exhumed, cremated and reburied in Glasnevin Cemetery and development progressed apace.[8] The site of the graveyard is now a car park, situated behind the hotel and alongside the road that now grants access to a housing development (see Appendix).[9]

Laura McAtackney has studied these buildings, considering how and where the traumatic histories of the laundries are remembered in appropriate 'sites of conscience'. She provides a useful account of their current condition. Only three of the ten laundries that operated in Ireland currently remain, and all are derelict.[10] These are the former Seán McDermott Street and Donnybrook laundries in Dublin, in addition to the Sunday's Well location in Cork. In recent years, all three sites have been sought after and/or bought by property developers (Appendix). Future plans are thus a crucial element of the discourses surrounding these structures and sites due to the aggressive and encroaching demands of commercial development. However, these sites pose a problem for the neoliberal development economy, a problem that needs to be negotiated and managed. In order to build, the developer has to excavate, and in excavating they risk raising the spectres of the past. Such excavation of the past in the present is at once necessary for, and a grave threat to, the neoliberal future.

The powerful activism of survivors and their families, of the Justice for Magdalenes Research organisation, investigative journalists and other media organisations has uncovered much of the horrors of this biopolitical and carceral regime: too much for the political and economic agents of neoliberalism to conceal. The projects became caught up in the very process of (un)covering itself. It is capital investment that occasions the exhumation at High Park. It is the sale of the land that triggers the release of the repressed, as the ground is disturbed and the bodies and debris of the past are uncovered. One of the gravediggers, Barney Curran, gives this perspective:

[8] Miriam Haughton, Mary McAuliffe and Emilie Pine, 'Introduction: Commemoration, Gender, and the Postcolonial Carceral State', in *Legacies of the Magdalen Laundries* (Manchester: Manchester University Press, 2021), 11.

[9] McGettrick et al., 171.

[10] Laura McAtackney, 'A Suitable Place to Remember? Derelict Magdalen Laundries as Possible Sites of Conscience in Contemporary Ireland', *Space and Culture* 25:2 (2022): 267.

> '[. . .] the nuns were trying to sell the place, and it was big money like, so they didn't want anyone to know what was going on. It was all hush hush. We weren't supposed to tell no one about it'.

About the remains discovered there Curran comments:

> 'I said there were more bodies buried there. And they said no, there is only 133 [. . .] we kept digging and digging until we dug out the whole lot and we ended up with 22 more that we didn't even know was there.'

They discovered many bodies with broken limbs: 'A lot of plaster of Paris, which was on their wrist, and their arms, their legs, their feet, their ankles'.[11] This is the remainder that neoliberalism confronts at Magdalene sites and which it needs to both raise and contain: dead bodies.

Ireland faces a double bind in relation to the ruins of its institutional regimes. Developing these sites for the national project uncovers issues that threaten development as well as the nation. The preferred solution has been affect management in the name of national – read as economic – recovery. Shame – the very emotion that underpinned the working of these institutions in the first place – is displaced from bodies once said to be shameful onto a more generally conceived 'national shame'. This functions to shore up the contemporary self/subject in abjection of past histories.[12] As Chloë K. Gott notes, the past becomes the container, 'the site of the trauma', so that the present can 'temporally distance' itself from that past. The present is one of progressive liberal prosperity that played no part in this horror and has moved beyond it, into the future.[13] Such temporal distancing is evident in contemporary political responses to the Magdalene Laundry system. In February 2013, the *Report of the Inter-Departmental Committee to Establish the Fact of State Involvement with the Magdalen Laundries* was published. The report, presented by Senator Martin McAleese, and popularly known as the McAleese Report, has been extensively criticised for the lack of attention given to the conditions in the laundries, as well as its refusal to take on the commercial motives of the religious orders themselves. Two weeks after publication, then Taoiseach Enda Kenny offered a public apology in Dáil Éireann, calling the laundry system a 'national

[11] Barney Curran, 'Magdalene Laundries: Our World', BBC News.

[12] Clara Fischer, 'Gender, Nation, and the Politics of Shame: Magdalen Laundries and the Institutionalization of Feminine Transgression in Modern Ireland', *Signs: Journal of Women in Culture and Society* 41:4 (2016): 832.

[13] Chloë K. Gott, *Experience, Identity & Epistemic Injustice within Ireland's Magdalene Laundries* (London: Bloomsbury Academic, 2022), 163.

shame, for which I again say, I am deeply sorry and offer my full and heartfelt apologies'. He noted that:

> Today we live in a very different Ireland with a very a different consciousness and awareness. We live in an Ireland where we have more compassion, empathy, insight and heart. We do, because at last we are learning those terrible lessons. We do, because at last we are giving up our secrets. We do, because in naming and addressing the wrong, as is happening here today, we are trying to make sure we quarantine such abject behaviour in our past and eradicate it from Ireland's present and Ireland's future.

It is evident here how 'national shame' is being harnessed to move the nation forward. The national self – experiencing and witnessing shame simultaneously – 'quarantines' the past, so as to advance from the slough of shame into 'a new dawn for all those who feared that the dark midnight might never end'.[14] Similar comments were made by then Tánaiste Joan Burton in 2014. Herself a survivor of Ireland's shame laundering regimes, Burton spoke out about the Laundry and Mother and Baby Home systems. She was put into a Sisters of Mercy Mother and Baby Home, Temple Hill in Blackrock, at two months old, and was subsequently adopted. In a BBC interview for 'Magdalene Laundries: Our World', Burton framed the atrocities, including her own personal experiences, very much along the neoliberal political lines, defending the McAleese inquiry and describing how people who knew her birth parents would keep describing the past as a very different time: 'things were so different then'.[15]

This is neoliberal Ireland, where time is money and there can be no time like the present. But this means, too, that there can be little time for the past. The forward-driving logic of neoliberal presentism, what Mary McGlynn terms our 'inescapable present',[16] moves to contain past exposures. There is an inherent tension between the present value of the sites and ruins, and the encroaching development that wants to unearth but also bury the things they contain. In response,

[14] Enda Kenny, 'In Full: Enda Kenny's State Apology to the Magdalene Women', *The Journal*, 19 February 2013. Clair Wills also makes a similar point about Kenny's speech in 'Coda: Edna O'Brien and Eimear McBride', in Eric Falci and Paige Reynolds, eds, *Irish Literature in Transition: 1980–2020, vol. 6* (Cambridge: Cambridge University Press, 2020), 295–304, 301.

[15] Joan Burton, 'Magdalene Laundries: Our World', BBC News, https://www.youtube.com/watch?v=ChDRDrb7e-U, 27 September 2014.

[16] Mary McGlynn, *Broken Irelands: Literary Form in Post-Crash Irish Fiction* (New York: Syracuse University Press, 2022), 41.

the process of uncovering the past is co-opted both to produce future profit and repurpose past shame. Neoliberal recovery projects – the development plans, political and governmental responses – double as shame laundering, time-management strategies, whereby the past becomes a commodity to be reprocessed and re-covered. The messiness of times past, their unruly traumas, are a thing to be managed on behalf of a brighter tomorrow. Temporal distinctions between past and present are firmed up, and the realities and experiences of women in the laundries, their lives inside the walls, are not given significant representation, remaining marooned in a past that is itself quarantined to enable the present to *move on*: an uncovering followed by a cover-up: a re-cover-up.

Still Life, Dead Time

If contemporary re-cover-ups rely on a quarantining of the past, then ethical interventions into this neoliberal ethos need to be crafted with an attention to temporality. The unravelling of divisions between past and present play an important role in such interventions, by refusing the temporal separation upon which the tactic of quarantining relies. For many Irish artists, the ruins of Magdalene Laundry sites themselves have the potential to disturb and intervene in this way. The ruin is the place of trauma – its irrevocable reality – the place of the ghost, the voice, the gravesite of those bodies, dead and living, that suffered under the regimes in its walls and grounds. As material remainders/reminders of the past, they have both ontological and epistemological *presence* in the contemporary landscape. Activist resistance to the redevelopment of the derelict laundry sites highlights the potential of the ruin to generate productive fusions of past and present time spaces. For Dylan Trigg, ruins belong 'to an undead realm: of the past, yet haunting the present; dead but in ceaseless motion; devoid of life and yet constitutive of life'.[17] The living dead of the ruin activates the disruptive potential of psychoanalytic time – of the *après-coup* – by which the past irrupts in the present. Unlike neoliberal time, this temporality moves in two directions at once: the past translates the present and the present translates the past. Both coexist in what Jean Laplanche terms 'a double movement'.[18] Crumbling edifices take the place of abject bodies as ghostly ruins, refusing an easy separation of past and present.

[17] Dylan Trigg, 'The Psychoanalysis of Ruins', *3AM Magazine* (December 2012).
[18] Laplanche, *Après-coup*, 55.

Hence Julia Kristeva and John Lechte's definition of the abject as 'something rejected from which one is not separated, from which one is not protected as is the case with an object'.[19] The tangible presence of the ruin – speaking to a very real history – refuses presentist fantasies of transcendence, demonstrating their vulnerability, unravelling their strategies. The derelict remains of the laundries dominate the contemporary popular imagination. They disrupt the quarantining processes of erasure, containment and abjection. Newspaper articles and television documentaries mark them as sites of horror and abjection. The buildings take on the symbolic resonance of their function as 'architectures of containment' for the women contained within their walls.[20] Witness this image of the Seán McDermott Street Magdalene Laundry in Dublin (Figure 1). Originally published in the *New York Times*, it was reprinted in the *Irish Times*. With its ominous sky and the darkened shades of the desolate structure, it gives a sense of terror and foreboding. It looms forth as a spectre of horror, speaking to a contemporary imagination of shock and outrage at the abuses that took place there.

Figure 1 The back of the derelict Seán McDermott Street former laundry site. © Paulo Nunes dos Santos, photojournalist.

[19] Julia Kristeva and John Lechte, 'Approaching Abjection', *Oxford Literary Review* 5:1/2 (1982): 127.

[20] James M. Smith, *Ireland's Magdalen Laundries and the Nation's Architecture of Containment* (Manchester: Manchester University Press, 2008).

The Magdalene ruins have also been captured to powerful effect by photographer Mark Davis. He has a collection of photographs of Sunday's Well, with images of both the interior and exterior of the space, registering the former laundry building as an abject site, a place of discarded and disassembled rubble and decay (Figure 2). Highlighting these structures as abandoned, derelict and forgotten, these photographs represent them as shells – empty vessels of a haunting past – with light and dark intersecting to construct a sense of haunting absence.

Of key importance, here, is atmosphere. As Davis notes, 'I love discovering the way light plays a key feature in determining the difference between an informative photograph over one that truly captures the atmosphere'.[21]

Alongside this horror, though, the aestheticisation of the image – its stillness – allows for an element of containment. It tempers the *après-coup*. As an attempt to display the abjection of the site, these images are static and reifying: freeze framed. This same aesthetic dimension is evident in a range of other image-based work on

Figure 2 'Oblivion'. An image of the ruins of the Good Shepherd Sunday's Well Laundry in Cork. © Mark Davis, photographer/author.

[21] Quoted in Claire Earley, 'Camera Club Profile – Mark Davis', accessed 24 June 2024. https://www.thetelegraphandargus.co.uk/news/17677545.camera-club-profile---mark-davis-i-love-capture-atmosphere-abandoned-buildings/

the derelict sites. For example, 'Good Sheperd Magdalene Convent, Cork' [*sic*] is a YouTube video of collated shots of Sunday's Well.[22] The building is captured in its extreme desuetude, crumbling and peeling. Hans Zimmer's song 'Time' plays as the dramatic mediator between image and viewer, the sole sound in a compilation that contains no subject, no body, no life. Such emptiness characterises another YouTube video, of the Donnybrook laundry site in Dublin, footage of which runs for over forty minutes, with no music or voiceover, just images of an emptied-out, broken and disused space.[23] The ruin becomes sites of fascination but not threat.

In his YouTube videos, such as 'Magdalene Laundry – Cork', Davis goes one step further. The ruins are more viscerally registered in camera walk-throughs, allowing the viewer to connect experientially with their abject past.[24] Finally, though, these video sequences present the same problem as the still images. Their content has the potential to trigger a return of the repressed, but their form precludes this irruption. The self-containment of these images, their marked separation from the historical moment in which they are produced, aestheticises them. They stage a haunting scene, but their stillness sections them off from the viewer, who peers in from the outside. They allow us to stare, unperturbed, at images (both still and moving). There is separation between the viewer and the object of their gaze. They mark these institutions as relics from another age. In doing so, they surrender their potential to stage the *après-coup* and offer unwitting solace to those who would quarantine the past.

Embodying Complicity: *Magdalen* and *Laundry*

The potential of *après-coup* is realised, by contrast, in the spaces of experimental contemporary drama by women. Embodying the ruins of the past in performance, the present is made very present, as derelict spaces are infused with vital energy. Form and platform really matter here, especially at the level of consumption, attention and potential drift. Theatre entraps you; YouTube videos do not. While Davis's photographs allow for the serenity of the gaze, as well as

[22] Sylwiakrupa, 'Good Sheperd Magdalene Convent, Cork', youtube.com/watch?v=4OZ5j73P5Yk

[23] thebettyfordclinic, 'Abandoned Magdalene Laundry in Donnybrook, Dublin, Ireland', accessed 24 June 2024, https://www.youtube.com/watch?v=YETH7W0yCBg

[24] Mark Davis, 'Magdalene Laundry – Cork', accessed 24 June, 2024, https://www.youtube.com/watch?v=NbPyvF9fnhg

its distancing, the plays I explore here demand that their audiences face questions of complicity and accountability. Erin Layton's 2012 one-woman play *Magdalen* disrupts the neoliberal process of quarantine, unravelling past–present separation in a work inspired by the High Park exhumations. Layton is especially interested in structures: 'There is something in the land, the soil, the heart of Ireland and something inside the walls of the abandoned Laundry buildings and the lost stories of these girls and women that aches to be heard'.[25] The play moves between two time periods: 1998 and 1948. The 1998 sections of the play are narrated from the perspective of Reid, a middle-aged man who runs a hostel for boys that was developed on the site of a former laundry. He also features as a child in the 1948 section of the play, which provides a series of narratives of women incarcerated in the laundry, including a young girl with a disability (who dies at the end), a sex worker who has literally been torn from her place of work, an unmarried mother and a zealous Child of Mary girl who hopes to become a Magdalene and receive the highest order of status (beneath the nuns, of course).[26]

In one of the play's early scenes, Reid comments on the derelict condition of the laundry building, in response to an unknown questioner (possibly the playwright herself in a metafictional creative mode):

> REID: All's I can tell you is . . .
> Well, it was an absolute fuckin' pigsty when we bought it from
> Them to make the . . . the . . . hostel.
> I wanted a place – for the boys –
> Backwards kids like myself who are only out roaming the streets
> Looking for . . . for trouble
> You know, give 'em some purpose, some food in their bellies,
> A place to call home
> Floors were cracked, caked on with dirt
> Doors were falling off their hinges

We are returned to the former state of the building in the play's penultimate scene:

> REID: Like I said before, the property was old and wasted when I bought it –

[25] Quoted in Charles R. Hale, 'Giving Voice to the Magdalene Women: A Review of "Magdalen", a Play by Erin Layton', *Irish Central*, 4 September 2014.
[26] A selection of the performance is available to watch here: https://vimeo.com/76731893.

the whole renovation took quite a bit of work . . . and money.
We got permission from the State to expand the property.
They gave us a nice size plot in the backyard.
We figured we'd use it as recreation space for the boys.
So, the contractors arrive – they had to dig up the property grounds to set down the new foundation . . .
I was out.
I don't remember where exactly,
and I see this call on my cell phone –
'I think you should come down here. Now'
The tractor had stopped dead.
And I see her –
a skeleton –
in the same drab uniform I remember seeing on the girls –
when I was a boy.
There were many of 'em – hundreds as a matter of fact . . .
stuffed like weeds.
No gravestones.
No death certificates.
There was nothing on them.
Some had been there for centuries . . .[27]

Reid takes on the language of redevelopment spoken through the myth of progress. The 'old and wasted building' is dug up and the past is unearthed: 'hundreds' of dead bodies. Even as he critiques the abuses of the past, expressing horror at the discovery of unacknowledged and discarded dead bodies, his position is rendered complicit. He is running a hostel, another institution, for boys with intellectual disabilities. Initially, he is shown to resist media questions about the history of the building (re-silencing the stories), as well as emphasising the 'cost' of development and the 'money' involved, echoing in many ways the nuns' own discourses about the running of the laundries themselves. He presents himself and his hostel as a beacon of light and hope, one of Sara Ahmed's 'well-meaning individuals',[28] but his words continue the very discourse that legitimated the Magdalene Laundries in the first place: representing them as refuges/places for those whom nobody wanted.[29]

[27] Erin Layton, 'Magdalen', unpublished manuscript.
[28] Ahmed, *The Cultural Politics of Emotion*, 109.
[29] See the 1990 RTÉ radio interview with the nuns and women in the Seán McDermott Street laundry: 'Close the Door – Magdalen Laundries', https://www.rte.ie/radio/doconone/646632-radio-documentary-close-the-door

Layton's play taps into the curious temporality of the *après-coup*. The site of the play, the disintegrating pile, condenses past and present, disrupting Ireland's preferred narratives about development as progress. Layton's ethical reckoning with the past of 1948 draws lines of continuity with the present of 1998, making two discrete moments speak with a single voice: Layton's own. By performing all the speaking parts in her play, Layton brings them together in one body. She personifies Reid's problem of complicity in herself. With this move, *Magdalen* unseats neoliberal logic, enveloping it within the more capacious and accountable dynamics of psychoanalytic time.

Similarly charged is the site-specific theatre production *Laundry*, part of Anu Productions' Monto Cycle trilogy, which literally gets inside the walls of Seán McDermott Street in a production staged in 2011. Audience members wait on the street outside and enter (individually) into the building. As they travel through the rooms, they encounter women in different performative vignettes and become engaged into the performance itself. Here, too, theatre is used to model complicity. We are compelled to think about what shame does to bodies, as Ahmed would have it.[30] One woman asks an audience member to help her escape (and the audience member can help her right out to the front of the laundry, where she runs away), another woman cries in pain with mastitis in a bathtub (some women died from complications from mastitis in both the laundries and the Mother and Baby Homes), another tells of how her husband told her to come back to the laundry after he died, another – Christina, she gives her name – dances and whistles in a small room, suffocating in its restrictions of her voice and movement. The stories recounted in the production are all taken from the direct testimonies of women and families connected to the Seán McDermott Street laundry.

Miriam Haughton has written very powerfully of her experience at the production: 'I was acting as witness to a history of human torture and despair [as] a complicit member of Irish society, asked to consider the limits of my own social responsibility and willingness to intervene.'[31] The past is structurally inhabited here by the present spectator/witness in a way that is visceral: immediate and interactive. It affects the individual in the present.[32] Boundaries are broken

30 Ahmed, *The Cultural Politics of Emotion*, 103.

31 Miriam Haughton, 'From Laundries to Labour Camps: Staging Ireland's "Rule of Silence" in Anu Productions' *Laundry*', *Modern Drama* 57:1 (21 January 2014): 77.

32 Ahmed, *The Cultural Politics of Emotion*, 102.

down in this performance. The use of Seán McDermott Street as the arena mobilises it as a charged space: performer and spectator encounter each other in affective relation. The performance unravels the psychodynamics of shame itself. It is implication in the events themselves that the performance establishes as a starting point for thinking through a history that still lives through an ethical encounter with the others of the past. The moving bodies within the space, both performers and audience members, allow for a powerful staging of bidirectional temporality and, with it, the phenomenology of *après-coup* that subverts the forward thrust of neoliberalism, entangling its impetus with the forces of psychoanalytic time.

We Don't Know What's Buried Here: Neoliberal Waste

Exploring these examples of the Magdalene Laundry sites in contemporary experimental drama reveals the ruin as a potential space of critique and interrogation that galvanises ethical resistances to neoliberal repurposing of shame. Grace Dyas's 2018 play *We Don't Know What's Buried Here* takes us further, as we unearth wasted lives. A powerful piece of protest literature, this play features two women-ghosts, Bernadette and Tina, both of whom are digging in Liberty Park, just outside the walls of the Seán McDermott Street laundry. Dyas's theme is the very act of unsettling the past, of digging up the earth: its graves, its secrets. They have recently heard of the Hotel Tokyo's plan to purchase the site and they frantically dig before it is covered up and over. Bernadette is searching for her baby daughter's body, while Tina – initially searching for her baby – is now searching for the reports, cover-ups and burials of the Irish state:

> We don't know what's buried here
> — **Buried here, here**
> — I am standing here
> — **With god knows what else, drug paraphernalia, a human shit, with pink toilet paper, soggy, left upon it, a human shit, it's buried here too, pages and pages of reports, reports on the inner city, reports on poverty, exclusion, drugs, the church, the magdalenes, the murders, the buildings, the traffic, the air, pollution, play facilities, community development, Michael Colgan, imagine it;**[33]

[33] Grace Dyas, *We Don't Know What's Buried Here*, unpublished manuscript.

In never-ending exhumation, they expose Ireland's shame, an exposure that they will not fill or cover over. The excavation both expresses the necessity of ethical recovery and parodies the neoliberal work ethic (Leo Varadkar is repeatedly invoked in the play for his 'early riser' work claims). Their refrain – almost chant – is: 'and so we must dig'.

However, there is nothing redemptive about this effort. In Dyas's play, in spite of Varadkar's exhortations, time is not well spent. Time is wasted: in continuous acts of digging. These ghosts waste their time dredging up the abject that Ireland does not want to deal with. Bernadette and Tina stage neoliberal rubbishing. They put it on stage. Their digging is linked to the pointlessness of painstaking reports into the abuses of Ireland's past, which are reinterred in the masses of information. The play offers an inconclusive vision, not unlike many of the reports they search for. At one point Bernadette says: 'Maybe someone else can do the digging and we can read the reports'.[34] The reports want to moralise the laundries then in order to materialise the value of the land now. They turn the past of the laundries into a spectacle of national shame responsibly dealt with. Against this, Dyas recovers unsettling between past and present. Dyas's ghosts are enmeshed with the abject site they are excavating, and condense a multiplicity of subject positions: Magdalenes, the homeless of post-Tiger Ireland, a drug-ravaged inner-city community, as well as complicit agents of neoliberalism's presentist agenda (authors of reports, capitalist workers):

— **We have to be kept away from everyone else.**
— We can't corrupt this place.
— **We are women who had sex.**
— Dirty sluts.
— **We are welfare cheats.**
— So kill us with cuts
— **We are the inferior race.**
— They did this because they couldn't kill us.
— **Now, they are waiting for us to die.**

Shame suffuses everything here, as the women articulate not just their abjection by society but their shaming by that society, a shaming that takes places both in the past and in the present, exposing the neoliberal repurposing project as a sham: the past was indeed bad, but so too is the present, and they unfold along similar biopolitical lines.

[34] Dyas, *We Don't Know What's Buried Here.*

The capitalist moment is not located solely in the present, rather it shows itself stretching back into the past, as a fundamental condition of the laundries themselves. As a site of industry, time in the laundry was intensely managed. The laundries were fundamentally about commerce, with women aggressively inscribed into a regime that maximised their bodies as resource. Dyas's play not only highlights pervasive interpenetrations of past and present, but also asks us to think of the abuses of the Magdalene Laundry system as part of a biopolitical continuum of (dialectically different) abuses across the multiple times and spaces of the Irish nation, but globally, too. Bernadette and Tina are the outcasts of a modernity that renders them as wasted lives.[35]

Dyas's refusal to demarcate past and present, then and now, here and there, is a call to action. Instead of cloistering the past, or having the present remade in encounter with it, she stages a multidirectional temporality that exceeds both self-other as well as the usual past/present/future distinctions. In this way, *We Don't Know What's Buried Here* offers an even more sustained interrogation of neoliberal temporality than the brilliantly effected *Magdalen* and *Laundry*. While these texts figure the site of the ruin as a space that enables an ethical witnessing of the past through an interweaving of the *après-coup*, engulfing neoliberal presentism, Dyas's play moves beyond the lure of the ruin into the earth itself, highlighting the pervasive rhizomes of capitalist biopower and the impossibility of escape from them. The wasteland functions as a metaphor (Bernadette and Tina both reflect on their digging as a metaphor) for both the abjected bodies on society's margins – past and present – and the systems that inter them in the material and discursive operations of biopower.

As I have argued in this essay, neoliberal temporality has been a dominant tool in managing – quarantining – the past horrors of these institutions. The contemporary repurposing of the laundries – which includes the actual and proposed building plans, in addition to the political discourses of a darker past – are part of the same project. There is a fault line here: an inherent tension. The ruins are an ambiguous spectre on the neoliberal horizon: they suggest a bygone era but they also haunt the present, giving the past new life. This is the disruption that we see in *Magdalen* and *Laundry*. These experimental dramas shatter the unities of time and space on stage to reveal how, under certain conditions, moving on can trigger a reckoning with the past in the *après-coup*. Dyas moves beyond psychoanalytic time

[35] Zygmunt Bauman, *Wasted Lives: Modernity's Outcasts* (Cambridge: Polity, 2013).

by moving beyond subjectivity – beyond ideas of self and other – as well as the usual distinctions between past and present. This disassembles neoliberal logic in a radical dispersal. Dyas's particular mode of spatial and metaphorical layering zooms out from any individual subject position (on which the self-other divide relies) to confront continuities between the Irish case and the wasteland of neoliberal biopolitics more generally. The play's final words are an act of intersubjective care across the ages. They imagine an ethics of affective connection beyond neoliberal self-interest. They gesture beyond the wastelands of neoliberalism, where another world may still be possible:

— Do you want me to watch your shovel while you sleep?
— **Thanks, that would be great.**
— Goodnight
— **Goodnight**[36]

Appendix

Seán McDermott Street: In 2017, the hotel chain Tokyo Inn offered Dublin City Council €14.5 million for the Seán McDermott Street laundry site, but after considerable activism and resistance, councillors voted in September 2018 to halt the sale. Over 10,000 people signed a protest petition calling on the council to vote against the sale. Dublin City Council did so overwhelmingly. Councilor Gary Gannon called on the government to listen to survivors and their families and recognise the 'social, cultural and personal history' of the site: 'This building provides us an opportunity to create a physical space where future generations can touch the walls and know that what occurred in these institutions were not exaggerated.' A new initiative, *Open Heart City*, was announced, involving academics in multiple disciplines and international architects. This would 'facilitate the emergence of a shared design for the Seán McDermott Street site, by paying attention to previous survivor consultation reports and through further consultation with those personally affected by the Magdalene Laundries'.

Sunday's Well: There was also resistance to a proposed apartment complex on the Sunday's Well site in Cork by Moneda Developments. In 2017, the Justice for Magdalenes Research organisation

[36] Dyas, *We Don't Know What's Buried Here.*

made a submission to Cork City Council. After deliberating, Cork City Council informed the developers that they must carry out a geophysical survey to identify any unmarked graves at the site. The council also said that 'research on the records of residents of the institution, numbers of recorded deaths and recorded burials including an assessment of the likely occurrence of undocumented burials of children are required in the context of evidence from comparable institutions in Ireland'. Despite much opposition, Moneda got permission for 202 apartments in 2018. With permission secured, the site was put up for sale in 2019, then taken off the market a few months later. At that time, Councillor Kenneth Collins called on Cork City Council to buy the site and construct elderly care facilities. As of September 2023, Sunday's Well was still owned by Moneda.

Donnybrook: The site of the Donnybrook laundry in Dublin, owned by investment firm Montlake, has also been proposed as an apartment complex, with plans to demolish the structure and redevelop the space. In 2016, JFMR made a submission to the council, which also took advice from archaeologists and other advocacy groups, amid concerns about unrecorded burials at the site. The developers withdrew their application in 2017, but then resubmitted in 2019, and a plan to develop forty-four apartments on the site was passed by the city council.[37]

This essay is dedicated to Kitty Costello, my wonderful Nana. Huge gratitude to Abby Bender and Mary McGlynn for their insights on drafts of this piece. Thanks also to the volume's editors, Seán Kennedy and Joseph Valente for their incisive and theoretically illuminating feedback and advice on the shaping of this essay. Additionally, my gratitude to Erin Layton and Grace Dyas for their gracious permission to quote from their brilliant unpublished manuscripts. And thanks to Mark Davis and Paulo Nunes dos Santos for permission to reproduce their powerful photographs for this essay.

[37] For these and further details of the three sites, see Claire McGettrick, Katherine O'Donnell, Maeve O'Rourke, James M. Smith and Mari Steed, *Ireland and the Magdalene Laundries: A Campaign for Justice* (London: Bloomsbury, 2021); Luke Byrne and Ryan Nugent, 'City Magdalene Site May Contain Human Remains, Expert Warned', *Irish Independent*, 6 March 2017; Kevin O'Neill and Rob McNamara, 'Anger as 200 Homes Approved for Good Shepherd Site', *Irish Echo*, 22 September 2018; Robert McNamara, 'Good Shepherd Convent Taken Off the Market; Site Was Earmarked for 200 Homes', *Irish Echo*, 18 September 2019.

Chapter 6

Shame and the Breastfeeding Mother in Ireland

Abby Bender

In recent years, there has been much discussion about why breastfeeding rates in Ireland are the lowest in Europe, perhaps even the lowest globally.[1] Hundreds of articles in newspapers and blogs signal how fraught the topic has become: that breastfeeding, or rather, its widespread absence, is presented as not just a fact but a crisis, and a site for national self-examination: Why, ask the newspapers, don't Irish mothers breastfeed? As medical literature and social movements in both Western and developing nations argue for the benefits of breastfeeding, there has been a great mobilisation, at both national and grassroots levels, to encourage Irish mothers to breastfeed. First Lady Sabina Higgins now organises an annual 'latching on' event to raise awareness of low rates of breastfeeding in Ireland, and in 2018 she said that the global movement for breastfeeding was 'probably the most important thing in the world'.[2] President Higgins has also been involved in the campaign, which included a 2016 presidential Christmas card depicting Mary nursing the infant Jesus.

Yet even in this period of 'latch-on' events, a nursing Madonna holiday greeting and the 'Breastfeeding Welcome Here' signs in city shops and cafés, a Nigerian asylum-seeker was denied the extra food she needed for herself to nurse her three-month-old child.[3] For

[1] Yvonne Hogan notes, 'We have one of the lowest breastfeeding rates in the world with just 49pc of babies being exclusively breastfed when leaving the hospital. By 12 weeks, just 16pc of babies are exclusively breastfed'. 'What I know about feeding babies', *Irish Independent*, 24 February 2020.

[2] Quoted in Damien Cullen, 'Sabina Higgins calls breastfeeding drive "the most important thing in the world"', *Irish Times*, 25 June 2018.

[3] Elaine Keogh, 'A mum living in Direct Provision was allegedly threatened with being transferred to another centre when she complained', *Irish Mirror*, 25 September 2016.

asylum-seeking mothers housed in Ireland's infamous Direct Provision centres – where families are often forced to live for years in institutional settings while awaiting processing – a ghettoised austerity inhibits breastfeeding. The 'Infant Feeding Guidelines for Direct Provision Centres' admits that immigrants 'from countries with supportive breastfeeding cultures' may have been given the 'impression that Ireland does not value or promote breastfeeding',[4] and indeed, this institutional discouragement of breastfeeding for those held at the margins is an echo of both past and present, in which breastfeeding was and remains a site of shame. Breastfeeding promotion in Ireland is, as in other first-world countries, represented in ways that are overdetermined by race and class.[5] The images of the Higginses' breastfeeding promotion events, with the ornate backgrounds of their formal reception rooms and privileged, white guests celebrating motherhood and breastfeeding with pride, should be read alongside the stories – current and past – of women whose feeding practices have been quite literally controlled and abjected by state institutions: Mother and Baby Homes and Magdalene Laundries in the twentieth century, Direct Provision in the twenty-first.[6] In other words, breastfeeding must be considered along with the other ways in which women's bodily practices in Ireland have been regulated, directly or indirectly – that is, through biopower, and specifically, shame – by the state: a state whose enshrining of motherhood in the 1937 Constitution reified, as Mary McGlynn writes, 'a longstanding effort to control unruly female bodies, transforming cultural and religious practice into state policy'.[7] Although we can read bodily regulation of women and children most explicitly in institutions that literally imprison them within 'architectures of containment', in James Smith's phrase, biopower of course works its way into every woman's body, whether her walls are gilded or crumbling. 'None of the building blocks of the shame-industrial complex was intrinsically Irish or intrinsically Catholic,' writes Caelainn Hogan, in her book

[4] 'Infant Feeding Guidelines for Direct Provision Centres in Ireland' (2005/7), 17. https://assets.gov.ie/119484/abfb02de-3cb0-4126-9005-b33adc0c37fb.pdf

[5] Martha Joy Rose, 'Breastfeeding in the Public Arena: The Deployment of Mixed and Contradictory Racialized Messages', in Roksana Badruddoja and Maki Motapanyane, eds, *'New Maternalisms': Tales of Motherwork (Dislodging the Unthinkable)* (Ontario: Demeter Press, 2016), 149.

[6] Ronit Lentin, 'Asylum seekers, Ireland, and the Return of the Repressed', *Irish Studies Review* 24:1 (2016): 3.

[7] Mary McGlynn, '"Embodiment, Abstraction, and Hidden Reproductive History", in Reproductive Justice and the Politics of Women's Health in Ireland', *Éire-Ireland: An Interdisciplinary Journal of Irish Studies* 56:3–4 (Fall–Winter 2021): 135.

Republic of Shame: Stories from Ireland's Institutions for 'Fallen Women'. 'But independent Catholic Ireland brought them to a sort of dark perfection'.[8]

Revelations, excavations and journalistic and literary examinations of these hidden histories have brought to light the experiences of women and children who suffered institutional incarceration and abuse. But even as reports are released, plaques hammered into place and apologies rehearsed by the state (if not the religious institutions most directly involved in the management and staffing of the homes and laundries), the damage persists, as birth, health and adoption records continue to be withheld from survivors and their children. Moreover, as activist writers and academics have been arguing for years, the carceral structures and experiences of twentieth-century institutions have much in common with the current system of Direct Provision. Nevertheless, a sort of historical blindness to the analogies persists.[9] Claire Bracken describes 'the forward-driving logic of neoliberal presentism' in former Taoiseach Enda Kenny's 2013 public apology for the Magdalene Laundries, a speech in which, Bracken notes, '"national shame" is being harnessed to move the nation forward':

> Today we live in a very different Ireland with a very different consciousness and awareness. We live in an Ireland where we have more compassion, empathy, insight and heart. We do, because at last we are learning those terrible lessons. We do, because at last we are giving up our secrets. We do, because in naming and addressing the wrong, as is happening here today, we are trying to make sure we quarantine such abject behaviour in our past and eradicate it from Ireland's present and Ireland's future.[10]

As Clair Wills points out, 'In this formulation violence against women belongs to the past; the present is superior to the past not only because we know more but also because we are willing to tell the truth about what we know. . . Kenny's faith in historical progress must surely give us pause, and particularly his idea that the present offers a vantage point from which the past can be judged, and "quarantined".'[11]

[8] Caelainn Hogan, *Republic of Shame: Stories from Ireland's Institutions for 'Fallen Women'* (Harmondsworth: Penguin, 2020), 29.

[9] Joseph Valente and Margot Gayle Backus, *The Child Sex Scandal and Modern Irish Literature: Writing the Unspeakable* (Bloomington: Indiana University Press, 2020), xvii.

[10] Claire Bracken, 'Laundering Complicity: Experimental Drama and the Temporalities of Irish Shame', this volume.

[11] Clair Wills, 'Coda: Edna O'Brien and Eimear McBride', in Eric Falci and Paige Reynolds, eds, *Irish Literature in Transition: 1980–2020, vol. 6* (Cambridge: Cambridge University Press, 2020): 301.

The inability of the state to recognise the ongoingness of this trauma has continued, and the 2021 final report of the Commission of Investigation into *Mother and Baby Homes Report* – 3,000 pages describing the horrors of this system – resulted in an immediate (and ongoing) outcry from survivors and activists about the report's attempt to again separate past abuses from present life.

The continued control of breastfeeding in Direct Provision exists in an Ireland that has also, of course, rejected some forms of state control over bodies by overturning the Eighth Amendment (legalising abortion) and approving same-sex marriage. In contrast, then, to the apparent discourse of a new, shame-free breastfeeding promotion that celebrates lactation is the underlying tension between the stated mission to increase breastfeeding rates and the absence of material change to make that possible for most women – and certainly those living in Direct Provision – to do so (parental leave, community/childcare support, understanding of long-term financial implications of stepping back from work). Equally important is the continued presence of shame around *both* breastfeeding and bottle-feeding. Breastfeeding in Ireland, and its current state of 'crisis', is not only about a shameful history of incarceration, the literal hiding away of the nursing mother's body in both domestic spaces of home and public institutional homes, but also the problem of feeding babies across today's neoliberal spaces, both public and private. Recent Irish writing from Emma Donoghue's *Room*, *The Wonder* and *The Pull of the Stars*, to Doireann Ní Ghriofa's *A Ghost in the Throat* all explore and enact the ambivalent responses to breastfeeding in Irish history, addressing directly the shame surrounding infant feeding, or repressing it, or recasting it, intentionally or unconsciously. Both in and beyond particular literary texts, past and present collide with ambiguous spaces that are both homes and incarcerating stand-ins for homes (Magdalene Laundries, Mother and Baby Homes, Direct Provision centres). By following personal, national and literary narratives as a single thread, we see that the 'crisis' of breastfeeding is not, as it has been popularly presented, the story of so-called 'Mommy Wars' and parenting styles (a narrative defined by conflict between women), but rather a more complicated expression of biopolitical control that involves Ireland's history of both direct and indirect control of women's bodies (a narrative about gender). In what follows I consider Irish women's breastfeeding (and bottle-feeding) as something, like shame, that connects us to the past rather than quarantining us from it.

Practice

Sabina Higgins spoke during a recent 'Friends of Breastfeeding' Awards Ceremony to address the remarkable reality that, in the 1970s, 'nobody seemed to know about breastfeeding'.[12] Novelist Mary Morrissy, recalling the pictures arrayed in her suburban Dublin 1960s home, notes one, Pieter de Hooch's *Woman Lacing Her Bodice Beside a Cradle*, that depicts a mother 'opening her bodice as a prelude to feeding the baby'. 'As a child,' Morrissy writes, 'I did not understand why the woman seemed to be in a state of undress – breastfeeding was not a common sight in the Dublin suburbs of the early 1960s'.[13] Historians have concurred that breastfeeding effectively died out as the primary mode of infant feeding in Ireland in the twentieth century. Higgins explained that, 'in the late 1940s, '50s and '60s the whole knowledge of breastfeeding stopped. In fact, the doctors were hardly able to say the word "breast" – they had become so conservative'. Higgins suggests that the cause of Ireland's infamously low breastfeeding rates seems to be related not only to the advent of formula feeding and its corporate promotion – well-known factors[14] – but also to shame: shame about the body, shame nurtured by the state and the Church, shame evoked in the popular discourse that has for generations described breastfeeding as 'dirty' or 'disgusting', or even, indeed, unspeakable.[15] Malignant shame – the postcolonial cultural inheritance that psychiatrist Garrett O'Connor diagnosed as inhibiting individual development and, particularly, relationships to others – is perhaps one explanation for the fraught state of nursing in Ireland, past and present.[16] The Irish history of wet-nursing, too, includes ambivalent, anxious narratives – both literary and cultural – of Irish breastmilk as dangerous and destabilising.[17] And, as I've written elsewhere, the history of famine imagery – and in

[12] Quoted in Cullen, 'Breastfeeding Drive'.

[13] Mary Morrissy, 'Four Paintings and a Cloakroom', in Rhona Richman Kenneally and Lucy McDiarmid, eds, *The Vibrant House: Irish Writing and Domestic Space* (Dublin: Four Courts Press, 2017), 53.

[14] Cullen, 'Breastfeeding Drive'.

[15] Aoife Rickard links body shaming instilled in the Irish people through the Catholic Church to low rates of breastfeeding. 'The Shame of Breast-Feeding? An Aspect of Irish Culture in Historical Perspective', *PaGes: Postgraduate Research in Progress* 4 (1997).

[16] See Chris Engel, 'From Malignant Shame to Resilience. From Addiction to Recovery', *Paces*, 27 June 2013. https://www.pacesconnection.com/blog/from-malignant-shame-to-resilience-from-addiction-to-recovery

[17] On wet-nursing in Ireland, see Jules Law, *The Social Life of Fluids: Blood, Milk, and Water in the Victorian Novel* (Ithaca: Cornell University Press, 2010).

particular, as Margaret Kelleher has shown, journalistic accounts of dead famine mothers whose infants try to nurse from empty breasts – includes colonial history in its trauma.[18]

We get a picture of the complexity and ambivalence around breastfeeding in contemporary Ireland in Lenny Abrahamson's ironically titled *Prosperity* (2007), set in the Celtic Tiger years. The teenage Stacey, giving her infant a bottle that has dropped out of a stroller and onto the street, is accosted by a drunk man, weaving unsteadily on the sidewalk, his face covered in blood and dirt. 'Use your own milk . . . healthy,' he leers. 'Disgusting,' she replies, clearly referencing the idea of breastfeeding, although the referent of the disgust seems purposefully ambiguous, as the man is most clearly here abjected, and the can of beer he drinks perhaps suggestive of his own morning bottle.[19] The scene, with its threatening male gaze, figures the mother within the matrix of biopower's shame: the insistence on total motherhood even while Stacey has no place to safely feed her child during the day while the hostel where she lives (emergency state accommodation) is closed. In contrast to older, economically stable urban mothers more likely to breastfeed, the single teenage mother is essentially homeless, literally walking the streets; she is one generation away from the Mother and Baby Home, and her spatially contained life is approximate to that of the Direct Provision centre. Although Abrahamson here is clearly placing Stacey, and her attitudes about breastfeeding, within a working-class milieu, disgust associated with breastfeeding also cuts across class. Anne Enright, writing in her essay 'Milk' in the context of upper-middle-class Dublin (lactation consultants, not formula), writes that 'The milk surprises me. It does not disgust me as much as I thought it would.'[20] She continues, with sharp honesty: 'So I feed the child because I should and resign myself to staying home. I never liked being around nursing women – there was always too much love, too much need in the room.' Enright recounts how, forty years previous, an obstetrical nurse explained to her friend's mother that 'the only women who breast-feed are

[18] See Margaret Kelleher, *The Feminization of Famine: Expressions of the Inexpressible?* (Durham, NC: Duke University Press, 1997), 2, and Abby Bender, 'Nursing the Revival: Patrick Pearse, Breastfeeding, and Sacrifice', in Joseph Valente and Marjorie Howes, eds, *The Irish Revival: A Complex Vision* (Syracuse: Syracuse University Press, 2023), 277–91.

[19] Lenny Abrahamson, director, *Prosperity* (2007), produced by Element Films: Ed Guiney, Andrew Lowe/RTÉ.

[20] Anne Enright, *Making Babies: Stumbling into Motherhood* (New York: Norton, 2013), 39.

doctors' wives and tinkers', noting her own sense of the 'similar distaste in the midwives, a couple of months ago, who were obliged by hospital and government policy to prod the child and pinch my nipple'.[21] Embarrassment about feeding in public was, in a 2010 study, the top reason Irish women gave for not breastfeeding, and the feeling seems to extend, as Enright writes, to spaces of privacy as well, the shame, perhaps, of 'too much love, too much need'.[22]

In a counterpoint that demonstrates the very recent shift from disgust to crisis (at least in certain social milieu), a young woman in the RTÉ2-produced television series *Can't Cope, Won't Cope*, sitting in a fancy coffee shop, is shamed *into* breastfeeding; here she is pretending to breastfeed her infant brother, out of embarrassment about feeding him a bottle. It's a scene that could have played out in New York as well as Dublin, and the pressure to breastfeed, even amidst continued hostility to public breastfeeding, is not unique to Ireland. Yet Ireland offers a particularly damning double bind. One Irish promotion claims that 'breastfeeding is the norm for infants and young children in Ireland', a patent untruth that is aspirational rather than actual, as the culture lacks the generational experience and support to make it widely possible – to say nothing of Ireland's hidden history of breastfeeding as site of bodily control.[23] In fact, it is now part of the discourse of the breastfeeding crisis in Ireland that encouragement of breastfeeding, that 'breast is best', is too adamant, or that this pressure itself is responsible for the resistance to nursing in Ireland. An opinion piece in the *Journal* is titled 'Fussing about low breastfeeding rates reeks of mother-shaming';[24] another, 'Hundreds of Irish babies were breastfed in public yesterday and nobody noticed'[25] (a 'non-event event' to demonstrate the normality of public breastfeeding). The continued ubiquity of breastfeeding-as-controversy narratives illustrates the ambivalence around it (as Joan Copjec writes of the eighteenth century – equally relevant today – breastfeeding advocacy, too, expresses a profound anxiety).[26]

21 Enright, *Making Babies*, 40.

22 See Roslyn C. Tarrant, 'Factors Associated With Duration of Breastfeeding in Ireland: Potential Areas for Improvement', *Journal of Human Lactation* 27:3 (2011): 262–71.

23 Tara Pollack, 'Calling to the Breast: Contradictions in Irish Breastfeeding Discourse', *Eye on Global Health*, 12 June 2019.

24 Adrienne Corless, 'Fussing about low breastfeeding rates reeks of mother-shaming', *The Journal*, 6 August 2018.

25 Michelle Hennessy, 'Hundreds of Irish babies were breastfed in public yesterday and nobody noticed', *The Journal*, 16 August 2015.

26 Joan Copjec, 'Vampires, Breast-Feeding, and Anxiety', *October* 58 (1991): 26.

Ambivalence characterises the outpouring of contemporary writing about breastfeeding in Ireland, and whether articles advocate for its promotion or question it, their writing also includes the language of discomfort, regret, pain, sadness, disappointment, pressure and shame. One article explains, 'I felt shame [about introducing a bottle at night]. . . by about 22 weeks, I finished breastfeeding entirely. I was sad, and a bit disappointed with myself for not getting to six months as an exclusive breastfeeder, but I was also relieved.'[27] Interestingly, a 2020 study that assessed Polish women breastfeeding in Ireland found little of the shame that seems apparent in Irish women's experience; the Polish women in the study described Irish attitudes to breastfeeding in public as supportive and positive, both in terms of facilities and attitudes, but not pressuring (as they felt it was in Poland); 'they described Irish mothers as having the choice and freedom'.[28] On one hand, the Irish crisis seems to be the same as that in the US, Australia and Canada: a feminist divide over whether to view breastfeeding as liberatory and empowering or an entrapment in traditional patriarchal gender roles. The Polish women's perspectives, though, also points to what Sabina Higgins diagnosed at her latch-in event: that the source of the shame around breastfeeding in Ireland, and its low rates, are bound up intimately in (and passed down through) Irish history and culture in ways that are both deep and invisible – that is to say, at least partly through the traumas of institutional abuse that are intertwined with the history of Irish communities and families.

Most commonly, the discourse around breastfeeding in Ireland is removed from its relationship to history and culture, and instead focuses on the superiority of breastfeeding to bottle feeding by medical criteria that are deemed 'factual'. Yet the medical model is attentive only to the needs of the child, rarely the needs of the mother. Before the advent of modern infant formula, it was true that choosing to feed a child 'by hand' with animal milk, or pap – bread or porridge mixed with milk, and insufficiently nutritious – indeed imposed dramatic odds of death in infancy. In Ireland, as in England, the system of wet-nursing would force socially precarious mothers to substitute their own child's health for another's, risking the wet-nurse's own child's death from starvation, as George Moore dramatised in his novel *Esther Waters*. Certainly, that's no longer the case. A recent study

[27] Hogan, 'What I know about feeding babies'.

[28] Elizabeth J. O'Sullivan, Agnieszka O'Grady, Karolina Pawlak and John M. Kearney, 'A Qualitative Exploration of the Attitudes and Experiences of Polish Breastfeeding Mothers in Ireland', *Journal of Human Lactation* 37:2 (2021): 376.

found that the best outcomes for infants are related to the intention to breastfeed, rather than the breastfeeding itself.[29] Glenda Wall, writing about the Canadian case, argues that medicalised rhetoric promoting breastfeeding functions to displace the mother as a subject; to make the mother 'invisible'; that 'the celebration of breastfeeding can also reinforce essentialist tendencies within gender discourse'.[30] Joan Wolf has argued, in an often-cited line, that 'medical journals are replete with contradictory conclusions about the impact of breast-feeding: for every study linking it to better health, another finds it to be irrelevant, weakly significant, or inextricably tied to other unmeasured or unmeasurable factors'.[31] Recent work by Peter Balint explores the possibility that breastfeeding campaigns may do more harm than good.[32] But these claims, too, have their counterclaims in scholarly work. For Penny Van Esterik, Wolf's charge is 'patently untrue' and an '[attack] on breastfeeding advocacy'. Formula, Esterik implies, is 'not safe'.[33]

As Adrienne Rich noted decades ago, 'Most of the literature of infant care and psychology has assumed that the process toward individuation is essentially the *child's* drama, played out against and with a parent or parents who are, for better or worse, givens.'[34] Psychoanalytic readings of the breast as central to infant development also come into tension with the realities of how biopower constructs the experience of the mother; they are problematic, like the medical literature, for a nearly exclusive focus of infant rather than maternal experience. Only perhaps Laplanche's enigmatic signifier encompasses the complexities that include the multiple meanings of the breast for mother as well as child ('it is conflict-full, conflictual, because it is enigmatic, unknown, hidden, it involves the repressed').[35]

[29] Kerri Raissian and Jessica Su, 'The best of intentions: Prenatal breastfeeding intentions and infant health', *SSM – Population Health* 5 (2018): 93.

[30] Glenda Wall, 'Moral Constructions of Motherhood in Breastfeeding Discourse', *Gender & Society* 15:4 (2001): 603, 604, 593.

[31] Joan Wolf, *Is Breast Best? Taking on the Breastfeeding Experts and the New High Stakes of Motherhood* (New York: NYU Press, 2011), 600.

[32] Peter Balint, 'State Power and Breastfeeding promotion: A Critique', *Contemporary Political Theory* 17 (2018): 306–30.

[33] Penny Van Esterik, 'Foreword: What Flows Through Us: Rethinking Breastfeeding as Product and Process', in Tanya Cassidy and Abdullahi El Tom, eds, *Ethnographies of Breastfeeding: Cultural Contexts and Confrontations* (London: Bloomsbury, 2015), xvii; xvi; xxii.

[34] Adrienne Rich, *Of Woman Born: Motherhood as Experience and Institution* (New York: Norton, 1995), 35.

[35] John Fletcher and Martin Stanton, eds, *Jean Laplanche: Seduction, Translation, and the Drives* (London: ICA, 1993), 23.

Yet, as Enright writes, echoing Rich, 'What I am interested in is not the drama of being a child, but this new drama of being a mother'.[36] In Ireland, the medical, cultural and psychosocial displacement of the mother also resonates with the history of women's disenfranchisement from control over their own bodies, and so it is women's experience that interests me here. Like issues surrounding childbirth and abortion in Ireland, breastfeeding must be read within the context of Irish history.

Spaces

What Ronit Lentin has called Ireland's 'breathtaking history of incarceration',[37] where biopower is most visible, seeps into the other spaces of the nation. Like the metaphor of impurity, or infection, the contagion of shame spreads out from the dehumanising abuses of women's bodies in the Mother and Baby Homes and laundries, so that shame comes home to everybody wherever it lives: we cannot, as Duffy had proposed, quarantine the past. Breastfeeding can then be seen as a way in which literal bodily control is made into self-regulating biopower. Clara Fischer writes that 'the politics of shame, which required mass institutionalisation as a means of preserving a desired national identity of moral purity, is worth assessing in terms of place and women's physical occupation of space'.[38] While the metaphor of shame – as Fischer writes, presented as nakedness that requires concealment, or hiding away – is literalised in institutional settings, it is by no means limited to them. Again, we think of the many women who describe embarrassment and shame that keeps them from nursing even in their own living rooms, their own bedrooms (and today's equal, if opposite self-regulation, as when the scholar Elizabeth Johnston notes the 'panopticon of censuring eyes' witnessing her bottle feeding in her essay 'Big Mother').[39]

The shame was there before, too. As Cara Delay writes, 'the containment of the sexualised female body predates both modern architecture

[36] Enright, *Making Babies*, 49.

[37] Lentin, 'Asylum seekers', 24.

[38] Clara Fischer, 'Gender, Nation, and the Politics of Shame: Magdalen Laundries and the Institutionalization of Feminine Transgression in Modern Ireland', *Signs: Journal of Women in Culture and Society* 41:4 (2016): 836.

[39] Elizabeth Johnston, 'Big Mother: Images of Breastfeeding in Popular Culture and Literature', in Ann Marie A. Short, Abigail L. Palko and Dionne Irving, eds, *Breastfeeding and Culture: Discourses and Representation* (Bradford, ON: Demeter Press, 2018), 17.

and the Irish state of the 1920s and 30s. Indeed, legends and narratives on childbirth consistently advocated the containment of the pregnant or post-parturient body, demonstrating how traditional agrarian societies such as pre-1930s Ireland effectively confined and controlled women without the aid of modern institutions.'[40] Folklore about young women being abducted to serve as wet-nurses to fairy babies shifted into a medicalised discourse of lactation as a site of physiological instability. As James Smith notes in *Ireland's Magdalen Laundries and the Nation's Architecture of Containment*, the Infanticide Act of 1949 posits lactation as a source of mental imbalance.[41] In one case he records, it is stated that 'the balance of [a new mother's] mind was disturbed by reason of her not having fully recovered from the effect of giving birth to the child or *by reason of the effect of lactation* consequent upon the birth of the child'.[42]

Like so much else, breastfeeding was handled in a dehumanising way in the Mother and Baby Homes, where unmarried pregnant women were sent to secretly have babies (and suffer for their sins), and then work off their 'debt' until their babies were adopted or sent on to state institutions (mothers would often be sent to more unpaid labour in Magdalene Laundries). While both breast and bottle feeding were enforced in certain contexts, these options were entirely decided by the nuns who managed the homes, in ways that seemed premised on expediency, cost and the disruption of bonds between mother and child. One woman who worked at the infamous Bon Secours Mother and Baby Home in Tuam, County Galway, described how 'the Reverend Mother would nearly starve an infant in order to force a mother to breastfeed. A doctor would have to certify that the woman was unable to breastfeed before a bottle would be granted', while others were not permitted to breastfeed their children.[43] A mother from Bessborough Mother and Baby Home in Cork recently recounted her experience of having her child taken from her – 'ripped from my breast' – in the very moment of breastfeeding:

> In the nursery we had to breastfeed facing the wall. You daren't look at the woman next door in case you caught a glimpse of her breast it was immoral. But the door was behind, now I know why. The day my son was ripped from my breast they creep up behind you and they snatch

[40] Cara Delay, 'Women, Childbirth Customs and Authority in Ireland, 1850–1930', *Lilith 21* (2015): 12.

[41] James Smith, *Ireland's Magdalen Laundries and the Nation's Architecture of Containment* (Manchester: Manchester University Press, 2008), 54.

[42] Quoted in Smith, *Ireland's Magdalen Laundries*, 58, my emphasis.

[43] Hogan, *Republic of Shame*, 130.

> the child that's how they do it. I ran down this corridor shouting where are you taking my child?, she was running faster than I was. And then she went through these two doors and that was it you are not allowed go any further [*sic*].[44]

The passage shifts into the present tense so that the memory of the baby's removal becomes an ongoing threat ('they creep up . . . they snatch the child . . . that's how they do it'), the dream-like narrative recalling the folklore of fairy abductions, which indeed had often described the sense of instability and threat around the lactating mother.

June Goulding, a midwife in Bessborough in the mid-1950s, describes girls sitting on milking stools, forced to directly nurse each other's babies and to pump milk to be given to other children. Goulding implies the link between the mothers and cattle, suggesting that both the economy of milk, and a pointed cruelty, were behind the intensely structured and monitored nursing practices that were enforced there. Indeed, what Goulding describes suggests a sort of brutalised inversion of the milk kinship or fostering traditions of an earlier Ireland,[45] in which strong traditions of fostering by wet-nurses enacted connectedness (and also created anxiety about cultural and political contagion between the Anglo-Irish elite nurslings and their native Irish wet-nurses). And yet the tradition of fostering (including wet-nursing) demonstrated what is perhaps a now-lost ideal of connectedness: 'breast milk as a substance standing for the openness and intertwinement of our embodied selves to and with the world', a 'compelled generosity'.[46] This intertwinement is perhaps precisely the opposite of what the homes created: isolation, austerity, a walled-off world that particularly refused the connection between mother and baby, whose contacts were highly limited, intensely surveyed and ultimately cut off completely; mothers were rarely allowed to keep their children, who were often illegally or under coercion sent for adoptions, frequently in the United States. Nursing practices and disallowances in the Mother and Baby Homes were, of course, just

[44] Seamus Whelehan, 'Bessborough the Secret Penitentiary', *Cork Views & News*, 21 October 2014.

[45] June Goulding, *The Light in the Window* (London: Ebury Press, 2005), 17.

[46] Sara Shabot Cohen, 'Edible Mothers, Edible Others: On Breastfeeding as Ambiguity', in Sara Cohen Shabot and Christinia Landry, eds, *Rethinking Feminist Phenomenology: Theoretical and Applied Perspectives* (London: Rowman and Littlefield, 2018), 20.

one aspect of bodily control that included, ultimately, the permanent separation of mother and child.

Miriam Haughton describes a striking scene in Anu Productions' *Laundry*, a site-specific performance in the former Seán McDermott Street Magdalene Laundry in Dublin, in which audience members encounter a young woman 'bathing in a bath of cold water mixed with what appeared to be breast milk, expressed by her leaking breasts'. The milk is a sign of separation from her child, who presumably would have been sent for adoption while she herself was transferred from one carceral institution to another. Haughton writes that 'being faced with a shivering, naked, vulnerable body and instructed to wrap and cover her breasts conveys the fragility of these women in this repressive place, and the policy of denying the evidence of their motherhood'.[47] Narratives of enforced, denied and otherwise policed breastfeeding in Mother and Baby Homes are only beginning to be represented; they include the shocking breast abscesses and dangerous mastitis for which women were denied antibiotic treatment, and, ultimately, the deaths of many babies through insufficient feeding.

The 2021 report from the Mother and Baby Homes Commission (and recent work by scholars and journalists, and particularly the historian Catherine Corless) reveals what had been known, at least to some degree, already: that the neglect was endemic and often fatal. In 1943 at Bessborough, 75 per cent of the babies born died within a year, many of them, the Commission of Investigation report suggests, as a result of inhumanely managed feeding regimens.[48] Chillingly, even before the report was released, Hogan spoke to forensic archeologist Niamh McCullagh about whether exhumed remains could reveal the infants' cause of death, and McCullagh suggested a likely cause: 'Malnutrition'.[49] These traumatising encroachments on bodily practice, motherhood and life itself circulated beyond the walls of the institutions, and inflected feeding practices of the women, their future children, their confidants. As Wills writes about these buried infants, 'They did not survive, yet they have not gone away.'[50]

[47] Miriam Haughton, 'From Laundries to Labour Camps: Staging Ireland's "Rule of Silence" in Anu Productions' *Laundry*', *Modern Drama* 57:1 (2014): 81.

[48] Yvonne Murphy, William Duncan and Mary Daly, *Final Report of the Commission of Investigation into Mother and Baby Homes*, chapter 18, 'Bessborough', 22.

[49] Hogan, *Republic of Shame*, 229.

[50] Clair Wills, 'Family Secrets', *New York Review of Books*, 16 August 2018.

One mother whose child died in Bessborough recalled the horrors of how prescribed feeding practices seem to have led to his death. Hogan recounts Bridget's story:

> [She] first noticed William was sick three days after he was born. She was made to sit on a stool in a cold corridor outside the nursery to breastfeed him. 'I said to Sister that he wasn't eating', she recalled. 'She snatched him from my arms and said I wasn't feeding him properly. She rammed the bottle down his little throat'. His medical record said he had difficulty swallowing. Bridget had abscesses on her breasts, but the Sister would push his little mouth to Bridget's nipple until he struggled to breathe. The harshness with which the children were treated horrified her. 'They weren't fit to look after children', she said of the nun.[51]

Following an inspection at Bessborough in 1941, as Conall Ó Fátharta notes, a report showed 'there was a "tendency to discourage breast-feeding" . . . that . . . may be partly responsible for the high infant mortality rate at the institution'. The nun in charge insisted that, in fact, 'women *are* forced to breastfeed when they feel disinclined to do so'.[52] In other words, the regimented rules around breastfeeding functioned to shame women for failing to provide adequate 'natural' nutrition even as breastfeeding – undertaken in a profoundly 'de-naturalised' format (women disallowed from the regular feedings that would establish sufficient milk supply, forced to pump milk and feed it to babies on spoons, prevented from breastfeeding at all or forced to do so) that undermined the very biological function itself. In most cases, breastfeeding and the often equally austere versions of bottle feeding were strictly managed by nuns with neither training nor experience in how to care for new infants and new mothers.

As we recall Sabina Higgins's claim that breastfeeding was simply not known about, we might account for the nation's unknowing with something like Guy Beiner's idea of social forgetting.[53] As Mary Burke has written of the repeated forgetting of women's and children's traumas, specifically the recurrent social and scholarly amnesia surrounding the existence of Protestant, versus Catholic, institutions for unmarried mothers and their children (and the non-Catholic children who suffered in them), 'the word that occurs

[51] Hogan, *Republic of Shame*, 236.
[52] Conall Ó Fátharta, 'Special Report: Nuns told don't co-operate as Bishop tried to thwart probes into Bessborough scandal', *Irish Examiner*, 23 November 2015. My emphasis.
[53] Guy Beiner, *Forgetful Remembrance: Social Forgetting and Vernacular Historiography of a Rebellion in Ulster* (Oxford: Oxford University Press, 2018).

is "disremember", a dialect term meaning "to forget", but that I [Burke] use here to refer to a continual failure to recall something of which one has been repeatedly reminded'.[54] What was forgotten and what was remembered in the shame and abuses around breastfeeding as a bodily practice? How did the history of breastfeeding and its disastrous management in Mother and Baby Homes inflect the patterns of breastfeeding across the general population, and did it also contribute to Irish women 'forgetting' how to breastfeed?

Historian Caitriona Clear suggests that the choice to bottle feed was a sign of mid-century Irish women's confidence, a sort of resistance to essentialism, in which women stood up to traditional Catholic counsel that advocated breastfeeding. Clear reads the turn away from breastfeeding as a rejection of biological determinism and the enforced domestic role of De Valera's cosy homestead – an argument which remains a powerful feminist position today (among the many, and contradictory, feminist positions on breastfeeding).[55] Empowerment was possible, as Cara Delay has written, despite the regulation of women's bodies: 'women themselves were hardly powerless. They came into conflict with family members, neighbours and priests as they attempted to secure a comfortable and autonomous place for themselves within their communities and within the centralising Catholic Church. As they created their own birth customs and rituals, women struggled with, negotiated or reworked, and in some cases rejected, both local norms and Church directives.'[56] Yet Clear recounts various sources that suggest a negative attitude to breastfeeding: its difficulty, its potential failure; interference with work; and perhaps most pointedly, the loneliness involved, for women would not even feed in front of their close family members.[57] A reading of empowerment through bottle feeding also leaves out the shame that seems to have informed these choices and made them the singular way out of literal spaces of confinement in the period, whether those spaces were private bedrooms or institutions.

Crisis

The failure of breastfeeding in Bessborough and other Mother and Baby Homes was literal, and fatal; babies starved to death under the

[54] Mary Burke, '"Disremembrance": Joyce and Irish Protestant Institutions', *Éire-Ireland* 55:1 (2020): 217.
[55] Clear, *Women of the House*, 142.
[56] Delay, 'Women, Childbirth', 7.
[57] Clear, *Women of the House*, 142.

regime of insufficient feeding overseen by untrained religious staff, and mothers were traumatised by the inability to sufficiently feed their babies (whether by breast or bottle). One inspection from August 1943 describes how only eight of twenty-seven babies between three weeks and nine months old were breastfed even partially, and how 'the greater number were miserable scraps of humanity, wisened, some emaciated and almost all had rash and sores all over their bodies, faces, hands and heads'.[58] Ó Fátharta, in reporting on these inspections and the subsequent responses (now included in the Commission of Investigation report), records the explanation for such limited breastfeeding as faulting the mothers, who are said to 'have plenty of rest, copious fluids and good nourishing diet. . . In the majority of cases the mothers are inclined to be fretful and have no love for their infants.' In other words, as Ó Fátharta writes, there is a 'bizarre attempt to lay the blame for the emaciated appearance of children on their mothers' lack of love'. Equally astonishing is the following passage from Bessborough's medical officer, Dr James O'Connor, explicating the causes of infant deaths there in the mid-1940s:

> Some infants saw a remarkable difficulty in digesting food [including breastmilk]. . . This is more remarkable in illegitimate children. . . It must be remembered that the period of Gestation of these children is far different to that of the married woman. The girl worries a great deal and is mentally upset over her condition. She is constantly trying to conceal the fact that she is pregnant, and in some cases every effort is made to get rid of the foetus. All this has undoubtly [*sic*] a most injurious effect on the developing foetus resulting in weak and defective children who have a poor resistance to disease and defective powers for assimilating food.[59]

The deaths, then, of three-fourths of Bessborough's babies is attributed not to malnutrition, or even starvation, of babies whose mothers had no control over how, when or what to feed their babies, but rather to the 'defective powers' of illegitimate children and their mothers. Yet alongside O'Connor's overdetermined narrative about the inevitability of these deaths, he articulates a biological reality about how maternal stress, malnutrition and trauma can lead to poor outcomes for children: a truth that ultimately reinforces how these women's lives and bodies were taken out of their control.[60] Whether breastfeeding was prohibited or forced, it was endowed with a sense of contradiction, shame and failure that seems to persist in Ireland

[58] Quoted in Ó Fátharta, 'Special Report'.
[59] Ó Fátharta, 'Special Report'.
[60] I'm grateful to Abby Palko for her nuanced suggestions about this passage.

today, despite attempts by mothers, and many good intentions by the state, to reverse course.

The traumatic failures – past and present – to support infant feeding make explicit the connection between the Mother and Baby Homes and Ireland's current system of Direct Provision. Fischer argues that, with Direct Provision, 'the culture of containment and shaming continues', and that, 'with regard to the specific shaming of women, there has been an extraordinary blindness to the legacy of normative assumptions around parenting and family structure'.[61] Like the disremembered abuses at Bessborough, Tuam and the rest, the difficulty that faces breastfeeding mothers in Direct Provision has been observed since its beginnings in 1999, when Patricia Kennedy and Jo Murphy-Lawless wrote that, although most women seeking asylum came from countries where breastfeeding was expected, the absence of material and social support in Direct Provision meant that breastfeeding was abandoned early. 'Women who found themselves sharing rooms with other women and babies often stated that they gave them bottles at night as they were trying to keep them quiet. In the accommodation we visited there were frequently unsafe facilities for bottle-feeding, with women having to boil kettles in already overcrowded bedrooms, and toddlers walking unsteadily among them. The diet required by lactating women to establish a good supply of milk was not easily available.'[62] A 2001 report on child poverty and social exclusion found similar: 'In some cases the absence of an adequate diet for pregnant women and mothers with young babies caused difficulties in breastfeeding. Women in hostels tended to give up breastfeeding within a few weeks of the birth of their babies. They were compelled to switch to expensive baby formula which they could ill-afford on direct provision. The result might be described as a vicious circle which further undermined their ability to care for their own needs.'[63]

The foreword to the Reception and Integration Agency (RIA)'s own 'Infant Feeding Guidelines for Direct Provision Centres in Ireland' addresses the intersection of different cultural histories with institutional, neoliberal practice:

> Despite the known benefits of breastfeeding, the majority of Irish parents currently choose not to breastfeed their babies. Residents in accommodation centres often come from countries with strong traditions of prolonged

[61] Fischer, 'Gender, Nation, and the Politics of Shame', 840.

[62] Patricia Kennedy and Jo Murphy-Lawless, 'The Maternity Care Needs of Refugee and Asylum-Seeking Women in Ireland', *Feminist Review* 73:1 (2003): 48.

[63] Angela Veale, Bryan Fanning and Dawn Connor, *Beyond the Pale: Asylum-Seeking Children and Social Exclusion in Ireland* (Dublin: Irish Refugee Council, 2001), 5–6.

> breastfeeding. However, mothers in Direct Provision Centres have the same right as Irish mothers to choose how to feed their infants. Irish research shows that the availability of free infant formula milk in these Centres is having an adverse effect on the prevalence, exclusivity and duration of breastfeeding among this group.[64]

The suggestion that free formula is the deciding factor in declining breastfeeding rates in Direct Provision centres seems especially facile, given the evidence of insufficient maternal nutrition and the challenges of shared living spaces. In 2019, a group of mothers in Direct Provision refused food to protest the inadequacy, catalysed by a centre's refusal of additional food for a breastfeeding mother.[65] In the same year, a position paper by the Faculty of Paediatrics at the Royal College of Physicians of Ireland called on the Direct Provision system to be abolished: 'When we look back in 10 years' time, we may ask ourselves how we allowed the system to exist. The debate sparked by the Tuam mother and baby story should prompt us to reflect on the manner in which all children are treated in Ireland, not merely citizen children.'[66] Given the shocks of excavated horrors at Tuam and Bessborough – and indeed, the Indigenous residential schools in North America – another ten years of reflection may not be necessary. The distance between Direct Provision's austerity and Dublin's nurse-ins is perhaps greater than that between Ireland's past and its present; or perhaps none of these things is very far apart at all. Perhaps substantive change – and not merely higher rates of breastfeeding, but less shame, anxiety and ambivalence around all feeding practices – requires conversations not only about health and parenting, but about Irish history, and what is buried there.

[64] *Infant Feeding Guidelines for Direct Provision Centres.*
[65] Carl Kinsella, 'Mothers in Direct Provision emergency accommodation refuse food in protest', *Joe*, August 2019.
[66] 'Children in Direct Provision: A position paper by the Faculty of Paediatrics', *Royal College of Physicians of Ireland*, December 2019. https://rcpi-live-cdn.s3.amazonaws.com/wp-content/uploads/2019/12/Direct-provision-position-paper-full-final-PDF.pdf

Chapter 7

'you: are you complicit?': Shame, Trauma and Gender in Susannah Dickey's *Tennis Lessons*

Alison Garden

Middle sister, the narrator of Anna Burns's Booker Prize-winning novel *Milkman* (2018), spends a significant amount of time ruminating on the curious nature of shame. '[O]ften [shame] was a public feeling,' thinks middle sister, 'needing numbers to swell its effectiveness, regardless of whether you were the one doing the shaming, the one witnessing the shaming, or the one having the shame done unto you'.[1] For middle sister, shame is deeply relational, enmeshed in social, cultural and national contexts. The preeminent philosopher of ethics, Bernard Williams, insists these relational contexts are crucial because 'the basic experience connected with shame is that of being seen, inappropriately, by the wrong people, in the wrong condition'.[2] This 'being [. . .] in the wrong condition' is not evenly experienced. In 'patriarchal societies', Clara Fischer cautions, the 'disciplining device' of shame 'operat[es] through structures of oppression, such as gender, but also class, race, ethnicity, sexuality, nationality, and related intersectional categories'.[3] The specific contours of national contexts that mark the Irish experience of shame shape the essays included in this volume. As an individual emotional response to publicly established norms, it is a form of self-disciplining or self-censoring: it is a community feeling that turns the individual into a witness against the self. Shame is, in Sîan White's words, a

[1] Anna Burns, *Milkman* (London: Faber & Faber, 2018), 53.

[2] Bernard Williams, *Shame and Necessity* (Berkeley: University of California Press, 2008), 78.

[3] Clara Fischer, 'Gender and the Politics of Shame: A Twenty-First-Century Feminist Shame Theory', *Hypatia* 33:3 (2018): 371.

'public feeling experienced individually'; for Caroline Magennis, it is 'a public emotion which is particularly corrosive to self-esteem, and which is monitored and policed by the community'.[4] What is more, shame is one of a number of 'invisible and insidious forms of harm' that, like trauma, might 'resist representation and thus communication'. Writing shame, then, poses writers with a particular challenge. How do you articulate an affect that demands both a subject and witness, or 'narrat[e] a harm that leaves no physical mark'?[5]

Here, I adduce a recent novel, Susannah Dickey's *Tennis Lessons* (2020), to illustrate how contemporary Northern writers are harnessing formal experimentation and literary playfulness to give voice to the individually depletive impacts of culturally produced affects. *Tennis Lessons* is a homodiegetic second person narrative, whereby the protagonist and narrator are the same: an unnamed *you* who guides the reader through the novel.[6] We follow *you* through childhood, adolescence and early adulthood through a series of diary-like vignettes, of which some are dated precisely, whereas others are dated vaguely by month and *you*'s age. The novel's intimate engagement and preoccupation with naming, and its absence, illuminates the primacy of language. It is worth highlighting that *you*'s narration reveals her to have an accomplished and dexterous command of language, something that she, and her mother, revel in during her earliest childhood years.[7] When she is six, *you* declares that her 'mother [. . .] seems to like [her] best when [she is] learning new words'.[8] After *you* makes a particularly sophisticated and amusing pun, *you*'s mother 'laughs [. . .] like a wind chime', much to *you*'s delight: 'You feel so happy you might burst' (T 9). This childhood precociousness, a source of much joy and pride, seems to surface only intermittently throughout the novel – in happy interludes with her closest friend Rachel, for example – which is further indicative of how deeply she is affected by her corrosive adolescent experiences.

Consisting of three parts, including a Prologue and an Epilogue, *Tennis Lessons* is written entirely in the present tense, with the

[4] Sîan White, 'A Hair–Trigger Society and the Woman Who Felt Something in Anna Burns' *Milkman*', *Genre* 54:1 (2021): 126; Caroline Magennis, *Northern Irish Writing After the Troubles: Bodies, Intimacies, Pleasures* (London: Bloomsbury, 2021), 141.

[5] Patricia Malone, 'Measures of Obliviousness and Disarming Obliqueness in Anna Burns' *Milkman*', *Textual Practice* 36:7 (2022): 1,167.

[6] Manfred Jahn, 'Second-Person Narration', in David Herman, Manfred Jahn and Marie-Laure Ryan, eds, *Routledge Encyclopaedia of Narrative Theory* (London: Routledge, 2005), 522. The second person narrative *you* will be italicised.

[7] Thanks to Joseph Valente for this, and for generous feedback on drafts of this essay.

[8] Susannah Dickey, *Tennis Lessons* (London: Penguin, 2020), 8. Hereafter (T page).

exclusion of the Prologue and Epilogue, which use the past tense to recall moments from *you*'s childhood. The chronological flow of the novel is disrupted by 'Part II', which has different formal properties calibrated to detail, at a month's distance, the rape she suffered as she turned seventeen. On this day, *you* decides not to turn up for the first exam of her A-levels but instead goes to the pub, where she watches her father on a date with another woman while still married to her mother; *you* gets drunk and subsequently crashes her car. The gradual unfolding of *you*'s traumatic sense of self in *Tennis Lessons* makes it clear that shame is a perniciously gendered form of violence: its corrosive effects can be seen in *you* well before her rape – 'you know you were strange and wrong from the beginning' – and stop her from seeking support for a decade (T 183).

The centrality of the external community or larger society to the experiencing of shame in *Tennis Lessons* asserts itself in a loud silence. Born in Derry, Dickey has elected, like many of her contemporaries, to withhold the sort of topical and topological references that would distinguish her story as 'Northern Irish'. Reflecting on her national identity, Dickey claimed, 'I don't want to speak to any ostensible uniqueness of becoming a person in Northern Ireland, because I never tried to become a person somewhere else, but it seems to me that so much was, and is, going unsaid.'[9] Dickey's attentive absence of naming thus works to unstitch the novel from a deterministically national reading, but does so along nationally characteristic lines.[10] Tying shame to gender is not an Irish phenomenon but there are particular Northern contexts that serve as inflection points. Dickey's careful framing of her novel situates it within and beyond these contexts; and, indeed, this idea of things 'going unsaid' calls to mind the careful lack of naming within Burns's *Milkman*.

'so much was, and is, going unsaid'[11]

In the hundred years since Northern Ireland's foundation, sexuality and gender have fundamentally conditioned the politics of shame in the six counties that constitute the statelet. Both northern and southern Irish states have been shaped by competing nationalisms that have been historically united in their reactionary desires to restrict

9 Susannah Dickey, quoted in Magennis, *Northern Irish Writing*, 181.
10 Magennis, *Northern Irish Writing*, 170.
11 Dickey, *On Intimacy*, quoted in Magennis, *Northern Irish Writing*, 181.

the rights of women and LGBTQ+ people.[12] Morally conservative religious values that insisted on the primacy of the heterosexual nuclear family, Catholic and Protestant, have been put to work in supporting and securing nationalist politics through the reproduction of the 'national family'. Kathryn Conrad notes that, while 'state and nationalist groups fight over geopolitical and ideological territory in the public sphere, they rely on the literal and ideological reproduction of their constituencies through the family cell in the private spheres'.[13] The effects of this have been far-reaching. Across the island, 'female sexual purity and chastity were regarded as being of the utmost importance', and 'there was no general acceptance of female sexuality expressed outside marriage'.[14] Access to contraception and reproductive rights has, until very recently, been fraught and, in many cases, criminalised.[15] Likewise, non-heteronormative sexualities have been pathologised and criminalised. Sexual activity between men was not decriminalised in the North until 1982 (although the age of consent was still higher than for heterosexual couples) and was not decriminalised in the Republic until 1993. Where the Republic has seen increasingly liberal social politics take root – two referenda, in 2015 and 2018, respectively, saw resounding support for both same-sex marriage and the provision of abortion services – this liberalisation has not taken place in the six counties. While both same-sex marriage and abortion were legalised in 2019 by an imposition from Westminster, access to vital reproductive services is still difficult, and there is still a distinct strand of homophobia within contemporary Northern Irish politics.[16] Through the 'heterosexualisation of nationalism', as Sally Munt terms it, divergent or

[12] Rob Kitchin and Karen Lysaght, 'Sexual Citizenship in Belfast, Northern Ireland', *Gender, Place and Culture* 11:1 (2004): 83–103; and Lisa Smyth, 'The Cultural Politics of Sexuality and Reproduction in Northern Ireland', *Sociology* 40:4 (2006): 663–80.

[13] Kathryn Conrad, *Locked in the Family Cell* (Madison: University of Wisconsin Press, 2004), 118.

[14] Leanne McCormick, 'One Yank and They're off: Interaction between U.S. Troops and Northern Irish Women 1942–1945', *Journal of the History of Sexuality* 15:2 (2006): 229.

[15] See Lisa Smyth, *Abortion and Nation: the Politics of Reproduction in Contemporary Ireland* (Aldershot: Ashgate, 2005).

[16] Kathryn Conrad, 'Queer Treasons: Homosexuality and Irish National Identity', *Cultural Studies* 15:1 (2001): 124–37. On restricted access to reproductive care, Olivia Dee, 'Three Families: abortion is now legal in Northern Ireland but more needs to be done so every woman has adequate access', *The Conversation*, 20 May 2021.

dissident sexualities and genders needed to be policed: shame is both a tactic and an effect of these efforts to police.[17]

The history of the contested Northern statelet has been marked by periods of intense violence, including the thirty-year conflict euphemistically labelled 'The Troubles'. This violence produced by the 'armed patriarchy' was not just physical but epistemic and emotional; for much of its hundred years, life in the North has been conditioned by a punitive and repressive culture.[18] Without wanting to propagate an artificially partitionist understanding of two statelets, there is an essential difference that marks the social, cultural and political fabric of life either side of the border. The 'postcolonial nation-building' that Clara Fischer reads as instrumental to the 'construction of the Irish nation' has not happened in Northern Ireland, a statelet that is still, legally, a constituent part of the United Kingdom.[19] While the relevance of terms like 'imperial', 'colonial' and 'postcolonial' are still debated in Irish historical, cultural and political studies – quite apart from what an uncritical use might do to flatten experiential realities across the island – there can be no doubt that the former (or continuing) 'colonial' antagonist, Britain, still structures much of life in the North.[20] Because of this complex colonial past, Patrick R. Mullen writes, 'the problems of the Irish struggle for freedom do not simply exist at the level of the state but extend to the intimacy of the erotic and pervade the social fabric'.[21] This has important repercussions for how shame, so often a gendered phenomenon, is generated, felt and thought about, and the literary explorations of this.

It is not just the sexuality of women and LGBTQ+ people that is deemed shameful, either, but their bodies too. Apart from the specific Irish contexts to this, noted previously and explored in more detail shortly, shame is intimately associated with bodies that deviate from heteronormative masculinity: women's and queer bodies become sites of shame and anxiety. Fischer points us towards Simone de Beauvoir's *The Second Sex* (1949) for confirmation that the onset of puberty and

[17] Sally Munt, *Queer Attachments: The Cultural Politics of Shame* (Aldershot: Ashgate, 2007), 57.

[18] Eileen Evason, *Hidden Violence: A Study of Battered Women in Northern Ireland* (Belfast: Farset Co–op Press, 1982), 73.

[19] Clara Fischer, 'Abortion and Reproduction in Ireland: Shame, Nation-building and the Affective Politics of Place', *Feminist Review* 122 (2019): 33.

[20] Stephen Howe, 'Questioning the (bad) question: Was Ireland a colony?', *Irish Historical Studies* 36:142 (2008): 138–152.

[21] Patrick R. Mullen, *The Poor Bugger's Tool: Irish Modernism, Queer Labor, and Postcolonial History* (Oxford; New York: Oxford University Press, 2012), 115.

menstruation is 'a curse' and marker of 'shame', because 'femininity signifies alterity and inferiority'.[22] The particular politics of the North have created a heightened culture of shameful stigma around women's bodies, queer bodies and bodily functions.[23] Perhaps nowhere was this revulsion towards women's bodies more apparent than in the public reaction to the 'No Wash' protest staged by the republican women prisoners of Armagh Gaol in the early 1980s. In solidarity with the male prisoners in the Long Kesh/Maze prison, who had been on a 'No Wash' protest since mid-1976, thirty republican prisoners of Armagh Gaol went on their own 'No Wash' protest in February 1980. In smearing their menstrual blood, as well as their faeces, on the walls of their prison cells, these women 'were seen as more disgusting and shocking than their male counterparts'.[24] The reaction to these strikes encapsulates the socially entrenched beliefs that women's bodies were a source of shame and should be disciplined; a wealth of scholarship has explicated how such attitudes are heightened during times of conflict.[25]

Shame is an epistemic and emotional form of violence that is often gendered, but it is also used to compound the effects of gendered violence including, in particular, sexual violence. The insidious effect of patriarchal ideas can lead to survivors of sexual violence feeling ashamed about what has happened to them. Reasons for this are complex and multifaceted but it is telling that sexually violent crimes have an appallingly low conviction rate. This is an issue that effects many national jurisdictions, although the problem is worse in Northern Ireland than in any other part of the UK and has historically been worse in the UK, and the Republic of Ireland, than the rest of Europe.[26] In 2003, a report written for Rape Crisis Europe declared that Ireland

[22] Simone de Beauvoir, *The Second Sex* (London: Vintage, 1997), 341; cited in Fischer, *Gender and the Politics of Shame*, 374.

[23] See Marian Duggan, *Queering Conflict: Examining Lesbian and Gay Experiences of Homophobia in Northern Ireland* (Farnham: Ashgate, 2012).

[24] Theresa O'Keefe, 'Menstrual Blood as a Weapon of Resistance', *International Feminist Journal of Politics* 8 (2006): 545.

[25] See Kathryn Conrad, 'Women Troubles, Queer Troubles: Gender, Sexuality, and the Politics of Selfhood in the Construction of the Northern Irish State', in M. Cohen and N. Curtin, eds, *Reclaiming Gender* (Basingstoke: Palgrave Macmillan, 1999), 53–68.

[26] See, for example, Rachel Killean, Eithne Dowds and Anne-Marie McAlinden, 'Sexual offence trials in Northern Ireland: the cultural and legal dimensions', in Rachel Killean, Eithne Dowds and Anne-Marie McAlinden, eds, *Sexual Violence on Trial: Local and Comparative Perspectives* (London: Routledge, 2021), 3–21; Alison MacKenzie, 'Why didn't you scream? Epistemic injustices of sexism, misogyny and rape myths', *Journal of Philosophy of Education* 56 (2022): 787–801; Anne-Marie McAlinden and Clare Dwyer, *Criminal Justice in Transition: The Northern Ireland Context* (Oxford: Hart Publishing, 2015).

had the 'lowest conviction rate' in Europe; as of 2009, 'more accurate data' revealed that, while the conviction rate was still 'among the lowest in Europe', it was no longer the lowest rate in Europe.[27] Of particular interest to us in our study of the literary and cultural representation of sexual violence and gendered shame is how these experiences are codified in representative terms in language or, perhaps more accurately, how they are not. Theresa O'Keefe, drawing on interviews conducted with Northern women who had endured sexual violence during the conflict, highlights how 'euphemisms [were] used in place of concrete terms' when talking about their experiences. She notes how words and phrases like 'inappropriate and that kind of thing bring it up to the next level [. . .] sexual interference' were used rather than explicit language.[28] This, O'Keefe asserts, is a common tactic for discussing 'all complicated subjects in the north'. In her stunning article on *Milkman*, Patricia Malone parses Burns's novel through 'the problematics of naming', which stem from 'the difficulty in naming a conflict so various in its valences'; after all, Malone asks us, '[w]hat does one do with a war that cannot be named as such?'. In *Milkman*, Malone argues, we have a 'speaker who has found a way to make what was unintelligible intelligible through the careful and precise use of language'. Dickey's *you*, I contend, is another such figure. In what follows, I explore how Dickey makes ingenious use of a literary device to narrate 'the shame-*status* that attaches to the very fact of existing' in a woman's body.[29] Shame is an affective wound, which, like other 'invisible and insidious forms of harm', as touched upon previously, 'resist[s] representation and thus communication'.[30] I argue that Dickey engages the second person narrative *you* to express the dissociative affect of shame and the silencing violence of shame in the face and aftermath of extreme harm.

The Relational Grammar of Shame

Tennis Lessons capitalises on the decidedly ambiguous nature – what Liz Constable calls the 'relational grammar' – of the second person

[27] Linda Regan and Liz Kelly, 'Rape: Still a forgotten issue. Briefing Document for Strengthening the Linkages–Consolidating the European Network Project', September 2003, 10. https://nokjoga.hu/wp-content/uploads/rape-still-a-forgotten-issue-2003.pdf.
[28] Theresa O'Keefe, 'Policing unruly women: The state and sexual violence during the Northern Irish Troubles', *Women's Studies International Forum* 62 (2017): 75.
[29] Bonnie Mann, 'Femininity, Shame, and Redemption', *Hypatia* 33:3 (2018): 403.
[30] Malone, 'Measures of Obliviousness', 6.

you narrative.[31] The use of 'you' is an extradiegetic gesture inviting the reader to place themselves in the text. The 'referential scope of *you* [. . .] may include real readers,' says Jamila Mildorf, an effect given greater power in Dickey's novel because her protagonist is unnamed and *you* is not capitalised.[32] The pronoun *you* seeks to interpellate the reader into an ambiguous relationship with the text leading readers to question who the subject might be and their relationship to this subject. *You* relies on an Other, whether this is an imagined Other, a heterodiegetic narrator to a *you* protagonist, or the making of oneself Other through temporal or another remove. In such a way, second person *you* generates a second perspective or external gaze: it produces a subject and another. Such an aesthetic choice embodies what Liz Constable terms the 'relational grammar' of shame, in recognition of shame's socially and individually constructed nature.[33] This aesthetic choice by Dickey neatly maps on to the intimate explorations of what it means to feel shame, especially as it relates to the experience of being a girl in an oppressively patriarchal society.

While there are some instances within *Tennis Lessons* that we might think of as 'acutely' shameful, we can also view this use of second person *you* as a direct effort to reflect the shame of *feeling* Other. Dickey's use of the second person *you* works to narrate the 'ubiquitous shame' of feeling Other: or what Bonnie Mann describes as 'the shame-*status* that attaches to the very fact of existing as a girl or woman, or of having a female body'.[34] Denise Wong suggests that the second person *you* produces what Jean-Paul Sartre 'describes as the realising gaze of the Other in the phenomenological structure of shame'.[35] Within white, Western patriarchy, shame is everywhere encoded in bodies and experiences which deviate from the heteronormative. The formal properties of *Tennis Lessons* enable Dickey to illustrate the depletive effects of shame through an unflinching internal monologue. *You* ruminates repeatedly about her feelings of difference and exclusion: 'you [. . . are] wrong, and strange, and different'; 'You're an aberration'; 'you know you were strange and wrong from the beginning' (T 37, 83, 183). Given that Dickey's *you* is a narrator-protagonist,

[31] Liz Constable, 'Introduction: States of Shame', *L'Esprit Créateur* 39:4 (1999): 4.
[32] Jarmila Mildorf, 'Second-Person Narration in Literary and Conversational Storytelling', *Storyworlds: A Journal of Narrative Studies* 4 (2012): 75.
[33] Constable, 'Introduction: States of Shame', 4.
[34] Mann, 'Femininity, Shame, and Redemption', 403.
[35] Denise Wong, 'Gazing beyond the fourth wall: shame and second-person narration in *Fleabag*', *Textual Practice* (2021): 14.

these utterances read like a punitive, self-shaming internal dialogue that actively and intimately places demands upon the reader. A sizeable proportion of *you*'s shame is directed towards her body. At one point, *you* laments feeling 'so obstinately different from what a nearly eighteen-year-old woman should be, should look like', and her internal monologue is relentlessly punishing: 'your new year's resolution is to be normal' (T 83, 51). When *you* gets her first period, it is a 'messy and public bloodletting' which seeps through her clothes, which 'mark[s her] out, again, as wrong' (T 36, 37). At sixteen, *you* decides to get to know her 'vulva', and the 'adult pleasure' it promises, but her early attempts at masturbation make her 'cringe', and she berates herself, asking 'why aren't you feeling anything?' (T 22). The narrator-protagonist of *Tennis Lessons* registers a general disgust with her body in addition to her specific anxieties about her body as gendered.

From the start, *Tennis Lessons* unfolds a powerful meditation on the myriad ways in which the very experience of being a girl can be a cause of shame in and of itself. At the midpoint of the novel, however, *you* is subject to a violent sexual assault which compounds the shame *you* feels about herself exponentially. In Part II, the section of the novel that most concretely depicts this attack and its aftermath, Dickey makes use of numerous devices to illustrate how the 'invisible and insidious' effects of this assault impact on *you*. The chronology of Part II is also unlike the rest of the novel: there is an extended account of the first half of 'May 16th (today)' – when *you* will get drunk, watch her father on an adulterous date, and miss her first exam – which is interrupted by a brief vignette of 'April 14th (one month ago)'. This vignette details *you*'s sexual assault. The language and grammar here are different from the rest of the novel: the sentences run on without full stops, forming fragmented and disjointed paragraphs. Such use of language suggests the overwhelming horror of the situation, where the rules of grammar and punctuation disintegrate under the weight of trauma. This flashback to her rape is a technique that Robert Garratt argues is characteristic of a 'trauma novel', fiction that 'employs [. . .] memories, flashbacks, dreams, and hauntings' to reproduce the neurological effects of trauma on the brain.[36]

This formal rendering of *you*'s traumatised state is mirrored in *you*'s narrative arc and actions. As noted previously, *you* had already developed a tendency to self-shame herself; after the assault, this punitive rhetoric morphs into physical punishment and destructive

[36] Robert F. Garratt, *Trauma and History in the Irish Novel: The Return of the Dead* (Basingstoke: Palgrave Macmillan, 2011), 5.

behaviour. This includes acts of deliberate self-harm like holding her hands under the hot tap until the 'skin on [her] fingers is repentant and stinging' (T 76). After drinking 'four double vodkas and lemonades', *you* crashes her car and misses an A-level exam; this depiction of violence against *you* exacerbates the brutality of her rape and gestures towards the self-destructive behaviour that sexual assault survivors can adopt (T 115). Dickey also records *you*'s distressed mental and physical state – 'You don't sleep much at all now' – as the character grapples with the aftereffects of the assault (T 76). The next vignette is dated in September, and an eighteen-year old *you* tells us she did not sit any of her exams, and will be returning to school to retake them. The second person *you* was chosen precisely because Dickey felt it 'most adequately captures the potential dissociative impact' and 'simultaneous distancing and closeness for writing trauma'.[37] How to adequately begin to convey trauma through language is something that writers have struggled with; after all, as Anne Whitehead declares, 'if trauma comprises an event or experience which overwhelms the individuals and resists language or representation, how then can it be narrativized in fiction?'[38] Dickey's rhetorical strategy of second person narration enables her to intimate the deleterious afterlives of trauma and the particular qualities of traumatic memory, marked by 'amnesiac estrangement' and dissociation.[39]

This assault is not just traumatic but a 'shame-event': an incident that generates 'unbounded shame'.[40] We know this because, in addition to the graphic portrayal of *you*'s rape, the events of Part II's 'May 16th' also involve a trip to a sexual health clinic, where *you* is unable to report her assault to the sexual health nurse. Instead of saying anything – 'You want her to know without you having to tell her' – *you* shows the nurse her infected ingrown toenail, smelling of 'egg and sulphur and musty laundry'.[41] This is, of course, a physical manifestation of the enormous pain that *you* is enduring. *You*'s decision not to report her attack is revealing, and research suggests that one of the primary deterrents to survivors reporting rape or sexual assault is shame. Karen Weiss maintains that survivors of sexual assault 'fear they will be blamed, disgraced, or defamed' and that this fear means

[37] Dickey, 'On Intimacy', in Magennis, *Northern Irish Writing*, 181.

[38] Anne Whitehead, *Trauma Fiction* (Edinburgh: Edinburgh University Press, 2004), 3.

[39] Joseph Valente, email to the author, 20 May 2023.

[40] Mann defines 'unbounded shame' as 'a thick, relentless, engulfing shame – often catalyzed by a shame–event', in 'Femininity, Shame, and Redemption', 403.

[41] Dickey, *Tennis Lessons*, 134.

survivors 'are often too ashamed to report sexual victimization'.[42] Dickey's inclusion of this scene is a potent demonstration of how shame warps and corrodes those dealing with the aftermath of sexual trauma. Research suggests that as much as 75 per cent of sexual assault survivors experience shame after their attack, and academics believe that such negative feelings are often the result of a combination of factors, including stigma, victim blaming and self-blaming.[43] Girls and women are more likely to feel shame after sexual assault.[44] Shame and trauma are affects that are usually generated through diametrically opposed processes, with shame wedded to shared externality and trauma deeply grounded in private interiority. In the case of sexual (and often other forms of) assault, however, the individual trauma of assault causes shame because of an internalised sense of external, social consciousness. This reveals the complicated dialectical entanglement between shame and trauma, and Dickey's second person narrative choice illuminates the toxicity of a culture where survivors are taught to feel ashamed for their own abuse.

It is crucial to clarify why survivors of sexual assault, particularly women and girls, might feel shame after being attacked. We might begin by observing that such shame depends and builds upon the existential shame that patriarchal cultures enjoin upon their female subjects, the shame status that attaches to the very fact of having a female body. In these repressive cultures, 'the persistence of restrictive norms that regulate female sexuality [. . . and] the expectation that it is women's responsibility to protect themselves from sexual dangers' means that 'when rape or sexual assault occurs, it is often the victims rather than the offenders who are blamed, humiliated, or defamed by these crimes'.[45] These restrictive norms are pernicious in Northern Ireland, as highlighted previously and discussed in more detail later with regards to a horrifying assault case that has become known as

[42] Karen G. Weiss, 'Too Ashamed to Report: Deconstructing the Shame of Sexual Victimization', *Feminist Criminology* 5:3 (2010): 286–310, 293.

[43] M. E. Vidal and J. Petrak, 'Shame and adult sexual assault: A study with a group of female survivors recruited from an East London population', *Sexual and Relationship Therapy* 22 (2007): 159–71; Prachi H. Bhuptani and Terri L. Messman-Moore, 'Blame and Shame in Sexual Assault', in edited by W. T. O' Donohue and P. A. Schewe, eds, *Handbook of Sexual Assault and Sexual Assault Prevention* (New York: Springer, 2019), 310.

[44] S. E. Ullman and H. H Filipas, 'Gender differences in social reactions to abuse disclosures, post-abuse coping, and PTSD of child sexual abuse survivors', *Child Abuse & Neglect* 29 (2005): 767–82.

[45] Karen G. Weiss, 'Too Ashamed to Report: Deconstructing the Shame of Sexual Victimization', *Feminist Criminology* 5:3 (2010): 289.

'The Belfast Rape Trial'. The religious and moral conservatism of the statelet – which disproportionately affects girls, women and queer folk – 'makes it more difficult to discuss sexual violence openly', leading survivors to internalise the trauma of violence, execrating feelings of shame and self-blame. There are also, as Rachel Killean, Eithne Dowds and Anne-Marie McAlinden make clear, a number of 'unique legislative, policy and professional challenges that arise when responding to sexual violence in Northern Ireland'; these can also deter survivors coming forward to report. In addition to the statelet's conservatism, Killean, Dowds and McAlinden proffer that 'the militarised role of the police' during the conflict, fear of paramilitaries and a particular piece of legislation which 'mak[es] it a criminal offence for any person to fail to disclose information relating to a relevant offence to the appropriate authorities without a reasonable excuse' all compound already existing anxieties about reporting sexual violence.[46] Dickey makes this painfully apparent through her construction of her behaviour after the attack. *You* is too ashamed to seek guidance and support in the aftermath of her attack, let alone report it, for over ten years. When *you* finally does confide in her friend Rachel, and does go to get tested for STIs, *you* reveals '[f]or a lot of your life you have been struggling against the force of the secret inside you' (T 222). Note that it is the 'secret' that our narrator-protagonist finds so oppressive; after she unburdens herself of this, she feels 'something akin to lightness, freedom'. But, as elucidated at multiple points in this chapter, shame cannot take root without a subject and witness. Dickey reminds us of this with her use of the second person *you*. It is a writerly act that 'asks of both its reader and its character: "You. Yeah, you: are you complicit?"'[47] In naming her teenage survivor of sexual assault *you*, Dickey forces her reader to confront whether they too might be part of a culture that shames women and girls into silence. *Tennis Lessons* suggests, then, that the pain and trauma of sexual assault is amplified and exacerbated by the shame that such attacks engender – a shame that is so pernicious it stops *you* seeking support. This shame is the true cost of gendered and sexual stereotypes.

#IBelieveHer: Misogyny and Gendered Violence

Tennis Lessons was published in 2020 in the aftermath of what is known as the 'Belfast Rugby Rape Trial'; this infamous case dominated

[46] Killean, Dowds and McAlinden, 'Sexual offence trials', 7, 8.
[47] Dickey, 'On Intimacy', quoted in Magennis, *Northern Irish Writing*, 181.

the news on both sides of the Irish border throughout the first half of 2018 and was a disturbing indicator of how matters of sex, consent and misogyny are viewed in Northern Ireland. Over nine weeks in spring 2018, two men, Paddy Jackson and Stuart Olding, formerly Ulster and Ireland rugby players, were tried and subsequently acquitted of rape; Jackson was also found not guilty of assault. Two other men, Blane McIlroy and Rory Harrison, were also acquitted of charges against them. McIlroy was found not guilty of exposure; Rory Harrison was found not guilty of concealing evidence and perverting the course of justice. The complainant was, at the time of the trial, twenty-one years old, and was legally entitled to anonymity: however, Northern Ireland is a small place and her name was soon public knowledge. The evidence in the case was exceptionally distressing and, despite pleas from the judge, Patricia Smyth, much of it was discussed on social media during and after the trial.[48] Over the course of the trial and its aftermath, numerous hashtags were used on Twitter, including #IBelieveHer, #NotMyCaptain – in reference to the appearance of Ireland rugby captain Rory Best in the courtroom – and #SueMePaddy, after Jackson's lawyers, KRW Law, threatened to sue Irish senator Aodhán Ó'Ríordáin for defamation.

The varied responses on social media were indicative of the mixed feelings the trial generated and, we could argue, the cultural conditions that led to the allegations in the first instance. Key evidence involved a number of extremely misogynistic WhatsApp messages from the defendants discussing the night in question, 27 June 2016. Writing in the *Irish Times*, Conor Gallagher suggested the defence argued that these 'texts were banter and immature boasting' but, '[f]or the prosecution, they were evidence of a complete lack of respect for women'.[49] Of course, these alternatives are anything but mutually exclusive. In an article for the *Guardian*, Susan McKay traced how the Irish public responded to the trial in a divided fashion. McKay spoke to Noeline Blackwell, director of the Dublin Rape Crisis Centre, who voiced concerns that 'the absolute lack of respect for women shown by these men might be widely shared within rugby culture'. One of the 'Belfast rugby fans' that McKay had 'sought out to ask [. . .] about the case' argued that 'Northern Ireland was so backward, so Presbyterian, so out of touch in an era of Tinder and casual sex'.[50] The trial raised

[48] See MacKenzie, 'Why didn't you scream?'; Gallagher, 'Inside court 12'; McKay, 'How the Rugby rape trial divided Ireland'.

[49] Conor Gallagher, 'Inside court 12'.

[50] Susan McKay, 'How the rugby rape trial divided Ireland', *The Guardian*, 4 December 2018.

awareness about the appalling state of, or total lack of, sex education in Northern Irish schools. In April 2018, Sir John Gillen was commissioned by the Criminal Justice Board to complete a 'Report into the law and procedures in serious sexual offences in Northern Ireland'. His final report, which totals 714 pages, was published in May 2019.[51] Gillen's report highlighted the potently immobilising effect of shame on rape survivors, who frequently cite shame as a deterrent that stops them reporting their attacks, seeking further support or making criminal claims.

The content of, and reception to, the 'Belfast Rape Trial' made it strikingly apparent how prevalent misogyny is within Northern society. This case provides important sociocultural context to *Tennis Lessons* and reflects the world within which *you*'s narrative is set. What's more, Gallagher's reporting on the trial highlights a moment of interest for the purposes of this chapter, and its exploration of trauma, storytelling and memory. During her cross-examination in 2018, the complainant was probed on inconsistencies in her evidence. She responded by declaring that, after being raped, 'You go into shutdown, it's incredibly hard to state what happened until you've actually processed it'. Throughout her testimony and cross-examination, the complainant insisted that her reaction to this extreme violence was natural: 'In that situation you don't scream or shout because you are so scared' [. . .] 'You underestimate the state of shock you go into after being raped'.[52] As Mackenzie has insisted, using this idea of 'inconsistent memory' to 'dismantle the credibility of the complainant' is a 'common myth, and devastating strategy' used against rape survivors. These myths persist despite the fact that research in 'human physiology, endocrinology [and] neuroscience' has demonstrated that, in the face of extreme danger or trauma, standard brain activity is significantly impaired: it is an evolutionary survival instinct.[53] Despite the accuracy of the complainant's retort, it was her use of the second person *you* that the barrister Arthur Harvey queried, and he 'asked, in suspicious tones, why the woman used the impersonal you in [her] statement[s]'. Harvey went on to add, 'It's almost as if you're [the claimant] repeating something you've read rather than your personal experience'.[54] In response to this criticism, the claimant was quick to counter Harvey's dismissal

[51] Sir John Gillen, 'Report into the law and procedures in serious sexual offences in Northern Ireland', 9 May 2019.

[52] Gallagher, 'Inside court 12'.

[53] Alison MacKenzie, 'Why didn't you scream?', 797.

[54] Gallagher, 'Inside court 12'.

and was said to have succinctly replied, 'I'm not going to argue with you over grammar. You're not putting words in my mouth'.[55] It is important that we recognise and remain sensitive to the vital distinctions between reporting a lived reality and creating a fictional narrative, such as Dickey's, but it seems significant that the second person *you* gave the complainant an avenue to give voice to her experience.

Tennis Lessons, like *Milkman*, is shaped by the North yet transcends a reductive reading that emphasises these local contexts above all else. This trauma could be read as deeply inflected by its particular Northern roots, but it is also perhaps just that of the 'perpetual attunement, the pervasive affective taste' of being a girl or a woman.[56] *Tennis Lessons* registers the psychic a/effects of the North's punitive culture and the self-censoring that individuals perform in a society where gendered shaming is pervasive. Dickey's work is part of a burgeoning wave of Irish women writing from the North but not necessarily, as Caroline Magennis argues, '*about* Northern Ireland in the same way as previous writing that engaged with the conflict and its aftermath'.[57] The North may no longer be an 'armed patriarchy', but it is still overwhelmingly dominated by patriarchal values, and so the 'disciplining device' of shame remains potent.[58] Once again, I reiterate that misogyny and violence against women, girls and LGBTQ+ people are far from an exclusively Irish phenomena, even as they are experienced in a distinct way in Ireland. The 'Belfast Rape Trial' must be read as coloured by both intimately local and global contexts, such as the transnational #MeToo movement. And, in an interview with Caroline Magennis, Dickey herself notes the various international sources of inspiration that utilise the second person *you* to express their trauma narratives: Joyce Carol Oates's *Rape: A Love Story* (2003) and Claudine Rankine's *Citizen: An American Lyric* (2014), which documents racial aggressions in the USA through the dichotomous play on intimacy/distance that *you* facilitates.

Such an ingenious literary tactic galvanises the duality of shame – an intimate, internalised affect generated by an external public culture – while also introducing this question of complicity that Dickey alludes to; more than just turning the self into a witness, shame turns the self into a hostile witness. This chapter has outlined how the use of second person *you* is particularly apposite when detailing traumatic

[55] Gallagher, 'Inside court 12'.

[56] Sandra Bartky, *Femininity and Domination: Studies in the Phenomenology of Oppression* (New York: Routledge, 1990), 96.

[57] Magennis, *Northern Irish Writing*, 172, italics original.

[58] Clara Fischer, 'Gender and the Politics of Shame', 371.

events, facilitating both intimacy and distance, and how second person narration articulates the affective power of shame. Although their genesis is different, as noted previously, the two are mutually reinforcing: trauma produces shame and shame produces trauma. Their conjoined status is epitomised in the boundary-blurring *you*. In using the second person *you* to focalise literatures of shame and trauma, writers force readers to assess their own involvement in shame-producing cultures. *Tennis Lessons* foregrounds that we are all complicit in creating and sustaining a culture where survivors of sexual violence are conditioned by insidious patriarchal values to feel ashamed about their own trauma. The messy, painful affects of shame are still deeply gendered, and Dickey has found a novel literary expression to 'narrat[e] a harm that leaves no physical mark'.[59]

[59] Malone, 'Measures of Obliviousness', 1,167.

Part IV

Shame and Disability

Chapter 8

Disability, Embodiment and Shame in Caitriona Lally's *Eggshells*

Kathleen Costello-Sullivan

In the Epilogue to the recent study *The Child Sex Scandal and Modern Irish Literature: Writing the Unspeakable*, Joseph Valente and Margot Gayle Backus cite what they identify as the 'ethico-political failings of Irish society toward its disabled and disempowered members and . . . its continued moral default in allowing their systematic erasure from the national story'.[1] The recent Commission of Investigation's *Mother and Baby Homes Report*, released by the Irish government in early 2021, corroborates this impression, noting that, while 'some women [in these homes] had mental health problems [or] an intellectual disability', such individuals were often either rejected by these facilities or hidden away elsewhere:

> Conditions in the county homes were generally very poor; this . . . was also true for . . . people with disabilities. [. . .] County homes admitted women with special needs, mental health problems, venereal disease or a criminal conviction, *who would be rejected* by a number of mother and baby homes. They also accommodated children who had special needs. . . The accommodation and care given to these children . . . was grossly inadequate; some of the descriptions are extremely distressing.[2]

The language of rejection, of what James M. Smith calls 'containment', runs throughout the report, signaling the greater vulnerability of Irish

[1] *The Child Sex Scandal and Modern Irish Literature: Writing the Unspeakable* (Bloomington, IN: Indiana University Press, 2020. 237).

[2] Yvonne Murphy, William Duncan and Mary Daly, *Final Report of the Commission of Investigation into Mother and Baby Homes*, 12 January 2021, https://www.gov.ie/pdf/?file=https://assets.gov.ie/118565/107bab7e-45aa-4124-95fd-1460893dbb43.pdf#page=null, 2, 6. My emphasis.

women and children with intellectual disabilities and their susceptibility to cultural erasure throughout most of the twentieth century.[3]

Given this disturbing history, it is interesting to observe the reception of Caitriona Lally's award-winning 2015 novel *Eggshells*, where critics often skirt in-depth engagement with protagonist Vivian's mental status. In her review in the *Irish Times*, for example, Sarah Gilmartin describes the novel as 'light on plot' but the main character as 'beguiling', and she suggests that *Eggshells* offers 'a clever ambiguity surrounding the narrator' that obscures '[h]ow much of her changeling status is fictional[,] the delusions of a *severely disturbed character*'.[4] This passing reference – and another wherein she observes that Vivian 'clings to language as a code to understand *a world from which she's excluded*' – round out her engagement with Vivian's mental status, as the bulk of the review focuses on the use of language during Vivian's travels around Dublin.[5]

Similarly, in her review in *The Guardian*, author Claire Kilroy notes that the novel, 'filled with wordplay', 'thrusts the reader into a guessing game' wherein we question, 'Is this woman merely ditsy, or is she mentally ill? If she is mentally ill, what is the nature of her condition? Is she autistic? [or] Does she suffer from OCD?' Not unlike Gilmartin, Kilroy ultimately shrugs off such questions as a 'clever technique'. Accepting that Vivian displays 'eccentricity' and is an 'odd voice', Kilroy ultimately concludes that the novel is 'inventive, funny, and . . . rather moving'.[6] This seems to suggest that only by dismissing or turning away from the question of Vivian's mental status can we ease into the comfort of the novel's quirky and entertaining voice.

Even Lally herself downplays this question. She perceives attempts to identify Vivian's behaviour as more than 'quirkiness' as both negative and constricting. In an interview with E. Ce Miller for Bustle.com, Lally calls Vivian 'a social misfit' and eccentric, but she also demurs, 'I don't mind what readers think, but I'd hate to think Vivian's *quirks* were being put into a narrow definition and judged accordingly.'[7]

[3] *Mother and Baby Homes Report*, 74.

[4] Sarah Gilmartin, 'Review: *Eggshells*, by Caitriona Lally: full of action and humour', *Irish Times*, 6 June 2015. My emphasis. https://www.irishtimes.com/culture/books/review-eggshells-by-caitriona-lally-full-of-action-and-humour-1.2238835.

[5] Gilmartin, 'Review', my emphasis.

[6] Claire Kilroy, '*Eggshells* by Caitriona Lally review – a daring debut', *The Guardian*, 12 September 2015. https://www.theguardian.com/books/2015/sep/12/eggshells-caitriona-lally-review-novel-debut.

[7] Lally cited in Miller. 'This Writer Works as a Janitor at the University that just Awarded her a Literary Prize', Bustle.com, 31 October 2018. https://www.bustle.com/p/eggshells-author-caitriona-lally-just-won-a-prestigious-award-from-the-university-where-she-works-as-a-janitor-13025835. My emphasis.

Her discomfort with the conversation seems clear. In reviews and interviews, then, we can observe two things. First, the boundaries between being 'autistic' and being 'mentally ill' seem to be elided – as they often are, too, in the *Mother and Baby Homes Report* – and second, the reading that Vivian might have a disability is treated not only as something troubling, but as implicitly undermining of her ability *also* to be 'offbeat' or 'whimsical'. Either she is 'beguiling', or she is 'severely disturbed'.[8] There does not appear to be any middle ground.

Eggshells posits a challenge to such dualistic readings. Through the ways she interacts with others, society and her environment, Vivian bears many hallmark symptoms of being on the autism spectrum. However, like the faeries with whom she identifies – who, in Irish myth, can be both *in* and *out* of this world – while Vivian may not perceive reality the same as everyone else, this does *not* mean, as Gilmartin supposes, that she is 'excluded' from this shared world. Rather, Vivian's differing way of experiencing that world is repeatedly linked not just to words, but also to her senses (particularly her sense of smell) and to her physical engagement with it. Vivian's way of *being* in the world is thus a question of interpretation, not presence. Both divergent and magical, it contrasts with how others see – or, perhaps more accurately, do *not* see – her surroundings, or for that matter Vivian herself, as they seek to measure her on a scale that can tolerate 'quirkiness' but not 'disability'. The impulse to make Vivian's difference a zero-sum game of inclusion or exclusion, beguiling or disturbed, thus belies the complexity of her experience, as well as her undeniable, insistently bodily presence in Irish society.

Written against the backdrop of the many ways that Irish society historically sought to hide people with disabilities and/or mental illness, moreover, *Eggshells* interrogates the fates of those in Ireland who, while no longer institutionalised and literally hidden away *per se*, are nonetheless still expected to fit the narrow confines of societal norms – or else to render themselves effectively invisible.[9] Vivian's apparent integration into society contrasts starkly with the tenuousness of, and resistance to, her assimilation; other characters' discomfort with Vivian highlights societal uneasiness with those who diverge neurologically from 'the norm' and perhaps also their awareness of the inadequacy of their own, and Irish society's, response.

[8] See Miller and Gilmartin, respectively.

[9] While I wish to recognise that, historically, autism has often been conflated with mental illness, I also want to reinforce the difference between them (and indeed, that they are also not mutually exclusive, any more than 'typical' neurological profiles and mental illness are). I will thus seek to recognise their conflation while insisting upon their distinctness.

Thus, despite her seeming integration, the troubling history of Ireland's past treatment of the disabled or neurologically atypical shadows Vivian's actions and interactions in the novel, as through her repeated references to and enactments of her own burial and in the uncertainty of her naming. It is a constant reminder of the fragile boundaries that separate Vivian from such a fate.

Foregrounding Vivian's sensory and bodily engagement with the world versus others' avoidant perceptions and expectations of her thus highlights not only her vivid imagination, but also her disability and vulnerability. *Eggshells* questions Irish society's effort to dichotomise these traits, as well as its current readiness – or (un)willingness – to integrate diverse neurological perspectives and citizens as it labours under the shadow of their shameful treatment in the past. As a result, the novel challenges how far Ireland has actually come from those dark times of mass institutionalisation and abuse to today, in its ability truly to see, and therefore to protect, the Vivians among us.

As many reviewers note, *Eggshells* follows protagonist Vivian's daily travels around Dublin, in a manner reminiscent of James Joyce's *Ulysses*, while she seeks a 'portal' to take her 'back' to what she variously describes as 'where I belong' or 'home'.[10] This belief comes from her impression that she is a changeling – for, as she suggests throughout, her parents 'used force to try and shunt [her] back to [the] Otherworld', to 'exchange' her, or to 'send [her] back' multiple times in her childhood (e.g. E 6, 7, 31, 250).[11] We come to learn toward the novel's end that these efforts translated into attempted acts of murder, either by drowning or burning – which Vivian survived, but whose cruel traces she carries on her scarred body (e.g. E 31, 238, 250).

The tendency to read Vivian as 'quirky', 'oddball' or 'beguiling', as we have seen, hails predominantly from her unique worldview, which manifests both in a constant use of metaphor and in her rampant personification of the objects around her – and, undoubtedly, Vivian's use of language is a delight. To Vivian, envelopes, numbers and beans can act 'smug' (E 5, 62, 163); vegetables can be 'jealous' of one another, and corn acts 'inscrutable' (E 74, 29). Streets can be 'take[n] . . . by surprise' (E 9), whereas verbs 'expect too much' (E 10). The Joycean evocation of Bloom's travels highlights the *un*familiarity

[10] Caitriona Lally, *Eggshells* (London: Borough Press, 2015), 6, 85, 112. On 'portals', see 66, 122. Subsequent references given as (E page).

[11] For a reading of the mythical implications of Vivian's abuse and attempted murder, see Molly Ferguson, 'The Changeling Legend and Queer Kinship in Caitriona Lally's Eggshells', *Irish University Review* 51:2 (Autumn–Winter 2021): 296–311.

of the Dublin that Vivian sees.[12] The many stone statues and faces staring down at her on the Dublin streets are emotive and expressive: one statue or stone head on a building might be 'on [her] side' (E 19), but others (many of which she names, like Anna or George) 'don't seem to care' or put her 'on edge' by 'staring' at her (e.g. E 87, 133, 93, 131). This tendency to personify objects also extends to the very furniture in her house: Vivian repeatedly frets over her household chairs, worrying that they will feel hurt, jealous or neglected should she sit on one over another (E 38, 46, 127).

Yet throughout, these personifications also suggest her vulnerability and kindness. Vivian chooses bruised fruit at the market, because it is the fruit 'nobody else wants', and she struggles to buy flowers because 'taking just one bunch would be like trying to separate puppy brothers' (E 162, 136). These linguistic gestures justifiably draw critical attention and lend to a sense of sympathy for, and amusement with, Vivian and her narrative, while also highlighting her vulnerability as she relates to these inanimate things.

It seems evident, however, that, in addition to being 'quirky' and sensitive, Vivian fits many of the commonly understood characteristics of those with autism spectrum disorder (ASD). According to the criteria delineated in the CDC's summation of the American Psychiatric Association's Diagnostic and Statistical Manual, Fifth Edition (DSM-5), there are several ways in which Vivian can be classified as on the spectrum. First, those so classified display '[p]ersistent deficits in . . . social communication and interaction'. These can include 'deficits in social-emotional reciprocity, ranging, for example, from abnormal social approach and *failure of normal back-and-forth conversation*; to reduced sharing of interests, emotions, or affect; *to failure to initiate or respond to social interactions*'.[13] Obviously, Vivian struggles socially. Her attempts at conversation are often scripted: she gives an 'exaggerated shiver' when 'one word seems a fairly meagre response', and she repeats 'what busy people . . . say' in her attempts to hold a 'normal' conversation (E 7, 89). At the airport, she considers that she should 'do something airport-appropriate [*sic*]' (E 91).

Many of Vivian's interactions are also performative: she glances at the sky 'the way . . . women do', to 'practice using [her] voice aloud' and to act 'how an invited person would look' as a guest (E 14, 25, 63). Vivian imitates how others order coffee by 'watching how the girl in front of [her] holds her cup' (E 122). Finally, Vivian

[12] On the novel's evocation of Joyce, see Gilmartin.

[13] 'Autism Spectrum Disorder: Diagnostic Criteria', Center for Disease Control and Prevention, https://www.cdc.gov/ncbddd/autism/hcp-dsm.html.

imagines that she has a limited word-trove upon which to draw in such encounters, fretting that she might have 'wasted [a] topic' that she preplanned; feeling 'pleased' when she's 'said [her] sentence' or 'words for the day'; or fearing that she has 'not enough words' to call upon (e.g. E 26, 88, 210, 124). This self-consciousness with language and her stilted social interactions clearly fit the ASD criterion and often leave Vivian feeling embattled and stressed.

Vivian also struggles to understand and interpret non-verbal communication. As the DSM-5 criteria secondarily notes, symptoms can include:

> Deficits in nonverbal communicative behaviors used for social interaction, ranging, for example, *from poorly integrated verbal and nonverbal communication; to abnormalities in eye contact and body language or deficits in understanding and use of gestures;* to a total *lack of facial expressions* and nonverbal communication.[14]

Vivian clearly struggles throughout to understand people's responses to her; she notes, 'people don't respond well to my words' (E 163). As a result, she is extremely sensitive to others' reactions and often uses metaphor to express her bewildered inability to identify their emotions. For example, when she encounters an angry man on a bus, she observes that he 'isn't looking at [her] in a pleasant way' (E 57). When she accidentally gives the impression that she has left her (non-existent) wheelchair-bound six-year-old twins home alone, she describes the grocery clerk's horrified response as, 'Her face is squeezed into strange shapes' (E 41). A cabbie's wife's voice 'sounds like jagged rocks' (E 114). While watching the cab driver and his wife together, she knows (only by deduction 'from watching television with the sound turned down[,]) that they're arguing' (E 113). Vivian struggles with such intuitive interpretation.

Sympathetic responses are equally disorienting to Vivian. When a cemetery worker realises that her potential customer is vulnerable and on her own, Vivian can only observe that the woman's 'face slackens a little' (E 139). And she struggles with her own affect, too: she has to '*try* to form an expression of extreme calm on [her] face' (E 48, my emphasis). Like her conversational constraints, then, this compromised ability to interact causes Vivian enormous anxiety: she begins sweating each time she fears that a conversation will lead to conflict (e.g. E 28, 67, 151, 158). Lastly, people with ASD can struggle to form or maintain interpersonal relationships, displaying

[14] 'Autism Spectrum Disorder', my emphasis.

> deficits in *developing, maintaining, and understand relationships*, ranging, for example, from *difficulties adjusting behavior to suit various social contexts*; to difficulties in sharing imaginative play or *in making friends*; *to absence of interest in peers.*[15]

Vivian thinks a lot about friendship. She notes that she 'can't explain' herself to 'people who peer out windows and think they know the world' (E 13); she dislikes visitors, noting that 'the house seems more menacing' after a representative from the Social Welfare Office visits (E 55). She even recoils from guests whom she has invited: '[A]fter a while, I start to resent Penelope's presence. I feel suffocated and vexed that I can't escape her to sit in my lone, twenty-tog silence' (E 107).[16] For Vivian, people can be taxing.

This behavioural disadvantage is also physical. Vivian recoils from hugs (E 30, 256); she repeatedly scares people when she is trying either to be gesturally playful or just to interact. As a result, Vivian terrifies the social worker, David, with a pretend gun while '*playing* at Job-hunters [*sic*]' (E 51–2, my emphasis), and she inadvertently gives a stranger the impression that she is physically threatening him with a knife (E 228). In reflecting on her only friend, Penelope, Vivian muses, 'I'm not sure if I genuinely like her or if it's the shape of her name that appeals to me' (E 254). Although Vivian craves friendship and kindness – longing for friends (E 75) and celebrating her connection with Penelope (E 145) – she is as often reduced to imagining such associations or pretending that fleeting connections constitute a real affiliation (e.g. E 92, 114, 247), because she struggles to maintain and foster such intimacy in reality.

Each of these traits – her difficulties with conversation; her struggles to read non-verbal cues; and her awkwardness with interpersonal contact and friendships – clearly signals that Vivian may well be autistic.[17] At the same time, the DSM-5's ratings for 'severity', which are 'based on social communication impairments and restricted, repetitive patterns of behavior', also flag Vivian as potentially on the spectrum.[18]

[15] 'Autism Spectrum Disorder', my emphasis.

[16] This also reflects her challenges with changes to routine – what the DSM-5 identifies as an 'Insistence on sameness [and] inflexible adherence to routines', 'Autism Spectrum Disorder'.

[17] I do not say 'may well' to avoid committing to my own reading. Rather, as I illustrate later, such uncertainty can be inherent to ASD itself – and yet it is fundamentally counter-indicated to the desired surety evinced by Irish society in the novel, and even in its critical reception.

[18] 'Autism Spectrum Disorder', 'To be diagnosed, a patient must fit all the symptom categories delineated above, as well as three out of four of those that follow' ('Severity'): Vivian appears to fit all four.

From her consistent use of 'idiosyncratic phrases' in her descriptions, which readers so often flag as 'quirky'; to her 'inflexible adherence to routines', such as her dislike for company, daily mapping of walks or insistent creations of word lists (e.g. E 74; 78; 86; 142; 167 – and this is not exhaustive!); to her 'excessively circumscribed or perseverative interests', as evidenced in her focus on her great-aunt's chairs; to the '[h]ighly restricted, fixated interests that are abnormal in intensity', which her relentless search for a portal evinces – Vivian has many markers for autism.[19]

Unfortunately, Vivian's challenges from what appears to be autism are compounded by the fact that she is also a trauma survivor. Molly Ferguson observes that Vivian's resort to the changeling myth is 'a coping mechanism for surviving trauma', because 'the changeling story is a coded testimony of family violence'.[20] Behind Vivian's occasional references to her parents' efforts to 'send her back' are other, more ominous observations: she admits that she was 'sorry when [her] parents were alive' (E 68); that she gladly would have 'given away [her] parents' (E 132); and that she 'didn't cry when [her] father died; [she] cried when he was alive' (E 137). Vivian suffers from frequent nightmares: she alludes to screaming (E 47), crying (E 55) and experiencing a sense of foreboding (E 161, 211) in her dreams. She notes, albeit offhandedly, that there is 'terror . . . in being alive' (E 43), and she wistfully observes, in learning of the flower by that name, that she 'would like to *dread naught*' (E 142, my emphasis). Finally, Vivian fears the sea, stating, 'I hope to die without ever having to set foot or hand in seawater again' (E 157). These comments form a troubling subtext to Vivian's relatively placid exterior.

When Vivian accidentally exposes her scarred back to Penelope, she acknowledges that her father tried to burn and drown her, but she is incapable of receiving or offering sympathy to or from Penelope, who appears to have traumas of her own.[21] Thus, just as she avoids the subject of her own abuse (E 250–1), Vivian sweats and trembles when such conversations threaten (E 160), and she also shuts down

[19] 'Autism Spectrum Disorder'. Naturally, these challenges cause Vivian difficulties not only in social interactions, but also in her employment prospects, as she herself notes: 'Employers won't hire me to work in their offices when they can hire a shiny woman who speaks in exclamation marks' (54).

[20] Ferguson, 'Changeling Legend', 296.

[21] Penelope's actual name is Elaine (158); this substitution marks her as a kind of traumatised changeling in her own right (Elaine is 'exchanged' for Penelope). For a reading of Penelope and Vivian's relationship as an example of 'queer kinship', see Ferguson, 'Changeling Legend', 299.

emotionally: 'I can't bear tales of abuse and neglect and unwashed corduroy trousers so I replace her words with candyfloss and sherbet fountains and cake with buttercream so smooth it slides down the throat like a greasy angel' (E 68). Vivian's frequent whisper to herself – 'safe safe safe' (E 14, 18, 110) – reflects the hyperarousal common to trauma survivors who are conditioned to expect threats at all turns.[22] Between her history of trauma and her likely autism, Vivian is a vulnerable woman indeed.

I want to return, then, to the question of Vivian's reception, both critically and by other characters within the novel. In a recent article, Joseph Valente notes that 'the decisive property' of 'outward diagnostic signs of autism . . . in aggregate, is their heterogeneity': in other words, the only consistently predictable facet of autism is its variability.[23] Valente convincingly argues that any diagnosis of autism functions on two levels within what he terms 'autypicality':

> On the one hand, autypicality would seem entirely antithetical to its familiar counterpart, neurotypicality. . . On the other hand, autypicality analogizes with neurotypicality in that it names the impetus to establish a stable norm of autistic being, an au-type, much as neurotypicality does for brain function in general. [As a result], [a]utypicality is the false consciousness that lends autism whatever consistency of being it possesses.[24]

This is significant for *Eggshells* in two respects. First, hesitation over 'labelling' Vivian as autistic implicitly demands a kind of diagnostic certainty which is inherently counter-indicated by the condition of autism itself, owing to its characteristic heterogeneity. This means that the 'guessing game' or 'clever ambiguity' which critics cite is itself merely a facet of the condition, rather than an obstacle to its diagnosis, whether literarily or in real life.[25]

Secondly, the dichotomy in reading Vivian *either* as delightful *or* as autistic – and the parallel tendency to lump 'mental illness' and autism together, as if they were synonymous – betrays the kind of oppositional relationship to neurotypicality that the very concept of a 'spectrum' is meant to belie. In this respect, resistance to recognising

[22] Judith Lewis Herman, *Trauma and Recovery: The Aftermath of Violence – From Domestic Abuse to Political Terror* (New York: Basic Books, 1992), 35–6.
[23] Joseph Valente, 'This Disability Which Is Not One: Autistic Intermittency in Mark Haddon's *The Curious Incident of the Dog in the Night-Time*', *Contemporary Literature* 62:1 (Spring 2021): 35.
[24] Valente, 'This Disability', 37, 39.
[25] See Gilmartin and Kilroy.

Vivian's markers for ASD ironically recreates the very bifurcation that historically made people like Vivian vulnerable in the first place – not only to the abuses of the institutional system, but also to the narrative containments proffered through myths like that of the changeling.[26]

Perhaps not surprisingly, this same tendency to seek surety, clarity, *normalcy* from Vivian adheres *within* the novel as well. Repeatedly, Vivian's interlocutors shut down, withdraw or even are fundamentally hostile as soon as Vivian becomes visible to them not in her generic anonymity, but in her distinctive difference.[27] Given her small social circle, this usually involves strangers – a man who 'clears his throat' and 'left quite abruptly' when small talk took an unexpected turn (E 143); a woman who 'eyes [her] with wary in her voice [*sic*]' (E 138). A bus driver, who initially 'smiles' at her, recoils just as quickly: 'He turns his gaze back to the road and says, "Yeah", but he has cut the word as short as it will go, his throat wrapped tight around it' (E 202). In all of these instances, it is as if Vivian has morphed into someone else owing to the revelation of her difference, the visibility of her non-conformity. Or perhaps it would be better to say that Vivian, the 'normal' citizen with whom they expected to interact, is magically and insidiously replaced before their eyes by someone identical but societally 'Other' – someone, or something, they cannot or will not recognise. In this respect, Vivian *is* a changeling of sorts.[28]

Vivian is nonetheless very much in the world – and her presence is most pointed in the highly sensory way in which she interacts with her environment, through sight, hearing, taste and particularly through her sense of smell. This heightened sensitivity reflects another common behavioural pattern of ASD: 'Hyper- or hyporeactivity to sensory input or unusual interest in sensory aspects of the environment (e.g. . . . *excessive smelling or touching of objects*, [and] visual fascination with lights or movement)'.[29]

Vivian lives intensively through each of her senses. Thanks to sight, her language is heavily metaphorical and imagistic: she describes a melon as 'the kind of yellow that seas should be made of' (E 27).

26 Vivian herself strays widely among myths, invoking, at various times, changelings, mermaids, banshees, elves, leprechauns and faeries, among others (e.g. E 72, 48, 100, 37, 110, 120).

27 My thanks to Joseph Valente for helping me to think through this dynamic.

28 Ferguson, 'Changeling Legend', 298. I am suggesting that *Eggshells* aligns the notion of the changeling with her likely autism and her tenuous integration into Irish society, while reflecting a similar desire to avoid what cannot – or will not – be understood.

29 'Autism Spectrum Disorder', my emphasis.

Yet she also engages quite literally with colours, throwing herself a 'blue party' by eating 'only blue foods' (E 40, 42); buying a goldfish because, she observes, 'I need some gold in my life' (E 43); using a red bowl because 'I need some red in my day' (E 17); and noting, 'I have enough green foods in my life, I should eat more pink' (E 162). Colour, for Vivian, is not something one notices in its exceptional moments, but rather a medium in which, and through which, she reacts daily. Vivian is thus *not* excluded from this world: rather, she is intensely, almost painfully immersed in it – not only in a bodily way, but in a manner inflected by her neurology.

Vivian also relies on taste and hearing to try to process her environment more than others regularly do. As she seals envelopes, she notes that her tongue is 'tasting the bitter end of gluey' (E 5), and she samples bubbles from the fountain in the College Green, because 'from their whiteness, [she expects] dry fluff, . . . but they taste sharp and clean' (E 76). Similarly, Vivian *listens* intently and uses sound metaphorically to make sense of her world. A kind woman has a 'voice that could knit a teddy bear' (E 101); shovelling sounds like 'a tennis match with the grating of metal on stone' (E 177). Even the gas stove can be 'soothing', for its '*swwssh* [*sic*]' is 'like a gentle breeze or a low brook' (E 246, emphasis in original).

Vivian occasionally also exhibits synaesthesia, which highlights both her tendencies toward metaphor and her thorough entanglement in the world of sense. She refers to 'Marshmellowed Silences' (touch and sound) and a fish store that smells 'bright' and 'hot' (smell, sight and touch) (E 20, 14). If Vivian's outsized sensory processing of the world around her signals her difference, it also reinforces how very present she is in that world, living in and through her body. More than with any other sense, however, Vivian lives most intensely through her sense of smell. As with her other senses, she uses it to try to make sense of her world, but beyond the ways one might consider 'normal' – recall, the tendency toward 'Hyper- . . . reactivity to sensory input [as in the] *excessive smelling of objects*'.[30] Thus, throughout the novel, she sniffs things as random as envelopes, pencil shavings, a 'mouldy fur' growing in her tea pot and even the toilet bowl (E 17, 20, 51, 176). Sniffing a 'petrol-puddle rainbow', she describes it as 'chemical and dreadful and gorgeous' (E 197); a shop smells of 'warm linoleum' (E 86), and vegetables smell, in a powerful and evocative image, 'of the world being born' (E 74).

[30] 'Autism Spectrum Disorder', my emphasis.

Vivian also uses her sense of smell to test and capture the safety of her environment. She warily notes that an annoyed-looking man's gas heater 'smells of warm evil' (E 78). Entering a bus, she sniffs the 'used, lived-in smell . . . of warm upholstery and passenger breath' and whispers 'safe safe safe' to herself in reassurance (E 92). Vivian 'sniffs the air' as she enters new houses or cars, like Penelope's, or even as she walks down the street (E 63, 148, 134). Above all, Vivian looks for the reassuring smell of home, which carries the comforting familiarity of her deceased aunt: 'there is still a faint waft of her in every room – of lavender cologne mixed with soiled underthings' (E 3). After a particularly taxing day, Vivian burrows into the familiar feel and scent of her aunt's chair for safety: 'I crawl in between the red chair and the cushion, and sniff the dust and feel the scratch of crumbs on my face. Although there is very little air, I feel like I can breathe for the first time today' (E 243). As we have seen, she also dislikes visitors in part because her house smells 'wrong' after their visits (E 54, 107). Vivian sniffs out safety, or its absence – a sign, again, of her neurological atypicality, her trauma and her bodily presence in the world all at once.

Perhaps most importantly, Vivian focuses on and cultivates her *own* smell for reassurance, comfort and familiarity. When she enters her newly inherited house, she notes, 'I catch the beginning of my smell, an earthy tang that I plan to grow into' (E 10). As she seeks to 'grow into' her smell (E 17), Vivian avoids bathing or washing her clothes, and, as she identifies her scent, her descriptions are notable for their consistent evocation of her own corporeality. She notes that a 'pleasant sort of lived-in smell comes from [her] body, of meat and sweat and damp newspaper' (E 36). Later, her description shifts to a 'homely smell . . . somewhere between old milk and red meat on the turn' (E 76), which progresses to describing her body as smelling like 'overripe meat' (E 144). Ultimately, when she sniffs under her blouse, she observes that it 'smells . . . like the butcher shop under here: a dull meaty thud of a smell' (E 214). Not unlike Veronica Hegarty's emphasis on the carnal body in *The Gathering*, Vivian's repeated use of the word 'meat' stresses her own physicality and corporeality, while also objectifying her.[31]

Vivian is thus present in her society in a way that cannot be ignored. The novel's insistence on Vivian's bodily reality reminds us that she is, indeed, both in and of this world – forcing us, like the characters around her, to reckon with her literal and figurative presence. At the

[31] Anne Enright, *The Gathering* (London: Jonathan Cape, 2007), 47, 219.

same time, the forceful foregrounding of her corporeality is a constant reminder of her vulnerability. The fact that her perceptions are both distinctive and linked to her likely autism and/or confirmed trauma undermines the 'either/or' attempts to understand her which are so rampant throughout (and about) the novel. *Eggshells* thus suggests that Vivian's bodily presence is an irrefutable reminder of her place in society and in the world, despite – or perhaps even because of – her neurological atypicality.

It is telling, then, to note how that society deals with her within the narrative. As we have seen, in instances where strangers encounter Vivian, their most common reaction is to recoil; Vivian struggles with these interactions because of her apparent autism and her post-traumatic vulnerability. More important in this novel, however, is the letdown of networks that should sustain her in the context of post-institutional Irish society.[32]

It is clear that Vivian struggles to function socially in daily life. Yet, in addition to her interpersonal challenges, there are more serious concerns whether Vivian should actually be on her own at all, simply in the context of her safety and well-being. First, her hygiene is lacking, to say the least: along with cultivating her 'smell', Vivian acknowledges that her 'hair hasn't been washed in a long while' (E 191), and we know this is noticeable, since her sister critically comments that she ought to shower more often (E 83). She also carries the marks of her trauma behaviourally in this regard. Along with the fear of conflict, resistance to sad tales and the need to self-soothe ('safe safe safe'), as we have seen, Vivian has a visceral, negative response to her own reflection, and so she either covers mirrors or makes a pointed attempt not to look in them (e.g. E 17, 101, 163, 193).[33] As a result, she notes, 'I haven't looked at my face in the mirror in a long while – I don't know what other people see that keeps them away' (E 97). Vivian is fundamentally lacking in basic skills of self-care from her disability, and is compromised by the shame generated from her abuse.

[32] Covid-pandemic society has led to renewed understanding of the ways casual contexts and associations sustain individuals' well-being. See Amanda Mull, 'The Pandemic Has Erased Entire Categories of Friendship', *The Atlantic*, 27 January 2021.

[33] Vivian's resistance to her own image signals the self-loathing and self-blame consistent with traumatic shame. K. J. Van Vliet, 'Shame and resilience in adulthood: A grounded theory study', *Journal of Counseling Psychology* 55:2 (April 2008): 233–45. On the impact of child abuse on shame and self-disgust, see Bessel Van der Kolk, *The Body Keeps the Score: Brain, Mind, and Body in the Healing of Trauma* (New York: Penguin Books, 2014), 212–13.

Her diet is also deplorable. Vivian consumes enormous amounts of sweets (86, 188) and cannot cook, so trying to make dinner is often disastrous. She does not know how to use the stove:

> I don't want to poison my guests with half-cooked meat, so I turn the oven to the highest setting and close the door. [. . .] Then I sit and watch the oven, but I don't know what I should be watching for. Food cooks in such a silent, devious way; I wish it screamed when it started to burn. (E 214)

Her consumption habits can be harmful or even dangerous. Thus, she sickens herself by eating too many snacks at her 'blue party', until her 'belly feels bruised inside' (E 42). She also self-medicates with both alcohol (with frozen peas to cool it) and with her aunt's pills (E 21, 45), at one point taking a dosage of sleeping tablets strong enough to cause her to pass out on the staircase (E 127–8). Obviously, her failure to understand moderation could have serious consequences.

In general, Vivian has no sense of domesticity at all.[34] When she finds that her kettle is full of mould, she uses the water in it to make tea regardless (E 51). (She also puts tea into hot water bottles (E 45)). Vivian does not feel the need to clean up dust or crumbs (46, 243), and she allows the house to be overrun with mice (E 104, 222). She is indifferent to maintaining her property – hoping, rather than discouraging, the intrusion of animals (much to her neighbours' consternation) (E 104). In what likely can be identified as hoarding behaviours, she clusters multiple chairs together haphazardly, crowding her rooms, and she dedicates an entire room (appropriately, the 'hoard-room') to childhood toys and treasures (E 38, 24).[35]

Finally, Vivian does not understand finances. In lieu of money, she offers to give lemons to someone who is begging (E 57); she randomly tucks bills into pockets at a discount store, even though she hasn't a job (E 98); and she cannot see the relationship between food in a cafeteria and its cost: 'It seems strange that if I don't have enough of these small discs, I can't have all the food on my tray, when there is no real connection between the two' (E 165). She is, in short, compromised in her ability to adhere to basic hygiene; to provide herself

[34] On Vivian as 'fail[ing] to internalize gendered norms of femininity', see Ferguson, 'Changeling Legend', 301.

[35] This is an example of how Vivian can have ASD and an arguable mental illness simultaneously. On hoarding as an obsessive-compulsive disorder, see 'What is hoarding disorder?', *American Psychiatric Association* website.

with a clean environment or healthy sustenance; and she is lacking in fundamental life skills. Vivian could use some help.

Despite the obvious challenges she faces, however, Vivian does not enjoy a safety net, whether familial, communal or societal. Obviously, her parents were abusive and are deceased; but her living sister treats her with tolerance at best, distaste at worst, and makes it clear that, when she refers to family, she does not mean Vivian (E 224). When Vivian considers buying a tombstone, she highlights her aloneness: although she has a sister, she acknowledges, 'I'm going to be buried alone' (E 138). Her sister finds Vivian's spontaneous calls distasteful and a visit even worse (E 22, 80). Instead, her sister seems wilfully to look away from Vivian's needs and vulnerability, demanding that she perform the 'normalcy' of which she clearly is not capable. Along with urging her to shower more (E 83), her sister criticises Vivian's manner of dressing; does not intervene with her disastrous cooking (only suggesting 'You should really use a cookbook'); and only appears to approve of her when she thinks that Vivian has found a friend (until she learns that Vivian actually advertised for one) (E 218–19). Vivian thus does not have family who will look out for or take care of her, even though they are clearly aware of her vulnerabilities: her sister sees her more as a social embarrassment than as a vulnerable sibling in need of help.

Vivian encounters the same failure of support in her community. Although her neighbours recognise Vivian's incapacity, discussing her and/or 'shak[ing] their heads' (E 16; also 127, 182) and referring to her as 'Poor Vivian' (E 18), they do not in any way try to intervene to help her. Instead, like the strangers she meets and her own sister, her neighbours try to force Vivian to conform – to perform the generic social role assigned to her.

Thus, when Vivian climbs a tree, her neighbour Mary admonishes, 'Ah, Vivian, would you look at yourself, a grown woman up a tree on a day like today' (E 37). When Vivian allows her yard to be overgrown, the neighbours do discuss it; however, their concern is not Vivian, but rather their property values: 'Their voices float in my direction and I catch "have to say . . . something has to be done . . . it's not right . . . bringing down the look of the place"' (E 104). Neighbour Bernie admonishes Vivian that she would 'do better to find a husband, never mind your hobbits' (E 173), and when Mary finds Vivian essentially burying herself in a giant hole, Mary only tells her that she 'needs to get a hold of' herself (E 182). Despite her obvious challenges, then, Vivian's community offers no meaningful support for her. Instead, they, too, look away with embarrassment and disapproval, insistently trying to impose a paradigm on Vivian which simply does not suit.

In the absence of family or community support, one would hope that at least there would be a societal structure to offer Vivian a safety net – but this, too, fails her. As mentioned earlier, Vivian does receive a visit from the Social Welfare office – and she is sensitive enough to its importance that she actually bathes and vacuums the house, much to her distaste (E 47–9).[36] It quickly becomes clear, however, that the representative, David, is not interested in Vivian's 'social welfare', but rather only in the need to arrange for her to obtain gainful employment. Even as he notes that Vivian 'appears . . . inappropriate' (E 52), he doggedly adheres to his script, trying to fit Vivian into the mould of an average job seeker and ultimately concluding, 'Right, I think we're all done here' (E 54). Like her sister, who wants Vivian to be a clean, neat, well-dressed, sociable person; and like her neighbours, who want a houseproud, tidy, suburban housewife as a neighbour, David looks away from Vivian's obvious fragility and social ineptitude, and pretends to see a qualified, potential job candidate in her stead.[37] None of them wishes to see the real Vivian; they each substitute an imaginary norm – a kind of harmless social changeling – in her place. As a result, they offer her no assistance, and in many respects, no recognition of who she actually is. Irish society in this novel, at all levels, looks away in embarrassment and distaste.

Needless to say, it is difficult, in seeing this narrative failure by family, community and state of a vulnerable woman with a probable disability, not to think of earlier times in Irish history, when such a person could realistically have found herself in an institution, such as in the Mother and Baby or County Homes cited previously. As James M. Smith observes in his oft-cited study of the Magdalene Laundries, 'Many families of former Magdalen women remain[ed] silent about their past abandonment of a daughter, a sister, a cousin, or an aunt, thereby refusing to recognize their role in supporting the

[36] Ireland's Social Welfare office is responsible for providing a 'Jobseeker's payment', which is clearly the cause for David's visit; however, the office also handles a 'Carer's Allowance' for 'people who are caring full-time for a person who has a disability or illness', so it is not unreasonable to hope that David could have noticed that Vivian was in need of help. See 'Social Welfare', Irish government website. https://www.gov.ie/en/category/social-welfare/.

[37] In the arena of mental health, too, social structures are inadequate. See Brendan Kelly, 'Ireland Must Tackle its Mental Health Services Deficit Disorder', *Irish Times*, 10 December 2019. My thanks to Molly Ferguson for pointing me to this article.

abusive conditions in these institutions.' In the same way, as Valente and Backus argue, '[t]he disabled, the institutionalized, and the abandoned . . . have not enkindled the same deep, passionate, and gnawing "grief and anger" as . . . the child sex victims of respectable and relatable middle-class families [have]'.[38] In such cases, individuals were subject to either wilful erasure or terrible neglect – and, often, to a societal determination not to see them.

When Vivian encounters a stranger outside 'the ruin of the [local] psychiatric hospital' who assumes that she was once a patient there, her response is revealing: 'I don't tell him that I often peek in when I'm passing . . . I don't want him to think I'm odd . . . I don't want him to think I'm a trespasser' (E 226–7). As Ferguson notes, 'the "ruin" of the psychiatric hospital looms ominously, symbolizing the lack of services for the mentally ill in today's Dublin'.[39] Yet Vivian's response also invites the seductive amnesia similarly proffered in the recent *Mother and Baby Homes Report*, in its troubling but repeated insistence that '*it must be acknowledged* that the institutions under investigation provided a refuge – a harsh refuge in some cases – when the families provided no refuge at all'.[40] By rendering the harshness of institutional life only parenthetically, the report implicitly justifies that harshness as somehow excusable or justifiable, given 'the conditions'. In the same way, by showing Vivian's vulnerability *outside* the hospital, *Eggshells* seductively invites us to ask, would she have been better off?

Vivian's own ruminations answer that question. Throughout the text, she consistently summons imagery of burial, of anonymity and of suffocation that provide a painful reminder of the fate of many women and children consigned to these national institutions. Thus, when she meets with social worker David, she asks, 'Have you ever pretended to be dead?' (53). As we have seen, she goes shopping for her own cemetery plot, noting that she will be buried alone. After her blue party, she notes, '[t]he underside of the table reminds me of the inside of a coffin lid, so I decide to practise being buried alive' (42–3). Vivian's death and burial are constant undercurrents in the text.

In a particularly harrowing scene, Vivian asks Penelope to help her dig a hole in which to bury herself, noting, 'If we keep digging until the hole is my height, I can be buried here standing up, with the

38 Smith, *Magdalen Laundries*, 186; Valente and Backus, *Child Sex Scandal*, 238.

39 Ferguson, 'Changeling Legend', 307. Again, Vivian's mental illness versus neurological atypicality is not clear.

40 *Mother and Baby Homes Report*, 1. Invocations of immediate families and the wider community, a species of 'whataboutism', occur repeatedly in the report.

grass lid pulled over my head like a stopper' (178–9).[41] The narrative is pointed in contrasting the possibility of her formal burial – Penelope asks, 'I thought you'd already bought your plot in Glasnevin?' – with this trial run of unsanctioned, unofficial burial (179). Vivian's invocation of the 'sound of peace and nothing', and her identification with worms and why they 'stay so secret and safe and hidden' (181, 177), again invokes the allure of anonymity provoked by shame.[42] It also speaks to a perceived safety in the grave – but it evokes a grave to which over 9,000 babies were consigned by the state and religious institutions that were meant to protect them, and for many of whom this meant interment without the decency of proper identification and burial.[43]

Vivian's sense of redundancy – her recognition that her sister 'was born first and has more rights to' the name they (weirdly) share than she does (15), also invokes the sense of her perceived expendability, as well as the many nameless children, institutionalised and alone, who were consigned to unmarked graves in Ireland's past.[44] Her willingness to be erased parallels their historical and legal erasure in Irish society. Having this constant echo of nameless burial is thus an insistent reminder of the past fate that other women like Vivian faced. Yet, it is also implicitly suggested that, in her familial, communal and state neglect, she is living a version of that *same societal treatment* in Ireland today.

In speaking of her belief that she is a changeling, Vivian repeatedly invokes the question of 'thin places' (e.g. 31, 33, 136, 123) – those spaces where the boundaries between this world and that of the Otherworld are most porous. Interestingly, some theories of autism use the very same language: Valente notes that 'a 'lack [of] depth' [is sometimes] consistent with the expert view, reiterated by science

[41] There are ironic echoes here of Cnoc na Riabh in Sligo, where Queen Medbh is colloquially said to be buried standing, 'as no man would dare approach her lying down', versus Vivian's profound vulnerability.

[42] See Van der Kolk, *Body Keeps the Score*, 104.

[43] About 9,000 children, 15 per cent of all incarcerated, died. See *Mother and Baby Home Report*, 4. On burial without proper identification, 27, 29–31. On counterproductive attempts to 'save' children in Irish religious institutions, see Valente and Gayle Backus, *Child Sex Scandal*, 12–18.

[44] It is unclear whether, publishing her novel in 2015, Lally was privy to the discoveries of Catherine Corless in Tuam in early 2014. Regardless, enough evidence of unnsanctioned burial had been substantiated by then to justify this recognition. See Smith, *Magdalen Laundries*, 105, 137, 162–3, 177. Vivian's redundant naming with her sister is never explained. However, that duplication, too, emphasises her expendability as a disabled child.

historian Ian Hacking, that autistics have 'thin' personalities'.[45] I do not believe that this echo is entirely accidental. Vivian's hold on her place in society is tenuous; the boundaries between her inclusion and exclusion are thin. *Eggshells* highlights the false dichotomy between being in this world and of it – the ways in which Irish society, which can claim no longer to excise those citizens who do not fit seamlessly, nonetheless does not offer the stability, the surety, of recognition and inclusion, what Fintan O'Toole has called 'our unknown known, always apprehended but never comprehended'.[46]

Quirky but also fragile, beguiling but disabled, Vivian disrupts neat polarities, societal and literary, that would demand she fit solely in one aspect of the world or the other. Her aggressive embodiment refuses erasure, even as her disability rejects normalising incorporation. *Eggshells* portrays the fragility of one woman living in the 'thin' spaces of society – but it also highlights the porousness of that society. In his oft-quoted and haunting 2009 op-ed for the *New York Times*, John Banville observed of Irish society, 'We knew, and did not know. That is our shame today.'[47] This novel considers that shame *today* – what was known; what was ignored – and what continues to be seen but unseen, known but unacknowledged. Like an eggshell, which protects its 'meat' but also readily accepts the colour and variety of dye, as well as the potential fracture of touch, society can 'keep out' what it can as easily 'let in': if only the conditions, and the willingness, are right.

[45] Joseph Valente, 'There's a Girl Inside', *Journal for Cultural and Religious Theory* 15:2 (Spring 2016): 119.
[46] Fintan O'Toole, Foreword in Valente and Backus, *The Child Sex Scandal and Modern Irish Literature*, xi–xiv. xiii.
[47] John Banville, 'A Century of Looking the Other Way', *New York Times*, 22 May 2009. https://www.nytimes.com/2009/05/23/opinion/23banville.html

Chapter 9

'that old shame trick': Mothering, Trauma and Neurodiversity in Emilie Pine's *Ruth & Pen*

Moynagh Sullivan

This essay explores shame in the context of Emilie Pine's contemporary novel *Ruth & Pen* (2019), which connects narratives of neurodiversity and women's reproductivity. Pine explores what it means to live a life in the shadow of the pronatalist imperative of what she describes as 'compulsory motherhood', extending themes about fertility so arrestingly treated in her bestselling 2018 memoir *Notes to Self*.[1] The eponymous Ruth, a psychoanalyst, is in her early forties, and in the process of evaluating her marriage to her husband, Aidan, in the wake of four unsuccessful attempts at IVF, while the nominative Pen, who is autistic and in her mid-late teens, is gathering the courage to ask her friend, Alice, on a romantic date. Pine is explicit about the 'totally conscious' gestures to James Joyce and modernist literature, which involve the remapping of Dublin in *Ruth & Pen*, as Joyce once mapped it in *Ulysses*.[2] Like *Ulysses*, and Virginia Woolf's *Mrs Dalloway*, the action takes place on a single day, Monday 7 October 2019, during which the protagonists cross the city as they both consider significant changes in their lives. Reviews of *Ruth & Pen*, focused on the architecture of the plot and precision of style, as well as on the more legible story of Ruth's reproductive trauma and grief, but were less positive, and even neuroshaming, when it came to Pen. The term autism is still pervasively freighted with ableist overtones.[3]

During the round of promotion interviews for *Ruth & Pen*, Pine was asked by one journalist why she chose 'to foreground an autistic character', and Pine answered, 'why not?'[4] Her answer, much like

[1] Emma Saunders, 'The Novelist Putting Autism Centre Stage', 4 May 2022, https://www.bbc.com/news/entertainment-arts-61227465; Emilie Pine, *Notes to Self* (Dublin: Tramp Press, 2018).

[2] Saunders, 'Emilie Pine'.

[3] See Edith Sheffer, *Asperger's Children: The Origins of Autism in Nazi Vienna* (W. W. Norton and Company, 2018).

[4] Moynagh Sullivan, interview with Emile Pine, UCD, December 2023.

the novel itself, refuses complicity in the ongoing marginalisation of autistic identities, as instanced in Rosemary Goring's review, which was 'unconvinced' by the foregrounding of an autistic protagonist:

> Less assured, or convincing, is the implied parallel between Ruth and Pen. Why she has chosen someone with autism remains unclear, unless it is to highlight that everybody struggles, a fact Pen recognises herself: 'even for people without sensory processing differences, emotions can be really hard to read'. Basically, thinks Pen, the entire rom-com genre is proof that feelings aren't easy.

I want to argue, against Goring, that the two stories and situations are 'very differently weighted'.[5] *Ruth & Pen* links gender and neuroequality by shaping and breaking maternal lines, to suggest a wider register of coded neurodivergent characters besides the openly identified autistic Pen. Pine disassembles the ableist/disableist binaries and hierarchies inherent in traditionally pathologising accounts of autistic/allistic differences.[6] By refusing to make Pen a foil for a neurotypical person to flourish, the novel affirms what Joseph Valente calls the 'heterogeneity' of autistic identities. It underscores Valente's observation that there is no typical autistic, only a set of contradictory, widely variable behavioural characteristics that occur across the spectrum into neurotypicality.[7] Hephzibah Anderson, in *The Guardian*, confirmed that 'Pine sidesteps many of the cliches that attend the representation of autistic characters in literature and film'.[8]

The text's reframing of dominant and inherited autistic tragedy tropes is clearly aligned with the adult autistic-led Autism Rights Movement,[9] and draws from what Mary Doherty calls 'autistic community wisdom and scholarship'.[10] This identity and rights-based movement is for

[5] Rosemary Goring, 'Ruth & Pen, by Emilie Pine, Hamish Hamilton', https://www.heraldscotland.com/news/20171907.ruth-pen-emilie-pine-hamish-hamilton/

[6] Hanna Rosqist, Nick Chown and Anna Stenning, eds, *Neurodiversity Studies: A New Critical Paradigm* (London: Routledge, 2020).

[7] Joseph Valente, 'This Disability Which Is Not One: Autistic Intermittency in Mark Haddon's *The Curious Incident of the Dog in the Night-Time*', *Contemporary Literature* 62:1 (Spring 2021): 35.

[8] Hepzibah Anderson, '*Ruth & Pen* by Emilie Pine review – A World of Joy and Pain', 15 May 2022, https://www.theguardian.com/books/2022/may/15/ruth-pen-by-emilie-pine-review-a-world-of-joy-and-pain

[9] AsIAm, Ireland's National Autism Charity, is also strongly aligned with autistic-led values https://asiam.ie/statement-on-applied-behavioural-analysis-aba-therapy/

[10] Mary Doherty, 'Viewpoint: 'Weaponized Heterogeneity Only Harms the Most Vulnerable Autistic People', *Spectrum | Autism Research News*, 17 April 2023. https://www.spectrumnews.org/opinion/viewpoint/weaponized-heterogeneity-only-harms-the-most-vulnerable-autistic-people/

the most part, situated within the frame of the neurodiversity paradigm, which understands neurotypes not in pathological terms, on an abnormal/normal binary, but simply as neuro-majorities and minorities.[11] Julie Singer, known as the 'mother of neurodiversity', originally conceptualised it in 1996, as a corollary to biodiversity, for affirming the variety of cognitive and sensory neurotypes that make up the human species.[12] Pen lives in a neurodiversity-affirming home supported with a range of survival strategies which are about accepting, not suppressing, her needs, and appreciating and managing her natural responses to stimuli – whether stimming, echolalia or other echopraxias.

Despite this, her life involves daily camouflaging of different intensities when in public spaces, and we meet her on a day on which she needs to 'save her strength for all the ways she will have to be not-like-herself today',[13] in order that the novel can explore the damaging disbursement of masking and camouflage from the point of view of someone surviving a neurotypical-shaped world. Pen is attending an Extinction Rebellion march, a trope that appears to walk Pen straight into what that Anna Stenning calls the autistic 'ecological saint' narrative, which 'presents autistics as ahistorical beings and as symbols of naïve, pre-Industrial attitudes to nature, rather than as historically and spatially enacted human beings'.[14] However, this stereotype relies on representing autistic people as 'precluding agency or introspection',[15] while Pine depicts autism as 'not inherently disabling'. Rather, it becomes a disability in certain contexts, particularly the social realm produced by a majority non-autistic world.[16] The novel's depiction of Pen's inner world view supports the autism-affirming idea that autism is congenital with unique but highly variable 'traits' and 'behaviours', as well as the neurodiversity-affirming position that such indices can also in part be understood as evidence of stress and trauma responses to neuronormative corralling such as the neurobullying endured by Pen, when she was tricked and locked in a wardrobe.[17]

[11] The neurodiversity paradigm includes autism, ADHD (where currently exists a 60–70 per cent overlap), OCD, Parkinson's disease, schizophrenia, bi-polar and many other conditions that 'diverge' from the neuro-majority.

[12] See Julie Singer, *Neurodiversity: The Birth of an Idea* (Kentucky: Singer, 2017).

[13] Emilie Pine, *Ruth & Pen* (Harmondsworth: Penguin, 2019), 62. Hereafter given as (RP page).

[14] A. C. Stenning, 'Misfits and Ecological Saints: Strategies for Non-normative Living in Autistic Life Writing', *Disability Studies Quarterly* 42:1 (2022).

[15] Stenning, 'Misfits'.

[16] Stenning, 'Misfits'.

[17] Jurgen De Wispelaere and Judy Walsh, 'Disability Rights in Ireland: Chronicle of a Missed Opportunity', *Irish Political Studies* 22:4 (2007): 517–43.

Ruth & Pen was published just one year after Ireland voted to repeal the Eighth Amendment, giving women reproductive rights for the first time in the state's troubled history,[18] and only one year after Ireland finally ratified the United Nations Convention on the Rights of Persons with Disabilities (UNCRPD) in March 2018.[19] The novel examines how the extractive logics of capitalism and colonialism reproduce themselves by instrumentalising the labour of others,[20] and how the pro-natalist and neurotypical norms of the Irish state operate to shame a woman/assigned female at birth (AFAB) whose body does not produce children, or children fit to represent the state. *Ruth & Pen* unpicks how re/productive shame is carried by the bodies of those whose value as citizens was not assured in the 1937 Constitution; Pen, who in Ireland is medically defined as disabled, would have been prohibited, until 2015, in Irish law from reproducing (under the 1821 Lunacy Act). The shame at work in the interpellation of the protagonists is not their own but, nonetheless, it marks how they occupy spaces including that of their own bodies.

Shame has, as Jacqueline Rose points out, 'a visceral quality about it' such that people are 'turned red' with it, 'flooded' by it, and she notes how Freud considered it a 'trauma'.[21] *Ruth & Pen* is built from acute observations of sensory experience as each character navigates her own 'big T' trauma; Ruth is in recovery from the repeated bodily violations inflicted by invasive reproductive technologies, while Pen is also in recovery from acute trauma experiences at the hands of bullies.[22] Each also shares the low-level trauma of living as AFAB in a state of hyper-vigilance due to the pervasive threat of sexual or verbal assault. Pen also endures 'small t' trauma of having to handle neuronorms and having a minority sexuality, and Ruth's infertility

[18] See Cara Delay and Claire Bracken, eds, 'Women's Health and Reproductive Justice in Ireland', *Éire-Ireland* 56:3 (2021): 5–20; Sinead Kennedy, '"No Country for Young Women": (Re)producing the Irish State', in Oona Frawley, ed., *Women and the Decade of Commemorations* (Bloomington: Indiana University Press, 2021), 267–83.

[19] De Wispelaere and Walsh, 'Disability Rights', 517.

[20] Ndlovu Sibonokuhle, 'Humanness and Ableism: Construction and Deconstruction of Disability', in Melissa Steyn, ed., *Decolonising The Human: Reflections From Africa On Difference And Oppression* (William Mpofu: Wits University Press, 2021), 65–85.

[21] Jacqueline Rose, 'Introduction: "Shame"', *On Not Being Able to Sleep: Psychoanalysis and the Modern World* (Princeton: Princeton University Press, 2003), 1.

[22] Lamora Ash, '*Ruth & Pen* by Emilie Pine – a tale of two lives', *The Guardian*, 19 May 2022. https://www.theguardian.com/books/2022/may/19/ruth-pen-by-emilie-pine-review-a-tale-of-two-lives

means she is chronically traumatised by the pervasive 'compulsory motherhood' narrative, the state *raison d'être* for women:

> She tries to enter the doctor's room smiling, because you have to pretend you don't hate this, don't hate sitting in your coat, too hot, too female, too scared to say anything other than yes and no. It must be strange for the doctor too, strange to have only patients with vaginas, strange to say, if you could just undress, to a parade of women, strange to have to pretend you can't see their shame. (RP 100)

Finding eye contact agonising is a common neurodivergent experience, and the novel highlights how eye-avoidance is also a normalised aspect of women's reproductive health experience.

Ruth & Pen creates a slippage between being a woman/AFAB and neurodivergence, through the vector of shame and, while the reasons for eye avoidance may differ, the actions overlap. Ruth notes how the women waiting for news about the health of their reproductive organs in the waiting room at the National Maternity Hospital avoid each other's eyes: 'the worst thing is to catch someone's eye, to share that tight grin that says, I see you and you see me and we will pretend that we do not see each other, that we do not share this thing inside us' (RP 99). A form of somatic communication saturates the room, in which shame is produced though the deferred action of being seen. Rose also points out that 'shame requires an audience [u]nlike guilt, which can fester quietly inside you, shame only arises when someone knows, or fears, they have been seen'.[23] The waiting room audience do not shame another because they confer on each other the dignity of not seeing, but are shame-faced nonetheless because the constitutional collapse of mother and child into the one person is reflected in the medical space in which maternity and gynaecological services are provided. Thus, the space of the National Maternity Hospital itself, standing in for the state, is the seeing audience where Ruth's most intense experience of shame occurs, and it also functions as a symbolic locus for the connections and breakages of the maternal intergenerational links the novel explores. For Claire, her most intense articulation of shame is also related to seeing and mothering, in her case, what she thinks of as her failure to see and be a 'good' mother: she feels 'ashamed of how long it took her to *see* [my emphasis]. Her lovely girl. Her difficult girl' (RP 109).

Claire's slowness to see that Pen is autistic gestures to the collective and historical inability to actually see autistic women and girls, because of masculinist biases in health care and sciences, and

[23] Rose, 'Introduction', 1

because women are socialised to be highly masking within patriarchy.[24] Pen is not high masking, but still feels acutely that she is 'not like other girls' (RP 10), while Ruth masks to conform to binary gender norms created by a set of practices that Judith Butler calls performativity. When Ruth 'feels suddenly aware of her make-up-less face' (RP 14) we are reminded by the novel that being feminine is associated with masking, and that it is also, fundamentally, a survival strategy, employed by those at a structural disadvantage. For, as [sarah] Cavar reminds us in 'The Queer Aut of Failure', masking, 'like other methods of "passing", is not a marker of privilege but an indication of embodied danger'.[25] Women/AFABs and girls are, after all, actually expected to 'mask', to daily make-up another face, to be placed on top of our own, in order to achieve 'femininity'. Joan Rivière's 'Womanliness as Masquerade' (1929) identifies a form of exaggerated femininity, especially evident in intellectual or otherwise high-achieving women, which hides rivalry with, and deflected retaliative behaviours from, men. From a neurodiversity perspective, this is suggestive of high-masking autistic women who camouflage to survive, and whose fear of retribution is not from men but from neuronormative society at large.[26]

Recent research that has taken women/AFABs as their subjects, along with neurodivergent-led community knowledge, has transformed understandings of autism from a narrowly defined 'disorder' and dis/ability associated primarily with white middle-class boys to seeing it as an aspect of a much more prevalent neurodivergent profile that is considerably under-assessed across all populations, especially women and girls, racialised minorities[27] and disadvantaged populations which have historically been more likely to have been diagnosed with various personality disorder and other antisocial behaviours, with negative outcomes that include early death, lack of employment, incarceration, institutionalisation and homelessness.[28] *Ruth & Pen*, by centring Pen 'when characters who are autistic are

[24] The Neurodivergent Woman, 'The History of Neurodivergence', 7 February 2002. https://omny.fm/shows/the-neurodivergent-woman/the-history-of-neurodivergence.

[25] [sarah] Cavar, 'The Queer Aut of Failure', *Lateral* 11:2 (Fall 2022):.

[26] Joan Rivière, 'Womanliness as Masquerade', in Russell Grigg, Dominique Hecq and Craig Smith, eds, *Female Sexuality: The Early Psychoanalytic Controversies* (London: Routledge, 1999), 172–82.

[27] Angela Willey, Banu Subramaniam, Jennifer A. Hamilton and Jane Couperus, 'The Mating Life of Geeks: Love, Neuroscience, and the New Autistic Subject', *Signs* 40:2 (Winter 2015): 372

[28] See Malcolm Matthews, 'Why Sheldon Cooper Can't Be Black: The Visual Rhetoric of Autism and Ethnicity', *Journal of Literary & Cultural Disability Studies* 13:1 (2019): 70.

more often than not male',[29] links to the radically paradigm-shifting, unprecedented and recent efflorescence of research on autistic woman/AFAB and girls,[30] which is being called a 'mental health revolution' and shows how neurodivergence in women can be hidden in plain sight. Stimming and avoiding eye contact are normalised within acceptable – and expected – behaviour codes of commodified femininity, especially white femininity. Because women are hypersexualised by patriarchal cultures, it is considered 'feminine' to look away and/or down as a mark of submission, while certain stims can be camouflaged by conversion into performative actions that signal availably or vulnerability, and conform to restricted and repetitive – what Butler calls 'iterative' – actions that produce binarised gender norms, such as flirty hand movements, hair-twisting and flicking, as of which have contributed to the under-assessment in women and girls with lower-support needs.[31]

In Rivière's estimation of the hyper-feminine masquerade, the subject was neither fully homosexual nor heterosexual. Today, she might be called queer. Centring Pen's character as lesbian challenges Simon Baron-Cohen's contested male brain theory of autism, in which the 'neuroqueer' dimension is under-researched. Baron-Cohen's model autism has been criticised for implicit gender bias and reification of the gender binary.[32] There is a statistically significant overlap between gender and neuro-diversity, and female-identified neurodivergent people have the highest rate of identifying as asexual.[33] Pen's crush, Alice, is asexual (ACE) and, although not openly identified in the text as neurodivergent, can be thought of as neuroqueer, as she says she 'felt *different* to everyone else' (RP 229), describing herself in tropes such as being alien,[34] adopted, a changeling,[35] or from another planet or

[29] Saunders, 'Emilie Pine'.

[30] In 2023, for the first time in the USA, autism among white children was assessed lower than other racial/ethnic groups. See 'Autism Spectrum Disorder'.

[31] Judith Butler, *Gender Trouble: Feminism and the Subversion of Identity* (London: Routledge, 1996).

[32] Simon Baron-Cohen, 'The Extreme Male Brain Theory of Autism', *Trends in Cognitive Sciences* 6:6 (2002): 248–54.

[33] Nick Walker, *Neuroqueer Heresies: Notes on the Neurodiversity Paradigm, Autistic Empowerment, and Postnormal Possibilities* (Fort Worth: Autonomous Press, 2021); Hilary Bush, Lindsay Williams and Eva Mendes, 'Brief Report: Asexuality and Young Women on the Autism Spectrum', *Journal of Autism Developmental Disorders* 51:2 (2021): 725–33.

[34] Emily Paige Ballou, Sharon da Vanport and Morénike Giwa Onaiwu, eds, *Sincerely, Your Autistic Child* (New York: Beacon Press, 2021).

[35] Caitriona Lally's *Eggshells* (New York: Melville House Publishing, 2017) has been read as a novel with a possibly autistic protagonist who see themselves as a

universe, terms that are familiar in the self-authoring of neurodivergent people, even those who are lovingly supported and affirmed.[36] When Pen 'could see Alice and her in the mirror at the same time', she noted that 'Alice smiled, a real smile, not like the fake- mirror-posse one' (RP 33), suggesting a pattern of camouflaging that resonated with Pen's own survival strategies. Moreover, even while sitting beside Pen, Alice prefers texting to talking to Pen; texting or exchanging voice messages can be a preferred mode of communication as telephone calls and face-to-face talking can be more exhausting and difficult. Although Pen admires Alice as the person she knows who 'least cares about what people think', Alice has still internalised the language of deficit and lack, indicated when she says, 'it's like the bit that connects looking to feeling doesn't, like, work in me' (RP 229). The novel orients the reader to Claire's parenting practices when Alice describes how her parents are not like Claire, but just made her keep a diary of her 'feelings as if it doesn't really matter' (RP 229).

The privileging of Claire's perspective and neuroaffirming mothering intervenes with the interfaces examined in Catherine Tan's *Spaces on the Spectrum: How Autism Movements Resist Experts and Create Knowledge*,[37] where the differing needs and experiences of parents and carers of autistic children come into conflict with adult autistic-led activism.[38] Claire is explicitly not an 'autism mom', and the novel counters the 'warrior mother' discourse so prevalent in the media, where autism is largely framed as a tragedy, penance and cross to bear for the embattled 'autism mom' who seeks to 'save' her child from autism.[39] To be a mother in a pro-natalist and industrialised culture who has 're/produced' a child who may not *produce* or *reproduce*, is implicitly shameful'[40] for not being 'enough' and not re/producing 'enough'; this powerful ideological conscription to patriarchal capitalism is resisted by the novel when Ruth is able to accept she is 'enough' in herself, challenging her fear that Aidan believes

changeling. See Molly Ferguson, 'The Changeling Legend and Queer Kinship in Caitriona Lally's Eggshells', *Irish University Review* 51:2 (Autumn–Winter 2021): 296–311, and Kathleen Costello-Sullivan's essay in this volume.

[36] Joanne Limburg, *Letters to My Weird Sisters* (London: Atlantic Books, 2021).

[37] Catherine Tan, *Spaces on the Spectrum: How Autism Movements Resist Experts and Create Knowledge* (New York: Columbia University Press, 2024), 12.

[38] Meghan Ashburn and Jules Edwards, *I will Die on this Hill: Autistic Adults, Autism Parents, and the Children Who Deserve a Better World* (London: Jessica Kingsley Publishing, 2023).

[39] Mary Barbera, *Turn Autism Around: An Action Guide for Parents of Young Children with Early Signs of Autism* (London: Hay House, 2021).

[40] Tan, *Spaces on the Spectrum*, 39.

'that without children she is not enough', and when Pen texts Alice to say, 'you are enough' (RP 172).

Claire and Pen's relationship is contrasted with the neurodivergent-coded shadow story of Ruth's fractured relationship with her mother.[41] The novel highlights a trauma-frame as Ruth digests instances of her mother's emotional abuse, but the episodes recounted intimate the trauma origin as Ruth's mother struggles to survive in a neurotypical world; Ruth's character is neurodivergently drawn. Her mother calls her a 'drama queen' (RP 75) and tells her there is '*no need to make everything a production*' (RP 3). Ruth's mother's 'thing' – which was 'not getting tea' in a café or elsewhere, because 'you couldn't ensure the water was just boiled or scald the pot or chose the mug' (RP 91), is suggestive of neurodivergent sensory experiences, and when Ruth describes her 'mother's constant fury' (RP 78), it indicates not only the meltdowns and anxiety that arise from negotiating neurotypical expectations, but also a compensatory parenting pattern to quell her fear that her daughter will suffer as she has, so she seeks to shame Ruth into neuroconforming,[42] as shown by this poignant account of the repression of Ruth's echolaliac joy:

> [Ruth] must have been about five, and she'd sung (delighted with herself) over and over, the song about the bear going over the mountain to see what he could see. But her mother had hated it, told her to shut up, and when Ruth had kept going, she had stopped the car, made her get out, told her to stand by the side of the road, 'don't move, now'. Ruth had not dared move, had only stood and watched as her mother had driven away. She'd come back, of course she had, but Ruth had learned her lesson. (RP 91)

Terrifying her daughter into suppressing her vocal stim, as well as dismissing Ruth's feelings as 'dramatic', all so that the family stage could be reserved just for acting out her own psychodrama, is illustrative of the intergenerational trauma load that can get passed down and imprinted via shame behaviours when parents are misunderstood, under-resourced and unsupported. Alison Kafer, in *Feminist Queer Crip* (2013), explores the shame carried by the body that 'echoes

[41] Devon Price notes links between ABA and the controversial 'Pray the Gay Away' therapy used to 'cure' homosexuality. Devon Price, *Unmasking Autism: Discovering the New Faces of Neurodiversity* (Oxford: Blackwell, 2022).

[42] Sara Gibbs documents the shaming labels she endured growing up autistic in *Drama Queen: One Autistic Woman and a Life of Unhelpful Labels* (London: Headline Publishing Group, 2021).

what nobody wants to hear',[43] and thus we can read the shaming that is involved in the extraordinary efforts: to repress, supress and reduce echolalia and repetition, the bodily self-soothing and expression of stimming to fit with neurotypical social interactions as a violating resistance to a set of knowledges – epistemologies and indeed ontologies – that disrupt, extend and 'queer' received knowledge of human value. Ruth's early trauma primes her to live in a body that seems to 'echo what nobody wants to hear', and she wrestles with being both 'difficult' and 'infertile', exceeding both designations, but not before she confronts what it could mean when Aidan called her 'not easy' (RP 172).

When Ruth muses that 'Aidan is right, Ruth has never figured that out, a way to be *easy* around others', it suggests that neurotypical socialising is hard for her, and her description of music as a 'shield' reads as a neurodivergent assimilation tactic that allows one to be in the group yet safely apart, because 'you were always liked if you could play an instrument, you were called on at parties, and you were given space and brought close, all at the same time'. Ruth wonders if 'music was a mask, like any other', and whether 'playing an instrument is maybe more of a shield than a mask' (RP 41), and she describes the 'pure joy of wholly being themselves with each other' when with Aidan (RP 173). Although 'masking' is the umbrella term most commonly used by autistic people, masking is more precisely considered a subset of 'camouflaging'.[44] Camouflaging is broadly comprised of compensatory behaviours such as using social scripts, suppressing neurodivergent behaviours and assimilation, fitting in with others to avoid the pain of social exclusion; not all neurodivergent people mask, and many simply remain their authentic selves.

Neurodivergent masking is differentiated from style shifting – the general social practices of assuming different behaviours in different contexts – because camouflaging involves hiding so-called deficits and unacceptable characteristics across all dominant neurogroup contexts. It involves a relentless cognitive and emotional cost. It is more akin to racial and cultural code-switching, where racially privileged socio-cultural norms are mirrored to avoid adverse consequences (which also means of course that masking black and brown neurodivergent people are even more adversely effected). When Ruth 'looks in the mirror, sees her still creased face, sees her body in the

[43] Alison Kafer, *Feminist Queer Crip* (Bloomington: Indiana University Press, 2013).
[44] Eva Silvertint, 'Embrace Autism', accessed 24 June 2024, https://embrace-autism.com/autism-and-camouflaging/

Navy suit, thinks, oh, this is who I am' (RP 4), she is guided by these external coordinates; her not asking for help 'was to do with shame, usually' (RP 54), as to do so would negate the point of camouflaging: the point of which is to hide so-called deficits. Ruth relies heavily on social and professional scripts and, as a psychotherapist, has an occupation that self-selects highly for neurodivergent people (human behaviour as a special interest).

Ruth's description of normally having 'more margin' (RP 70) suggests the edge of autistic burn-out, and while her realisation that 'she has no clothes for who she is meant to be today. Counsellor. Patient. Wife' (RP 3) might suggest code-switching, her internal musings tend more towards 'not losing face'/mask, when she tries to 'summon the calm face, the blank canvas, the friendly manner' (RP 44), and she 'hates' that she is 'caught out' by Lisa, when 'a flash of worry' crosses 'her face' (RP 127). Ruth also displays multi-sensory engagement: 'her clothes still feel strange on her, reminding her of the body underneath' (RP 115); she wakes up with a 'sticky after-feeling' (RP 1) and notes that 'the hand soap dispenser feels sticky' (RP 144); she 'listens to the growing boil of the water' (RP 18), her hairdryer 'roar' (RP 4) and enjoys the huge sensory hit from her food, which is 'crispy, salty, cheesy'; she demonstrates a strong sense of smell, noting 'the scent of olives or spices' (RP 18). She seeks out windows, which provide not only a source of natural light but also a multi-sensory corrective to the assault of fluorescent and artificial light on the body/mind of neurodivergent people, and as Ruth keeps vigil with her dying mother she thinks 'still it was nice to be by a window' (RP 81). Moreover, Ruth directs herself through the day with an internal monologue comprised of instructions, imperatives and exhortations. When she crosses Pen's path, Ruth is pleased 'with acting on feeling' (RP 87), which not only implies she acts a lot 'on script', but also insinuates that she felt an inter-bodily recognition of a familiar neurotype.

When, in *Divergent Mind: thriving in a World that Wasn't Designed for You*, Jenara Nerenberg wrote that 'women walk around with unnecessary amounts of shame, guilt, depression, and anxiety [since] our reality has not been properly validated',[45] she referred to the health cost carried by generations of women shamed for multiple health issues, many of which now increasingly appear to be related to neurodivergence: the pain in a woman/AFAB's 'mind' now appears to be 'in the body' after all. Research on the nervous and sensory as well as the musculoskeletal systems has identified co-occurring conditions

[45] Nerenberg, '*Divergent Mind*', 33.

due to the actions of myelin and collagen in the bodies of neurodivergent people that suggests a whole body and brain structural design. For instance, autistic communities fondly refer to 'T-Rex arms', a signature neurodivergent way of holding the hands which relieves the unconscious sense that shoulders may be dislocating due to joint lability; researchers are now also exploring how the different collagen structures of neurodivergent bodies and brains may account for signature cognitive patterns.

The high co-occurrence of Ehlers–Danlos syndromes, as well as generalised joint hypermobility, with neurodivergence, is being explored as a common aetiology for seemingly unconnected endocrine and gynaecological conditions such as endometriosis, fibroids and unexplained infertility (as experienced by Ruth), auto-immune diseases, fibromyalgia, CFS/ME and chronic joint pain.[46] Ruth, who isn't described as hypermobile, does do 'Yoga' (RP 91), has 'fibroids' (RP 90–1) and is hyper-aware of her joints and her flexibility: when Ruth wakes up, 'Her right hip is stiff, knuckles massage the part where the edges – is there something wrong with it? With the bone, the socket, the joint? (RP 3) and, in the National Gallery, her 'neck is sore from being bent back' (RP 14), where she not only looks at the paintings but also finds herself in them. In the gallery, Ruth has a full-body encounter with Mainie Jellett's painting *Decoration* (1923), where she 'imagines herself in it, being held within it'. The novel spotlights the gallery artwork label, which includes the detail that it was bequeathed by the stained-glass artist and painter Evie Hone in 1955. Ruth finds herself enfolded in this 'painting that looks like a collage, like the outline of a house, like the inside of a person' (RP 152), which, like much modernist art and writing in its time (like the queer woman artist who painted it), challenged inherited norms. When first exhibited it was called 'subhuman art',[47] by George Russell (aka 'Æ'). Inti Guerrero, curator of the 2018 EVA International biennial, noted that Russell's medicalised language is comparable to '[degenerate] art, the pathology given by the Third Reich to modernist artists'.[48]

Ruth's synesthetic response to this 'de-generational' picture with its historical and eugenic undertones of sub-humanity, its materiality noted – made from tempera, an egg medium – as well as the neuroqueer echo-phenomena of the window art of Hone (Jellett's partner)

[46] See Barb Cook and Michelle Garnett, eds, *Spectrum Women: Walking to the Beat of Autism* (London: Jessica Kingsley, 2018).

[47] George Russell, 'Irish Statesman', 27 October 1923, 207–8.

[48] Sarah Bochiccio, 'The Female Painter whose Modern Art Shocked Ireland', *Artsy*, 18 April 2018.

all contribute to what Melanie Remi Yergeau terms 'resonance'. This autistic-led concept describes a multimodal form of communication or recognition, a form of 'interbodily knowing' and 'reverbing', a perceptibility that is also expressed by Pen when she says that 'people vibrate too' (RP 204).[49] Jellett's argument, in 'An Approach to Painting', also 'reverbs' in this moment: her view that the 'artist' was 'a special person, an exotic flower set apart from other people is one of the errors resulting from the industrial revolution',[50] parallels the increasing marginalisation of 'un-productive' or un-abled – read neurodivergent – people since industrialisation. 'Resonance' can extend the interpretive paradigms available to readers of cultures, visibilising autistic experience while refusing to partake in the patronising and illusory 'unified field paradigm of autism: whether social first theories (like theory of mind or mirror neuron), phenomenological theories (like weak central coherence), or neurosensory theories (like intense world syndrome)',[51] so powerfully identified by Valente. 'Resonance' operates as a counter to symptomatic thinking, and constitutes what Yergeau calls an 'autistic heuristic',[52] with its refusal to excise the body from the picture, and it draws on Sara Acevedo's theory of 'embodiminds',[53] which opens the possibility of representing neurodiversity while resisting the reliance on the dehumanising and contradictory lists of what Valente has termed 'symptomatic markers'.[54]

Claire's parenting could be read as an example of what Valente calls the 'normativity Mom', who, by 'shifting to a celebration of the triumphant aspects of autism itself', makes a 'more explicit gesture in the direction of neurodiversity',[55] but given Claire's slowness to 'see' that Pen is autistic, it could equally have been because she didn't relate 'neurotypically' to her daughter. In other words, perhaps Claire didn't 'notice' because associational and interbodily reverberation created a 'resonance' with each other in the relationship they

[49] Melanie Remi Yergeau, *Authoring Autism: On Rhetoric and Neurological Queerness* (Durham: Duke University Press, 2017).

[50] Mainie Jellett, 'An Approach to Painting', in Angela Bourke et al., eds, *The Field Day Anthology of Irish Writing, Vol. V, Irish Women's Writing and Traditions* (Lawrence Hill, Derry, Northern Ireland: Field Day, 1991–2002), 1,085–6.

[51] Valente, 'This Disability', 37.

[52] Yergeau, *Authoring Autism*, 302.

[53] Sara M. Acevedo Espinal, '"Effective Schooling", The Age of Capital: Critical Insights from Advocacy Anthropology, Anthropology of Education, and Critical Disability Studies', *Canadian Journal of Disability Studies* 9:5 (2020): 265–301.

[54] Valente, 'This Disability', 35.

[55] Joseph Valente, 'All Better? Recovery Anxiety in the Writing of Autism', *Journal of Literary & Cultural Disability Studies* 12:4 (2018): 493.

shared.[56] Increasingly, neurodivergence is identified as a heredity, and so neurodivergence is likely to be a pattern in Pen's family. The playwright Jody O'Neill, who served as a consultant on Pine's novel, and whose plays include *What I (Don't) Know about Autism* and *Yellow*, has spoken how, while 'researching autism on account of her son's diagnosis in 2016', she 'became fascinated with the subject and saw similarities between herself and her child'. O'Neill 'describes her own diagnosis of autism at the age of 39 as an overwhelmingly positive experience',[57] and this follows an increasingly common pattern whereby parents of neurodivergent children come to an awareness of their own, as well as ancestral, neurotypes, through their children's assessments. Claire makes her living through having a professional special interest ('SpIn'). It is not a leap to describe academic specialisation as a version of 'hyper-fixation', given the hyperfocus and niche interest that is needed to complete a PhD, or subsequent research, and this seems a more likely alignment with neurodivergent monotropism[58] than with the wider, more consistent and less intense range of evenly distributed neurotypical interests and cognition.

Claire is highly trained in 'reading', in decoding and seeing the patterns across texts and subtexts, and *Ruth & Pen* abounds with literary self-reflexivity – Cristin Leach obverses that it's a story of 'things misheard, not heard, not said, and misunderstood',[59] ironically, a description that appears to reflect the array of supposedly autistic deficits in communication that still form part of the diagnostic processes today, but which also leads us into the terrain of literary criticism,[60] particularly post-structuralist-inflected literary criticism, in which all readings are misreadings. Claire notes that Pen is better at English literature than her school teacher, and 'Pen thinks of the way words touch the surface of things, sliding across the world and your tongue. Some words can make you feel loved and soft, and others dent and damage' (RP 23). But far from mishearing, not saying and misunderstanding, *Ruth & Pen* resonates and ripples with meaning. Claire wishes she 'could change' the other people, not her

[56] Damian Milton, 'On the ontological status of autism: the "double empathy problem"', *Disability & Society* 27:6 (2012): 883–7.

[57] Jody O'Neill, 'In the arts, more and more people are presenting as neurodivergent', *Irish Examiner*, 13 June 2002.

[58] A. Grissom, E. Fink and E. Zane, 'Verbal Fluency and Autism: Reframing Current Data Through the Lens of Monotropism', *Autism Research* 17:2 (2024): 24–337.

[59] Cristín Leach, 'Book of the Week', RTÉ, 4 June 2022. https://www.rte.ie/culture/2022/0604/1302320-book-of-the-week-ruth-and-pen-by-emilie-pine/

[60] Julie Brown, *Writers on the Spectrum: How Autism and Asperger Syndrome have Influenced Literary Writing* (London: Jessica Kingsley Publishers, 2009).

daughter; Claire's name relates to 'illustrious', being clear and bright, and she dares us to shame her beloved daughter, warning us too not to 'fall for that old shame trick'. As an English professor and professional interpreter of texts, she provides perspective and serves as an orienting point of view for the reader, when she asserts that, as far as Pen's life is concerned, 'all she can do is watch' (RP 111); on her 'watch', she guards against and deflects the shame willed on her daughter by 'other people' – who turn out to be us. She not only neurodiversifies the world for her daughter, but also does the same for her students, the 'aliens' (RP 108) in the classroom, and for us as readers. As a literary scholar, she functions to emphasise the need for narrative refiguring so that readers in the future will be less likely to ask 'what's the point of having an autistic character'.

The recurrent motifs of windows and mirrors highlight what can be made visible in inherited interpretative epistemological frames. When Ruth and Pen's paths cross, Ruth asks to take Pen and Alice's photo – on her camera phone, a technology that reproduces images via refraction of light through a window onto a mirror (RP 86–7). Although, when the 'the girls move into frame', Ruth has no intention of keeping the picture thus framed, and we are moved into a new unframed space (RP 87) which represents the ongoing resituating of knowledge via bodies and space, tallying with Rebecca-Eli M. Long's argument that 'neurodiversity should not only refer to many types of "embodiminds", but also a diversity of knowledge-making practices, including cripistemologies [. . .] made at moments of crises'.[61] In *Ruth & Pen*, when each embodimind makes their way through the spaces of Dublin, cripistemologies are created at moments of epistemic crises, and the city is neurodiversally remapped (quite differently from *Ulysses*) and the metrics of their steps aligns with Stenning's exploration of walking as a form of embodied autistic cognition.[62] The novel invites us off the two-dimensional flat page of the book into multi-dimensional spaces, including the National Gallery, where Ruth sensory merging with Jellett's contemporaneously transgressive painting and Pen's nervous system reset represent moments of deshaming.

The text thus reads as the novelistic corelative of Jos Boys's and Zoe Partington's 'DisOrdinary Architecture', which aims to redesign

[61] Rebecca-Eli M. Long, 'Security Blanket: Neuroqueer Knitting in Pandemic Times', *Lateral* 11:2 (2022).

[62] Anna Stenning, 'Autism and Cognitive Embodiment: Steps Towards a Non-ableist Walking Literature', in David Borthwick, Pippa Maryland and Anna Stenning, eds, *Walking, Landscape and Environment* (London: Routledge, 2019), 149–67.

urban and built space to accommodate those currently disabled by public environments.[63] The novel pays unusual attention to the spaces between bodies and objects, substituting the more usual prepositions and persons/people terminology: Ruth is acutely aware of 'no other bodies in the building' (RP 74), Claire, 'looking at the bodies in front of her' (RP 108) and Claire 'puts an apple on the table in front of [Pen's] body' (RP 12). Each character 'misfits' environments, and while herself in space remaps norms by proprioceptively remapping their own embodimind in the city's spaces.[64] For instance, Ruth may wish to be the 'home' Aidan comes home to, her final choice not to continue with the IVF, makes her unhomely, unheimlich, according to the coordinates of woman and home in articles 41, marginalised and misfitting, as does the medical language about her womb, that designates it a 'hostile environment' (RP 196). Ruth becomes home to herself, and her relationship, as the novel 'unravels experiences' of 'architectural misfitting across built, conceptual and disciplinary spaces reveal shared patterns of invisibility and marginalization, as well as differences and tensions in how othering is made concrete',[65] demonstrating Yergeau's argument that including the phenomenological as an 'autistic rhetoric' extends our range of understanding of multiple planes of communication.[66] *Ruth & Pen* remaps not so much the spaces of Dublin but knowledge making through multimodal communications across its spaces, creating cripistemologies that have potential to undo the binary on which what Valente calls the 'auttype' can continue to produce harm.

63 Jos Boys, 'Call to Action', *Journal of Architectural Education* 74:2 (2020): 171.
64 Stenning, 'Misfits'.
65 Boys, 'Call to Action', 171.
66 Yergeau, *Authoring Autism*, 302.

Part V

Psychoanalytic Shame

Chapter 10

The Shame of Ireland's Mother and Baby Homes

Eve Watson

In February 2021, the much-anticipated *Final Report of the Commission of Investigation into Mother and Baby Homes and Certain Related Matters* was published upon completion of the commission's investigative work into the treatment of unmarried mothers and their children in state- and religious-run homes since Irish independence.[1] It was lauded as an important step in bringing to light difficult truths and the importance of documenting and historicising the institutional treatment of women and their children between 1922 and 1998. Testimony from over 600 witnesses with direct experience of Mother and Baby Homes was heard by two committees, a Confidential Committee and an Investigative Committee, in addition to the collection and review of substantial documentary evidence. The *Final Report*'s publication was, however, met by a storm of protest and disquiet, and its principal failure was deemed to have been its inadequacy in handling and reporting the witness testimonies. There were also objections to its refusal to provide adoption and burial records to adoptees and survivors, and the claim that women were generally not coerced into homes, nor were their children forcibly removed. Survivors criticised how their testimony was collected as they were never provided with a transcript, and they objected to the commission's decision without notice to destroy audio tapes of all testimonies, in addition to the disregard of the testimony of 550 witnesses given to the Confidential Committee. Witness accounts heard by the Investigative Committee that were included in the *Final*

[1] Yvonne Murphy, William Duncan and Mary Daly, *Final Report of the Commission of Investigation into Mother and Baby Homes*, 12 January 2021, 1–2,865. https://www.gov.ie/en/publication/d4b3d-final-report-of-the-commission-of-investigation-into-mother-and-baby-homes/

Report were erroneously and inaccurately represented, and witnesses were, in a judgement by the Irish court, unlawfully denied the right to review a transcript of their testimony prior to its publication.[2]

Drawing from a psychoanalytic framework, I explore the context and significance of the *Final Report*'s failure and specifically the mishandling of the witness testimonies, which (given the *Final Report*'s place in a two-decades-long succession of reports and the fact the commission was directed by a judge who served on previous Commissions of Investigation into child abuse in state institutions, a leading Irish historian and a lawyer with expertise in child protection and human rights law) is both discouraging but also interpretable. Analysis of the report's tone, described by historian and archivist Catriona Crowe as hectoring, at times defensive, at times cryptic, sometimes all three,[3] and the mistreatment of witness testimony, anathema to psychoanalysis, a field in which the analysand's speech is treated as 'holy writ', is supported by a consideration of the role and value of shame in the contemporary world. Shame is a psychical factor and is an affect that traverses both the individual and the social. It properly locates the obscene and is important in organising socially agreed-upon values, limits and accountability.

The failure of the *Final Report* and its astonishingly insouciant treatment of witness testimony, which should have been its highest priority, signifies a resistance to accounting for a dark history of misogyny, bigotry, indoctrination, ignorance, collusion, greed, silence and hatred. Bearing witness is an important intersubjective practice that is a necessary first step in reconciling with the past and is a logical precipitant to responsibility-taking and restitutive work. The inaccuracies, mistakes, lacunae and reproachful tone of the *Final Report* can be understood as denoting an impasse of shame at the level of the social body as public and social discourse today does not easily permit shame which confronts us with our worst selves, a point of pure abjection. A discourse that bespeaks the moral incompleteness of the speaking-being is one that keeps a check on narcissistic hubris and the enjoyment of the drives. Giving voice to and naming the histories of witnesses and survivors of Mother and Baby Homes will not

[2] Ellen O' Riordan, 'Findings of Mother and Baby Homes 'at odds' with Testimony, High Court Hears', *Irish Times*, 17 November 2021. https://www.irishtimes.com/news/crime-and-law/courts/high-court/findings-of-mother-and-baby-homes-report-at-odds-with-testimony-high-court-hears-1.4731252

[3] Catriona Crowe, 'The Commission and the Survivors', *Dublin Review* (Summer 2021). https://thedublinreview.com/article/the-commission-and-the-survivors/

introduce base qualities into the world because they are already there, but it can animate a limit to their compulsive repetition.

The *Final Report* in Context

A Commission of Investigation into Mother and Baby Homes and Certain Related Matters was established in 2015 to comprehensively investigate and record the treatment of unmarried mothers and their children in state and religious care since Irish independence, between 1922 and 1998.[4] The commission's work drew from a wide range of state, county, diocesan and health authority records, as well as the testimonies of over 600 witnesses. Precipitating the commission's establishment were shocking revelations of mortality rates and burial practices in Mother and Baby Homes which arose from the exhaustive research of historians and advocates such as Jim Smith, Catriona Crowe, Catherine Corless and Caelainn Hogan. This included the uncovering of a mass grave of almost 800 undocumented babies in Tuam, County Galway.[5] The *Final Report* followed in the footsteps of previous reports – the Ferns Inquiry (2005), the Ryan report (2009), the Murphy report (2009), the Cloyne report (2011) – which documented systemic failures to protect children in Church and state care in industrial schools, orphanages and dioceses during the twentieth century. These reports, while encumbered by the limitations of their terms of reference and archival support, were important in initiating and supporting a process of historicising a catastrophic and shameful legacy of abuses of children in Church and state care and establishing frameworks for restitution.

The commission's investigation extended to examining living conditions and care in fourteen Mother and Baby Homes, in addition to rates of mother and child mortality, the extent of compliance with relevant ethical and regulatory standards, pathways in which children exited the homes, the welfare and protection of children,

[4] 'S.I. No. 57/2015 – Commission of Investigation (Mother and Baby Homes and certain related Matters) Order 2015', https://www.irishstatutebook.ie/eli/2015/si/57/made/en/

[5] Sorcha Pollak and Patsy McGarry, 'International Reaction to Mother and Baby Home Revelations', *Irish Times*, 4 June 2014; Catherine Corless, *Belonging: A Memoir of Place* (Hachette Books Ireland, 2021); Caelainn Hogan, *Republic of Shame* (London: Penguin, 2019); James M. Smith, 'Knowing and Unknowing Tuam: State Practice, the Archive and Transitional Justice', in Katherine O'Donnell, Maeve O' Rourke and James Smith, eds, *Redress: Ireland's Institutions and Transitional Justice* (Dublin: University College Dublin Press, 2022), 356–82.

procedures for obtaining consent of mothers and the extent of mothers' decision-making in respect of adoptions.[6] Testimonies were given to two committees, a Confidential Committee and an Investigative Committee, which heard and recorded the testimonies of a total of 613 survivors of the fourteen institutions who formed a representative sample of the almost 113,000 women and children estimated to have resided in Mother and Baby Homes between 1922 and 1998. The representative sample isn't really a representative sample, as it aims to represent at least 56,000 women and 57,000 children who went through these homes, and it is unavoidably skewed in representing those who resided in these institutions towards the latter period of their operation, from the 1960s onwards. The significance for survivors of telling their stories and the importance of allowing their stories to be told was written into the *Final Report*:

> For all kinds of personal and public reasons, some witnesses still felt it was necessary to tell their stories, sometimes against their own families who, petrified by shame, mortification, fear of parish scandal and neighbours' blame, had jettisoned them at a time when help and solidarity were most needed.
>
> However, in all groups, the depth and honesty of what witnesses revealed to the Committee about what had happened to them having left the mother and baby homes, was startling. To tell these stories and have them noted by the Irish state, took courage, and of that there was plenty.
>
> The Committee is very grateful to all those who came forward to tell of their experience in the mother and baby homes. For some it was the first time they had revealed their feelings and thoughts of their time there. The Committee wishes to acknowledge how difficult that was for them.[7]

The power of words matters and was categorically acknowledged. But for all that the *Final Report* did not observe the commission's own acknowledged significance of the value of witness testimony nor adhere to generally accepted methods of research and data collection and publication. This failure was unwittingly written into the *Final Report* by way of an elision, which in psychoanalytic terms is the kind of mistake where the truth of matter is likely to be found. The various sections list their main sources of evidentiary support as Department of Health files, local authority archives, congregational records, diocesan archives but not the testimony of the survivors, despite stating

[6] For details, 'S.I. No. 57/2015', https://www.irishstatutebook.ie/eli/2015/si/57/made/en/

[7] Murphy, Duncan and Daly, *Final Report*, 2,583.

that survivors' testimonies are expressed largely in the words of the individuals themselves.[8] The *Final Report* thus acknowledges the use of witness testimonies but does not list them as one of its sources. What is to be made of this strange omittance, and what is to be found in the place of its absence?

Truth Can Be Refound[9]

Let us consider that any process of accounting for individual experiences and testimonies and historicising them is necessarily fraught because the result will always be partial; the past cannot be fully re-collected and represented. But the *Final Report* is not a partial and incomplete report of the survivors' accounts. It failed, in the words of appellant and survivor Philomena Lee, to impartially and fairly investigate and establish the truth.[10] This impartiality, as a turning away from the truth, can be inferred from the handling of the testimonies. In her evaluation of the retrieval practices, the supporting documentation, and follow-up statements and documentary support of women who gave interviews to the Confidential Committee, Catriona Crowe has concluded it is probable the investigators relied on notes taken during their interviews with the witnesses and not the taped recordings of each interview. The reason for relying on these notes, Crowe proposes, is the tapes were mislaid, lost or destroyed. While the commission has acknowledged it destroyed all recordings of the interviews for legal and moral reasons, it cannot, Crowe concludes, be clearly established if the tapes were destroyed prior to the writing of the *Final Report*. Given the level of error, inaccuracy, omission and misrepresentation of witness testimony, it is unlikely they were used in the published report.[11]

The *Final Report* is therefore a compendium of what was heard and documented by the interviewers and is not a synopsis of what witnesses actually said. Not surprisingly, the *Report* contains errors,

[8] Murphy, Duncan and Daly, *Final Report*, 2,405; Crowe, 'The Commission'.

[9] Jacques Lacan, 'The Function and Field of Speech and Language in Psychoanalysis, or Reason Since Freud', in *Ecrits*, translated by Bruce Fink (New York: Norton, 2006), 215.

[10] Ellen O' Riordan, 'Rights of eight mother and baby home survivors breached over report, State says', *Irish Times*, 19 December 2021. https://www.irishtimes.com/news/crime-and-law/courts/high-court/rights-of-eight-mother-and-baby-home-survivors-breached-over-report-state-says-1.4758041

[11] Crowe, 'The Commission'.

inaccuracies and lacunae, as it is challenging for interviewers not to ascribe emphases and pick and choose what to include and omit, especially if they were unaware at the time of the witness interviews that their notes would be adopted as a primary source in the *Final Report*. We can also surmise that the witness testimonies were painful and difficult to hear and had a high emotional charge. The stories, some of them traumatic and devastating, were being told by witnesses, some for the first time, to interviewers who may have been affected by their telling. It is impossible to know to what extent this impacted interviewers' notetaking, but we can infer some impact in what resulted: inaccurate and erroneous re-presentations of the testimonies. In psychoanalytic terms, good (evenly suspended) listening is incompatible with the analyst's immersion in the affective dimension of the analysand's speech.

The missing tapes and the over-writing of witness testimonies with interviewers' notes suggests a crucial psychical factor at stake in the process of accounting for the distressing histories enunciated by the witnesses. This is the affect of shame which in psychoanalysis is privileged as a direct, unadulterated expression of truth. Being open to the past as shaming and shameful offers a place for the truth to speak and to be realised as part of a restitutive and responsibility-taking process. In an analysis, this is the analysand's responsibility-taking for their own desire and modes of drive enjoyment. In the social realm, this also involves honest responsibility allocation for actions, non-actions, deeds, misdeeds, silence and censorship, including those of previous generations. The report's failure can therefore be contextualised in terms of a derogated place of shame in contemporary Irish society and the absence of the necessary condition of probity, which supports shame.

This has not always been the case; the Other's shaming force was well-nigh throughout the twentieth century in Catholic doctrine which privileged shame in its teachings and instrumentalised it at all levels – socially, politically and ideologically – in shoring up its sphere of influence. This institutionalised deployment of shame, however, had the effect of curtailing its probative function as a regulator of the obscene. That is because shame properly locates the obscene/perverse, but within this doctrine practically all sexuality was deemed shameful, especially women's, which meant that the real obscenity could take place away from the social gaze taken up with policing ordinary sexuality and (unattainable) sexual norms. Off-scene, obscenity found unencumbered expression in the abuse of children and the vulnerable in state and Church institutional care. In the deeply patriarchal and misogynistic culture of post-independence Ireland, dominated by a church obsessed with the sexual hygiene of the populace, it was unmarried mothers and their children who served as scapegoats of impossible sexual and social norms and deflected the social gaze away from the Church itself.

Irish Shame: 'Unmarried Mothers' and Their Children

In a social body, shame supports values, ideals and aims that collectivise and unify it. In functioning as a policing tool that causes individuals to conform to collective aims, it is a point at which the social bond and the individual psyche traverse. As Cathy O'Neil puts it, it is administered by a collective whose rules and taboos are etched into our psyches and is borne of the conflict between an individual's desires and the expectations of a group.[12] Shame thus occupies an important and detested place at the same time. The experience of shame is painful in aiming at our being, or rather our lack in being, and no one wants to feel ashamed. As a mortifying revelation of the limitations of humanhood and the obscene enjoyment of the drives, shame actuates potentiality out of the precariousness of human subjectivity itself, something out of nothing or rather lack. The revelation of the obscene is subjectively constituted and is not the domain of others in so far as we displace it there. This can only happen when there is an Other that looks and causes the onlooker to become ashamed.

As a social force, it is important that shame be collectively deployed in a balanced way, serving certain agreed-upon limits and values. It must not function solely as an instrument of power. Since the late 1990s and into the first decade and a half of this century, shame actuated a national conscience in support of survivors of abuse while in Church and state care which has led to the convictions of perpetrators and the provision of reparation and redress. Prior to that, shame was a component of a social doctrine that O'Donnell, O'Rourke and Smith describe as an architecture of containment,[13] instrumentalised by the political and ideological aspirations of Catholic Church authority to demarcate a 'legitimate' Catholic national identity that took its coherence from 'illegitimate' elements within Irish society

[12] Cathy O'Neil, *The Shame Machine: Who Profits in the New Age of Humiliation?* (London: Allen Lane, 2022), 6.

[13] Katherine O' Donnell, Maeve O'Rourke and James Smith, eds, *Redress*, vii.

representative of immorality and transgression. This social doctrine mandated that even procreative sex and maternity were shameful emanations of sexuality that ought to be kept hidden. In the words of one woman, speaking in the mid-1950s, 'there is something repulsive about it [sex] and nothing will get that out of my system'.[14] Children, women and the disabled functioned, in the words of Valente and Backus, as a release valve for the social and economic stress imposed on the Catholic citizen-subject,[15] shameful figures who embodied sexual and spiritual impurity and who were banished to homes, asylums or the emigrant train and their children to industrial schools, laundries or illegal adoptions.

A society that enforces shaming practices on its citizens can be understood, as the psychoanalytic commentator Renata Salecl puts it, to be desperately seeking to sustain the fiction of itself as a constant and consistent Other, and it reveals its own inconsistency in needing the buy-in of people and communities to sustain its authority.[16] In the Irish context, this inconsistency is revealed in a doctrine obsessed with the moral cleanliness of the populace and marshalled through an ideal of the nuclear family, an ideal that is enshrined in the constitution and legitimated against fallen women and their illegitimate children. The ideal of the nuclear family, which was also measured against our supposedly less family-oriented neighbours (the UK and the continent), only came into question in the 1980s,[17] and it was not until 2015, with the advent of equal marriage, that this ideal expanded to include gay families.

In the language of Pierre Bourdieu, a habitus of unquestioning servitude, inculcated over generations and built upon silence and censorship, was added to by the shaming doctrine of what Valente and Backus describe as absolute ecclesiastical authority.[18] That an entire community – family members, relatives and neighbours, with the support of law and order and welfare personnel – participated in the voluntary and the involuntary committals of transgressors shows, as the historian Catherine Cox puts it, that the construction of deviance which operated across society was not confined to the state or the

[14] Diarmaid Ferriter, *The Transformation of Ireland 1900–2000* (London: Profile Books, 2005), 519.

[15] Joseph Valente and Margot Gayle Backus, *The Child Sex Scandal and Modern Irish Literature* (Bloomington, IN: Indiana University Press, 2020), 19.

[16] Renata Salecl, *Choice* (London: Profile Books, 2010), 139.

[17] Ferriter, *Transformation*, 5.

[18] See Pierre Bourdieu, *The Logic of Practice* (Stanford: Stanford University Press, 1990); Valente and Gayle Backus, *Child Sex*, 20.

Church. She notes, however, this should be understood in the context of the paucity of alternative, meaningful, non-institutional therapeutic and welfare provisions, and the cacophony of lay and religious expertise advising on the efficacy of institutions.[19] The effort to rid the social body of sexuality required certain subjects – unmarried mothers and illegitimate children – to embody the obscene and localise transgression within certain bodies and practices. Shame, in this social sense, was an effective support of Catholic authority and nationalistic ideology. Given its role in generations of suffering, it is hardly surprising that the pendulum has swung in the opposite direction and there is little appetite for shaming forces today.

The *Final Report*'s failure – its inaccuracies, misrepresentations and lacunae – tellingly and symptomatically reveal success in another area, the ongoing investment in the ideal of the legitimate nuclear family. A disinvestment would require confronting several painful and difficult truths. A first truth, in Foucauldian terms, is neither the absence nor the repression of sexuality under the dominant twentieth-century doctrinal regime of legitimacy but its busy presence throughout the social fabric. The focus on unmarried women and their children obscured real obscenities which could take place out of sight. Moreover, the Church's deeply attenuated relationship to celibacy and sexual conformity masked its prurient interest in the sexuality of its congregants, a point taken up by Valente and Backus, who outline how the policing of eroticisation became eroticising activities (voyeurism; sadism; enjoyment of disgust, chastisement, stigmatisation, internment). This was indicative of a reflexive turn of erotic energy in the disavowed jouissance and the pretense of mastery of sexuality itself.[20]

This leads to a second truth: the displacement onto unmarried mothers and their children of the social body's disavowed sexuality and its discursive reinforcement and iteration by socially sanctioned and enforced practices of shame. This disavowed sexuality includes, by definition, obscene and perverse forms, and is the shadow that underlies civilised morality and sexuality. Freud, after all, defined neurosis as the negative of perversion, not the other way around.[21]

[19] Catherine Cox, 'Institutional Space and the Geography of Confinement in Ireland, 1750–2000', in Thomas Bartlett, ed., *The Cambridge History of Ireland, Vol. IV* (Cambridge: Cambridge University Press, 2018), 698.

[20] Valente and Backus, *Child Sex*, 27–8.

[21] Sigmund Freud [1905], 'Three Essays on the Theory of Sexuality', in *The Standard Edition of the Complete Psychological Works of Sigmund Freud*, Vol. 7 (London: Vintage 2001), 165.

In other words, we are neurotic/normal because our perverse disposition has been repressed. The shadow of this repressed sexuality was cast upon single mothers and their children as placeholders of immorality and perversion. The imposition of the Other's shaming gaze meant they were forced to carry it under a veil of silence and censorship.

A third truth is that these practices required the participation of the full social body, from institutions to state officials, clergy, communities, families and individuals. Facing up to these truths brings its own shame and the revelation of wide-scale societal participation and worse, an enjoyment in the displacement of obscene jouissance onto unmarried mothers and their bastard children. History facilitates such a displacement as female sexuality has long been fantasmatically linked to shame and is a feature of the patriarchal culture that Ireland continues to instance. Marie Collins, a veteran Irish campaigner for the protection of the vulnerable in Church care, complained that the 2021 Vatican penal code does not go far enough, and she was hoping that the Church's attitude that children and women were temptresses would be 'dead and gone'. It was not, she said; that attitude was still there.[22] 'Shame lurks in repressed thoughts and unspoken fear. Secrecy is its habitat, even its greenhouse. To take it on, we need truth.'[23]

The process of properly situating the obscene and brokering justice and reconciliation is one that will require bearing witness and taking responsibility for the entire social body's treatment of unmarried mothers and their children, including their treatment by Church, state and local institutions, as well as by individuals. The *Final Report*'s failure to properly treat the women's voices and stories goes beyond the inevitable challenges of accurately reproducing a history. It damningly suggests a repetition. It is a repetition of the historical silencing of unmarried mothers and their children and the role of improper record keeping in their systematic mistreatment. This repetition is both a truth and a resistance to the truth. It is a truth as it reveals the shaming value of the testimonials in so far as they continue to be resisted and disallowed. This resistance is locatable in the *Final Report*'s emphasis on the homes as places of refuge and in principally blaming Irish society, notably absent fathers' and mothers' families, for the treatment of unmarried mothers and their

[22] Vivienne Clarke, 'New Vatican document 'very disappointing', says campaigner', *Irish Times*, 2 June 2021, https://www.irishtimes.com/news/social-affairs/religion-and-beliefs/new-vatican-document-very-disappointing-says-campaigner-1.4582009.
[23] O'Neil, *Shame Machine*, 204.

children without contextualising the prevailing ideological and social conditions.[24] As Crowe put it, the casual minimisation of the whole topic is breathtaking.[25] Blaming does not offer a reconciliatory and restitutive path as it leads to denial, defensiveness, silence and secrecy and attacks of outrage, misunderstanding, hurtfulness, bullying and humiliation. Blaming puts a wall up to confronting the past as shaming and shameful. Walls hide the truth and shame is seeing the truth. To take this process up in terms of the famous fable 'The Emperor's New Clothes', this is akin to the advent of the townspeople's shame which develops not on seeing the emperor has no clothes but when the little boy cries out and exposes their obscene enjoyment. Shame emanates from the Other which, in looking, shames the onlooker by revealing their enjoyment.

Shame as a Psychical Factor, Still?

Shame, in psychoanalytic terms, supports the organisation and socialisation of the drives by demarcating the realm of the obscene and delimiting the subject's capacity to enjoy, thereby contributing to a capacity for honesty, humility and modesty. Freud centralised shame in socialising the component infantile drives and facilitating their sublimation into socially acceptable pursuits such as work, love and art that bind individuals in a community together.[26] Lacan added to this and advanced shame as bearing on the limitation of drive jouissance. Jouissance refers to a dimension of enjoyment that goes beyond satisfaction; it is what enjoys and disturbs us because it is anti-social and self-serving. Jouissance, Lacan proposes, is foreclosed by the process of languaging and the constitution of desire. In undergoing castration, which is the installation of language, we are separated from and must live with a limited jouissance.[27] Shame plays several roles in this. It supports the Other in dignifying the abjuration of jouissance by valuing certain practices and behaviours and designating others as shameful, obscene, perverse. It also disposes

[24] Murphy, Duncan and Daly, *Final Report*, 6.

[25] Crowe, 'The Commission'.

[26] Sigmund Freud [1929], *Civilization and its Discontents*, in *The Standard Edition of the Complete Psychological Works of Sigmund Freud*, Vol. 21 (London: Vintage, 2001), 97, 108.

[27] Jacques Lacan, 'The Subversion of the Subject and the Dialectic of Desire in the Freudian Unconscious', in *Ecrits: The First Complete Edition in English*, translated by Bruce Fink (New York: Norton, 2006), 696–7.

us to thinking that the jouissance we have given up resides in others who are imagined as enjoying what we have relinquished. We take revenge on them by shaming them. In Ireland, this was the fate of fallen women, who were deemed to have immorally transgressed and who were punished. Many ended up in Mother and Baby Homes, pushed to the very margins of society as objects of shame, shamefully objectified and often ashamed.

Here, some etymological support may be useful. The etymology of the word 'obscene' reveals that it comes from the Latin *obscenus*, which means 'offensive', especially to modesty. It also refers to filth, and it is linked to *ob*, which refers to 'in front of'. Later, it came to be associated with sexual impurity, indecent and unchaste. Shame is linked to the revelation or appearance of the obscene. In psychoanalytic terms, it is the affect that signals the proximity of the drive and its obscene enjoyment, and it operates as both a sign of and defence against it. Shame is installed by the Other in its demands that limits be imposed on the child-subject. If we take toilet training as paradigmatic in structuring the anal drive within certain limits, faeces and shame become co-mingled in a process of organising the child's drive enjoyment by the Other who trains the child. Faeces become filthy and offensive. Similarly, the child's polymorphously perverse sexual drives are organised by the demands of the Other and delimited to socially acceptable variations.[28] Shame in this aspect regulates and limits the drives and pre-Oedipal jouissance.

This is not without a certain degree of consequence and tension when it comes to the social field, as the Other doesn't have to do much; it can simply tap into the individual psyche which is already structured by shame in delimiting enjoyment. In this, Lacan connects shame to the gaze, to the Other that looks and exposes jouissance or the jouissance we perceive as obscenely enjoying. The Other's shaming gaze produces the affective experience of shame in the subject, and this is how the process of shaming and the subjective experience of being ashamed are interlinked. What is unmasked by the Other's shaming gaze? It is our lack-of-being inaugurated by the entry into language whereby we gain languaged existence in exchange for relinquishing jouissance of being. Lacan describes shame as a haunting and mortifying return of excessive self-serving jouissance to the subject, a hontology which is a play on the French word *une honte*, which means 'shame'. We are haunted by the fact that we are mortal lacking beings and are not morally whole, but the assumption

[28] Freud, 'Three Essays'.

of this estate counter-intuitively confers dignity and meaning to a life. This is what is meant by Lacan's assertion of a shame of living.[29] We can understand this as allowing us to empathetically connect with injustice by undergoing a shaming recognition of it. This kind of shame, which can range from victimhood to privilege, urges action and impedes cynical inaction. It is underpinned by a humility grounded in outrage, impelled by the Other's gaze which draws from the humility of being outlined by Lacan.

Where then does this leave the individual subject when it comes to practices of social justice that aim at addressing harmfully shameful practices and separating them out from the ordinary shame of limited being? While Lacan emphasised psychoanalysis, any practice that centralises the role of the signifier and naming and insists on facilitating the Other who sees, shames us into living.[30] Such a commitment to the signifier and to an ethic of a shame of living emanates in Catherine Corless's memoir *Belonging*, which details her journey of naming the 798 undocumented babies buried in a mass grave between 1925 and 1961 beside the Tuam Mother and Baby Home in County Galway. Her book is an incitement to produce proper signifiers, to give names to the babies and the necessary role of shame in a truth- and change-making process. Highlighting the role of shame in dignifying the relationship between the Other and the citizen-subject, Corless calls upon the reader to take on the mantle of being ashamed and to allocate shame appropriately. Corless wants her own acknowledged shame in not recognising the Tuam Mother and Baby Home to be everybody's shame. She writes:

> for all the world, any one of those babies could be you or me. We are only as strong as the society we are born into. The people who make up that society, who decide the rules. Who decided who gets to live or die. Who is loved, and who is shamed. We are all responsible for this, every day. The world that we create, that affected every other living creature on the planet.[31]

Corless is seeking to transpose shame from author to audience and in so doing evokes a narrative of universal shameful responsibility for everyone. This is open to critique and falls into the trap of contemporary blaming and shaming practices. But it's also open to further

[29] Jacques Lacan, *The Other Side of Psychoanalysis: The Seminar of Jacques Lacan 17 1969–1970*, translated by Russell Grigg (London: Norton, 2007), 180.
[30] Lacan, *The Other Side*, 193.
[31] Corless, *Belonging*, 446.

analysis. If we think of shame as subjectively singular for everyone resulting from the lamguaging/socialising process, leaving aside Corless's generalised impugnation of everyone, might she be tapping into what psychoanalysis understands as a bedrock of individual shame and mortification which her approach implies has the potential to impel collective action, redress and restitution? This is hopeful and is in tension with Lacan on the currency of shame.

Lacan proposed in 1970 that there was no longer any shame, and his authorised successor, Jacques-Alain Miller, writing thirty-six years later, agreed. He describes this as a disappearance of the Other's gaze, castrated of its power of shame and the advent of a new permissiveness, a prohibition of prohibiting that has resulted in the dissolving of shame.[32] He adds that we are at the point where the dominant discourse enjoins one not to be ashamed of one's jouissance anymore. Ashamed of all the rest, yes, of one's desire, but not of one's jouissance. Under a gaze that enjoys rather than looks, he proposes that the value and meaning of life itself has disappeared.[33] This is the result of late capitalism, whose signifiers organise us as consuming rather than enjoying and overwrite the singularity of the subject with sameness. What separates living beings is no longer a master signifier which uniquely delimits desire and enjoyment and gives meaningfulness to life or transcendental purpose; rather, we are separated at the level of consumption and acquisition, and what distinguishes is what we have. The enjoyment of consumption or consumptive objects, which has no limit, has made the role of shame as a force of limit increasingly redundant, and there seems little today that meaningfully induces shame.

This rather alarming assertion benefits from some qualification and analysis. We are certainly castrated of the Other's gaze by the underwhelming quality and overwhelming politicisation of representations of the Other by the various forms of media and social media. This is the promotion of looking for the sake of spectating and generating outrage rather than the disturbances of being that the gaze occasions. This denigration of the Other's gaze, which has become ubiquitous and all-consuming, is a fact. It is complicit in the decline of the institutional gaze and its replacement, as Foucault identified around the same that Lacan was decrying the supposed disappearance of shame, by regimes of surveillance which have a

[32] Lacan, *The Other Side*, 182; Jacques-Alain Miller, 'On Shame', in Justin Clemens and Russell Grigg, eds, *SIC 6: Jacques Lacan and the Other Side of Psychoanalysis* (Durham, NC, Duke University Press: 2006), 12–13.
[33] Miller, 'On Shame', 27, 15, 18.

disunifying and exploitative aspect.[34] In Irish terms, we can think of this as the decline of the supervalent gaze of Church and state institutions and its replacement by what O'Neil calls the shame machine, which is to be distinguished from shame's affective vital power. This shame machine is an apparatus of disunification and humiliation, deployed primarily for profit and exploitation by corrupt politicians, predatory corporations, especially big tech, and state healthcare and welfare systems. They shift responsibility for social problems from institutions to individuals. Modern shame, she says, consistently flubs its unifying mission; instead of creating healthy opportunities, it punishes people and punches down on them.[35] She draws attention to contemporary shame's disunifying function and argues that it no longer draws a community together via a shared value system but permits a toxic shamescape of individual scapegoating for all social ills and an unending cycle of punching down through aggression and humiliation. This mislocates responsibility for inequality and is how the poor are disproportionally blamed for their own poverty and why the disenfranchised are blamed for their own exclusion.

She argues that the current shame machine supports a rigged status quo and a value system of shared norms based on apartheid, meritocracy, oppression and inequality.[36] Guy Debord's conceptualisation in the late 1960s of the society of the spectacle, and his assertion that the very triumph of the spectacular system would lead to a spawning of an insincere apologetics of the spectacle, can be mapped onto today's society of the screen with its incessant performing, posting, instagramming and TikToking.[37] From the words, actions and buffoonery of political figures to celebrity misdeeds, there seems no act, statement or misdeed that occasions shame. The importance of telling the truth by those in power has been replaced by swaggering egotism, vapid talk, false promises and lies. This fits with Lacan's assertion of the degeneration of social values such as honour and honesty, and by Miller as the rise of impudence and immodesty. In our spectacular and post-truth era, they argue that modesty has become hopelessly *de rigueur*, and it is difficult for a truth to win out when the concept of truth has become mired within menus of supposed alternatives.[38] When things go wrong, there are excuses, regrets, pardons, repentances, as Miller

[34] Michel Foucault, *The History of Sexuality*, Vol. 1. (London: Penguin, 1976), 42–6.
[35] O'Neil, *Shame Machine*, 9, 12.
[36] O'Neil, *Shame Machine*, 203–4.
[37] Guy Debord, *The Society of the Spectacle* (London: Rebus Press, 1967), 108.
[38] Lacan, *The Other Side*, 180; Miller, 'On Shame', 18.

puts it, but there is no longer a shaming Other who could be looking with a shame-bearing gaze.[39] In its place is O'Neil's shamescape of outrage, inaction, divisiveness and cynicism which is the opposite of a shame that unifies around collective ideals of truth-seeking, taking responsibility and making amends.

The current variation of shame, which is more akin to prestige-seeking by humiliation and jealousy, weaponises people against each other and generally disunites while at the same time it offers endless consumerist remedies as salve, serving corporations and wealthy individuals, and a reprieve to states and governments for their dishonourable or ignoble actions or misdeeds. Taoiseach Enda Kenny's apology to survivors of Mother and Baby Homes in 2012, while an important first step in validating survivors, should have been a starting point, not an end point for the state.[40] The *Final Report* reflects this shift away from state responsibility and it also reflects the current blamescape in leaving the state off the hook and blaming the Irish people, specifically absent fathers' and mothers' families, for the treatment of unmarried mothers and their children.

Miller asserts that the disappearance of shame alters the meaning of life because it alters the meaning of death.[41] Life without honour, Lacan states, is an ignoble and unworthy life which takes refuge in blaming others for life not living up to its promise. This is why mortification is linked to shame.[42] To be mort-ified is to be exposed as lacking, obscene and mortal. This, in psychoanalytic terms, can be an important impetus to action and a progenitor of change. The political and socio-cultural climate of blame, however, is antithetical to shame, and this appears to have factored into the *Final Report* not only in its failure to properly treat and represent the witness testimonies, which would have been a first step in assuming this shameful past, but in its blaming tendencies which close the door on accommodating shame and mortification and allowing it to be a progenitor of change. The fact that the *Final Report* generally blames Irish society without adequately explaining or contextualising it leaves survivors as both cause and effect, discounted and discarded (again) as the shameful waste products of a society that is still not ready to permit the truth to shame it into taking responsibility and providing justice.

[39] Miller, 'On Shame', 11–12.

[40] Enda Kenny, 'In Full: Enda Kenny's State Apology to the Magdalene Women', *The Journal*, 19 February 2013. https://www.thejournal.ie/full-text-enda-kenny-magdalene-apology-801132-Feb2013/

[41] Miller, 'On Shame', 18.

[42] Lacan, *The Other Side*, 182–3.

Where then does this leave projects of social justice and indeed of psychoanalysis, both practices of the signifier? They remain pivotal to projects of truth-telling and the task of going beyond the status quo and easy truths which are all the more important nowadays given the challenges to truth-telling and the derogation of the Other's gaze. But they are up against it on two fronts. First, there is the work of distinguishing and segregating blamescape practices from a properly subjectifying project of historicising and dignifying accountability. This is difficult and painstaking work, and it hinges on ways of articulating and listening: speaking with, hearing and listening to the other side without rancour and blame. This has the effect of negating an infantile factor. Infantile egocentrism intractably sees everything from its side and blames the other. Resisting this is not easy when it is actively supported by today's culture of 'it's not me, it's them'. Lacan's and Miller's assertion that shame has disappeared can thus be read as a provocation, as a warning shot across the bow of infantilising influences within dialoguing practices which must be resisted by an insistence on the articulation of individual truths (truths in the plural here) and ignominiously engaging with shame on a real level. This is a process of delimiting and punctuating the obscene by virtue of naming it. This is how the work of inscription ennobles and dignifies human experiences.

Conclusion

> The more unworthy you are [. . .] the better off you are.[43]

> We project onto others the shame of our repressed sexual desires which reflects first on us as humans with all our polymorphous perversity, as well as the influence of a Jansenist church and the ludicrous ambitions of a political class pretending we weren't like pagan England.[44]

There is no shame without obscenity, as obscenity marks where shame begins. There is little reason to doubt that the histories and testimonies of the survivors of Mother and Baby Homes carry terrible and unassimilated truths. If we make room for them, there is the possibility of shame. The *Final Report*'s failures demonstrate that we are some way from this, which would mean assuming our unworthiness, collusion and dishonesty in how vulnerable women and children were

[43] Lacan, *The Other Side*, 183.
[44] Anonymous source.

treated. No one wants to confront a hole in moral wholeness and, as Miller puts it, to face the ignominious, the disgraceful loss of a good name.[45] Such a truth of naming is a practice of the signifier that intervenes on false knowledge by opening up a hole in which the truth can be inscribed into the Other. This is the work of inscription and historicisation taken on by Corless, Crowe, Hogan, Smith, O'Rourke, O'Donnell, the contributors to the *Alternative Report* (outlined in the next paragraph) and hopefully others to come. This good work indicates shame has not altogether disappeared.

Some months after the publication of the *Final Report*, an *Alternative Report* with a re-written executive summary was published by a group of academic specialists in human rights law, family law, criminal justice, equalities, social welfare law, legal history and histories of institutionalisation. This document was their response to the *Final Report* and its aim was to show that the commission could have come to different conclusions using the same evidence. What is striking about the *Alternative Report* is its scope and tone. It emphasises women's rights and gendered experiences and draws attention to mechanisms of power and assesses the culpability of the Irish state. Importantly, it does not take a blaming approach and is instead a nuanced and comprehensive summary of the commission's findings, including a discussion of the legal status of illegitimacy, the bottom-up and top-down culture of secrecy and shame, consideration of human rights violations, harms of family separation and degrading treatment, the role of poverty and detention, and the institutionalisation of unmarried mothers and their children. The report writers acknowledge that we cannot discuss the institutions' 'welfare' functions without acknowledging that they reinforced this wider culture of shame and secrecy around unmarried and pregnant women and girls.[46]

Rather than offering an alternative set of conclusions, the *Alternative Report* simply concludes by setting out the differences between their findings and those in the *Final Report*, leaving it to the reader to come to their own conclusions and refraining from blame-gaming. Notably, the first difference is listed under the category of responsibility, with a distinction drawn between the *Final Report*'s placing of responsibility primarily with the fathers of children and mothers' immediate families, and the *Alternative Report*'s placing of responsibility on the

[45] Miller, 'On Shame', 23.

[46] Mairead Enright and Aoife O'Donoghue, eds, *Mother and Baby Homes Commission of Investigation Report, Draft Alternative Executive Summary* (*Alternative Report*) (2021), 15.

state through its institutions, its laws, its delegation of key public functions to religious bodies and in its assertion that the state was aware of constitutional and human rights abuses in the institutions. Its main recommendations include access-to-records legislation, national education and memorialisation measures, statutory rights to compensation, a comprehensive state apology to all those affected, and state action to ensure that religious orders and Church authorities participate in making reparations for the harm caused by Church's treatment of unmarried families.[47]

The simplicity and tenor of the *Alternative Report*, with its comparatively presented conclusions and the scope of its recommendations, which aim to supplement rather than replace the *Final Report*, highlights the challenges at stake. Together, the two reports reveal a shameful history of misogyny and bigotry that will require a united effort from all stakeholders, from the state to individuals, to integrate this expurgated history. A necessary first step is to facilitate those with direct experience of Mother and Baby Homes in speaking of their experiences and for them to be foregrounded, properly recorded and memorialised. Any further investigation into Mother and Baby Homes must insist on giving a full account and making a new survivor-centred mode for this inquiry.[48] This has been comprehensively addressed by O'Donnell, O'Rourke and Smith in their recent book *Redress*. There, Smith notes the ongoing problem of the coupling of historical amnesia and the erasure of witness testimony in the state's response when confronted with historical abuses. The result is what he describes as a cultivation of unknowingness.[49] The abdication of state responsibility is in its refusal to facilitate access to archival material and documents necessary to a full accounting and truth-telling, and this stands in the way of establishing the fundamental building block of reparation for historic abuses. Smith's analysis of the Commission of Investigation into Mother and Baby Homes' mis-assignment of responsibility away from the state is clear:

> The state understood the ramifications of the knowledge in its possession. It chose not to make that knowledge public. Yet again it prioritised limiting the state's liability and attempted to consolidate its own power rather than to empower survivors and family members to understand their loved ones.[50]

[47] Enright and O'Donoghue, 62, 67–8.
[48] Crowe, 'The Commission'.
[49] Smith, 'Knowing and Unknowing', 357.
[50] Smith, 'Knowing and Unknowing', 383, 385.

A dimension of human rights is one in which the value of life is prioritised. This is supported by a process of truth-telling and bearing witness to lives lived in peril and to the experiences of those whose human and constitutional rights were violated. But *how* we do this is vital. This process should involve all – victims, perpetrators, agents, silent abettors. It will mortify all including those who bear witnesses. To be ashamed means we can't look away from the misdeeds and the obscenities which stare back at us and shame us. We must speak them and hear them. Nothing less will do for this history to be given its proper place and so it does not find new repetitions: what is unresolved in one generation is destined to repeat in the next. This may give us a chance to impede the projecting onto others the shame of our repressed sexual desires. We are all guilty of enjoying our polymorphous perversion. Shame keeps it in check. It operates to the extent there is an Other that threatens to expose our baser selves and peers into our very being. This is an Other that keeps watch even when no one is there. The form this takes has changed, as Foucault and Lacan each noted, with one asserting its disappearance and the other its transmutation into surveillance, and how we respond to it will be significant. That we continue to respond and whether room can be made for the Other's shaming gaze is a question. But isn't a question always a place to start?

Chapter 11

'then die of shame': Reading Beckett's *Not I* with Lacan

Alexandra Poulain

For nearly two years, in 1934 and 1935, Beckett underwent psychoanalysis with the young Wilfred Bion at the Tavistock Clinic in London. In December 1935, Beckett decided, without consulting Bion, to interrupt the sessions, and returned to Dublin to live with his mother, whom Bion had been exhorting him to keep at a distance, given her deleterious influence on his physical and mental health. In his 1992 book, *Beckett et le psychanalyste*,[1] French psychoanalyst Didier Anzieu argues that Beckett's subsequent oeuvre performs the continuation of the treatment as self-analysis, and he offers a compelling reading of Beckett's major works of fiction, with their emphasis on soliloquising voices addressing more or less evanescent, and often silent, listeners, as variations on the relationship between patient and psychoanalyst. Though he comments briefly on the full-length plays, Anzieu claims that Beckett's theatre rests 'on a different basis',[2] and he does not mention the short plays, except for a few paragraphs about *Come and Go*. Subsequent commentators, however, have pointed out that a number of Beckett's 'shorts' can be read productively as re-workings of the analyst–patient relationship, although this relationship is rarely staged as a successfully therapeutic one.[3] A case in point is *Not I*, in which the analytical situation is reduced to its most basic components: a disembodied but explicitly female 'Mouth' spills out what appears to be her life story at breakneck speed, in the presence of a silent, gender-neutral 'Auditor' – who may be only a figment of Mouth's imagination, and is often omitted

[1] Later republished as Didier Anzieu, *Beckett* (Paris: Gallimard, 1998).

[2] Anzieu, *Beckett*, 225.

[3] Stéphanie Ravez, 'Beckett et la psychanalyse', in Elisabeth Angel-Perez and Alexandra Poulain, eds, *Tombeau pour Samuel Beckett* (London: Aden, 2014), 98.

altogether on the stage, after Beckett himself allowed the character to be dropped in the first productions of the play that he directed. Most notably, the 1973 production at London's Royal Court Theatre, featuring Billie Whitelaw as Mouth, and the 1975 French premiere at the Théâtre d'Orsay in Paris, featuring Madeleine Renaud.

The title of the play, *Not I*, indicates its point of departure from, and radical subversion of, the psychoanalytic contract: Mouth's insistence on telling her story in the third person, her refusal to acknowledge that the events she relates happened to her. On five occasions, her logorrhoea is interrupted by what seems to be an inner voice, audible only to her (the voice of the Auditor/analyst, real or imagined?), apparently suggesting that she use the first person pronoun, to which she responds, invariably but with growing vehemence: 'what? .. who? .. no! .. she!', thus relegating the unutterable 'I' to the paratext of the title. If we read Mouth's story as her own, as we are invited to do by the violence of her own denial, it is tempting to see her as a figure of alienation, and to understand her rejection of the first person as her failure to avail herself of the therapeutic potential of the 'talking cure', to achieve a sense of self and to enter the social sphere of interpersonal exchange – as suggested, perhaps, by Auditor's repeated gesture of helplessness. In this paper, however, I ask what it is that Mouth resists by resisting identification and suggest that her refusal of the 'I' may be productive to some degree. More precisely, I read *Not I* as a paradoxical performance of shame, in which the excruciating, defacing experience of shame leads not to self-reconstruction, but to the possibility of fictionalising, a possibility which arises from within the place of shame. I offer this reading in the light of Lacan's lifelong elaboration of the notion of shame, usefully collected and glossed in David Bernard's book *Lacan et la honte* (2011).[4]

The dramatic composition of *Not I* is uncannily suited to a psychoanalytic reading along the lines that Anzieu proposes. As David Lloyd points out in *Beckett's Thing*, *Not I* belongs in a set of plays 'that radically and unprecedentedly exploit the possibilities of darkness in the theatre rather than assuming that the visible space of the stage is to be maximised and filled with action and gesture'.[5] Out of the darkness a mouth emerges, 'faintly lit from close up and below',[6]

[4] David Bernard, *Lacan et la Honte. De la Honte à l'Hontologie* (Paris: Champ Lacanien, 2011).

[5] David Lloyd, *Beckett's Thing: Painting and Theatre* (Edinburgh: Edinburgh University Press, 2016), 208.

[6] Samuel Beckett, *Not I* in *The Complete Dramatic Works* (London: Faber & Faber, 1986), 376. Hereafter given as (NI page).

an orifice which we know must be attached to a body that nevertheless remains invisible. This paradoxical image of a hole cut out of the dark gives heightened visibility to what usually goes unremarked, the frantic workings of the lips and tongue of the actress, covering and uncovering the teeth, an image blown up uncomfortably in the television and film versions of the play, which show the mouth in close-up.[7]

Following Freud, Lacan describes the unconscious as the discourse of the Other, that which speaks through the subject, evading the control of the ego, and constitutes the subject as an effect of the signifier.[8] In Seminar 11, *The Four Fundamental Concepts of Psychoanalysis* (given in 1964–5), Lacan departs from the Freudian conception of the unconscious as a text which exists below the surface of consciousness and may be retrieved, and describes it instead as 'a gap' in the subject's discourse: 'Thus the unconscious is always manifested as that which vacillates in a split in the subject, from which emerges a discovery which Freud compares with desire'. The unconscious opens and shuts, and it is the analyst's task to become attuned to 'the rhythmic structure of this pulsation of the slit'.[9] The text of Mouth's soliloquy, with its verbal fragments interrupted by silent gaps materialised by suspension marks, provides an aural image of this 'rhythmic structure', which is redoubled visually in the frantically opening and closing lips: a striking image of the 'pulsation of the slit' in the speaking subject. While the dramatic situation – or what remains thereof, a Mouth speaking, an Auditor auditing – conjures up (and distorts) the psychoanalytic setting, the aural and visual images produced on the stage provide uncannily apposite metaphors of the Lacanian unconscious as pulsating gap in the subject, from which the subject's desire may eventually emerge. As I have suggested already, this is not to say that *Not I* is a dramatic metaphor of the analytic process, since Mouth's rejection of the first person completely subverts the structure of self-narrative and self-reconstruction on which psychoanalysis is predicated.

[7] Whitelaw's reprise performance of *Not I* was broadcast on 7 April 1977 as part of BBC2's programme 'The Lively Arts. Shades, Three Plays by Samuel Beckett', directed by Donald McWhinnie and Anthony Page. Neil Jordan's film *Not I*, starring Julianne Moore, was released in 2001 as part of the Beckett on Film project produced by Michael Colgan and Alan Moloney for RTÉ, BBC4 and the Irish Film Board.

[8] Jacques Lacan, 'The Subversion of the Subject and the Dialectic of Desire', in *Ecrits*, translated by Bruce Fink in collaboration with Héloïse Fink and Russell Grigg (New York and London: Norton, 2006), 671–702.

[9] Jacques Lacan, *The Four Fundamental Concepts of Psychoanalysis. The Seminar of Jacques Lacan, Book 11*, edited by Jacques-Alain Miller, translated by Alan Sheridan (New York and London: Norton, 1998), 27, 32.

Mouth's soliloquy does not provide a stable, coherent life-narrative, but rather proceeds – much like the ever-wavering, repetitive speech of the psychoanalytic patient – by aggregating fragments and silences, hesitations, self-corrections and inconclusive narrative loops which are abandoned and picked up later in slightly modified versions. The story that nevertheless emerges tentatively starts literally at birth, a premature birth ('before its time') envisaged as a violent expulsion. Mouth's first intelligible word is 'out', marking birth, according to the familiar Beckettian trope, as a traumatic experience, and programmatically shaping Mouth's whole life as one of enduring marginality – of always being on the outside, feeling socially inept and experiencing excruciating shame in all her social interactions. She is portrayed as a completely disenfranchised character, so that at one level, her shame may be rationalised as the shame of the marginal and vulnerable. She comes across as an ageing woman, 'coming up to seventy' (NI 376), an orphan, 'parents unknown' (NI 376), with obvious issues of mental health. Other textual hints also allow us to surmise she might be Irish: she mentions 'Croker's Acre', a place near Beckett's boyhood home in County Dublin (NI 380). One particularly acute moment of shame in *Not I* occurs on the 'rare occasions' when she suddenly starts speaking after a lifetime of near complete silence and comes up with 'half the vowels wrong' (NI 382), causing people to 'stare at her uncomprehending' (NI 379). This episode – repeated and modified several times in the script – suggests she has internalised colonial and classist preconceptions linked to accent, according to which only the English middle-class version of the English language is right and respectable. *Not I* thus returns to issues of accents and class which Beckett had previously experimented with in his early radio play *All That Fall* (1957), his grim satire of post-Treaty Irish Protestantism. In *Not I*, we are given no explanation for Mouth's lifelong silence, but at one level it is an index of her subaltern status: she cannot be heard, and so literally gives up speech.

While the personal history of Mouth remains enigmatic, the play resonates with the history of the Irish Free State (and later Republic) and the way in which it resolutely marginalised its internal others, predicating the Irish nation on a strictly monitored paradigm of normalcy to construct 'fallen women, queers, republicans, vagrants, asylum seekers' as the nation's abnormals, who were accordingly abjected outside the pale of nationality.[10] As Sally Munt

[10] Seán Kennedy, 'Here All Is Strange: Beckett Beyond the Normal', in Seán Kennedy, ed., *Beckett Beyond the Normal* (Edinburgh: Edinburgh University Press, 2019), 9.

has argued, shame played a decisive role in this project: 'Contrary to the commonsense view, nationalisms are not invested solely in pride, sometimes they are intractably linked to feelings of shame. Nationalist ideology is sustained by shaming those it considers to be external to its real and imagined borders, but it saves special regard for the repudiation of its internal others, those who are considered to be supplementary to the nation's need, that it would prefer to make invisible or expulse.'[11] As the Irish state sought to consolidate its alliance with the Catholic Church and to promote its ideal of Irish morality and sexual 'purity', it placed a special burden on women, who were confined to their role as wives and mothers (as expressly stipulated in the 1937 Constitution) and devoted exorbitant energy to the shaming of single mothers, who were criminalised as sexual deviants regardless of the circumstances of their alleged sin (for instance, it did not matter if they were victims of incest or rape), while the men involved in the conception of illegitimate children were routinely exonerated.

This process of criminalisation was enforced largely through what James M. Smith has called Ireland's 'containment culture' – the systematic incarceration of single mothers and their children in an extensive network of state- and Church-run, as well as private, institutions such as Mother and Baby Homes for 'first offenders' and Magdalene Laundries and County Homes for 'recidivists' – according to the terminology of the Local Government (Temporary Provisions) Act 1922, as well as orphanages.[12] As Clair Wills has shown in her analysis of the *Final Report* of the Commission of Investigation into the Mother and Baby Homes set up by the Irish government in 2015 in response to the finding of a mass infant grave in Tuam, the Irish state failed to protect and provide for the children just as it did the single mothers. Typically, the children were either adopted at birth or brutally separated from their mothers after two to three years of incarceration, causing trauma to both parties, and placed in industrial schools, where 'physical, sexual and emotional abuse was endemic' or fostered in conditions which sometimes 'amounted to

[11] Sally Munt, *Queer Attachments: The Cultural Politics of Shame* (London: Routledge, 2017), 55.

[12] James M. Smith, 'The Politics of Sexual Knowledge: The Origins of Ireland's Containment Culture and the Carrigan Report (1931)', *Journal of the History of Sexuality* 13:2 (2004): 208. Una Crowley and Rob Kitchin, 'Producing decent girls: governmentality and the moral geographies of sexual conduct in Ireland (1922–1937)', *Gender, Place and Culture* 15:4 (2008): 356.

baby farming, as foster parents maximised their income from subsistence payments'.[13]

While nothing can be established about Mouth's personal history with any degree of certainty, it is certainly possible to read her status as an orphan, and her subsequence lifelong experience of inaudibility, in this context, as the beginning of the play suggests:

> parents unknown . . . unheard of . . . he having vanished . . . thin air . . . no sooner buttoned up his breeches . . . she similarly . . . eight months later . . . almost to the tick . . . so no love . . . spared that . . . no love such as normally vented on the . . . speechless infant . . . in the home . . . no . . . nor indeed for that matter any of any kind . . . no love of any kind . . . at any subsequent stage . . . so typical affair (NI 376)

'Absence of love' is said to be 'typical', and although with classic Beckett cynicism Mouth adds that she was at least 'spared that', it is clear that it has caused enduring trauma and social maladjustment. The gaps in the text of the play leave open for speculation the possibility that Mouth may herself have been a rape victim in one or another of the institutions of containment intended for parentless children, or at a later stage in life, as suggested perhaps by the enigmatic episode of the field:

> wandering in a field . . . looking aimlessly for cowslips . . . to make a ball . . . a few steps then stop . . . stare into space . . . then on . . . a few more . . . stop and stare again . . . so on . . . drifting around . . . when suddenly . . . gradually . . . all went out . . . all that early April morning light . . . and she found herself in the – . . . what? . . who? . . . no! . . . she! . . . [Pause and movement 1.] found herself in the dark (NI 376–7)

Whatever happened in the field, the story is brutally interrupted by the first iteration of the sequence which justifies the play's title. A clue perhaps resides in the signifier 'cow*slip*', which encodes the suggestion of a repressed slip or *faux pas* – the latter signifier resurfacing in the French title, *Pas moi*. That the interrupted memory is followed by a sense of being in total 'darkness' certainly suggests the aftermath of trauma, and the impossibility of verbalising it.

Such an (avowedly speculative) reading in turn resonates with the later episode of the courtroom, when Mouth recalls having to appear

[13] Clair Wills, 'Architectures of Containment: Ireland's Lost Children', *London Review of Books* 43:10 (2021), https://www.lrb.co.uk/the-paper/v43/n10/clair-wills/architectures-of-containment

in court and finding herself incapable of performing adequately: 'that time in court . . . what had she to say for herself . . . guilty or not guilty . . . stand up woman . . . speak up woman . . . stood there staring into space . . . mouth half open as usual . . . waiting to be led away' (NI 381). The question 'guilty or not guilty' remains unanswered, and, of course, we never find out what it was she was being tried for – or even if the trial was real or a fantasy, a psychic dramatisation of her perpetual stigmatisation as a subaltern subject. Mouth's soliloquy registers the magistrate's injunction to 'stand up' and 'speak up', included in free direct speech as the intrusion of the voice of authority in her psyche, yet the extensive body of legislation passed by the Free State to enable the criminalisation of Ireland's abnormals – among whom unmarried mothers and the mentally ill featured prominently – ensured that their speech was delegitimised, and the architecture of containment deployed to separate them from society (which also included psychiatric hospitals) for prophylactic as well as punitive reasons ensured that they were *de facto* rendered inaudible. The double bind demonstrates Mouth's inability to defend herself, which results in her stupor in the courtroom.

At another level, however, Mouth's radically disenfranchised status is precisely what makes her an allegorical figure of shame, to whom we can all relate, however estranged we may feel from her circumstances. In this sense, she is not unlike Sufiya Zinobia, the mentally 'retarded', unwanted girl who comes to embody the shame of Pakistani society in Salman Rushdie's 1983 novel *Shame*.[14] As with Sufiya, shame is the only emotion known to Mouth, and her whole life is remembered as an extended performance of public shame. In her book on Beckett and hysteria, Pascale Sardin notes that Mouth (like many other Beckett female protagonists) manifests almost all the clinical symptoms of hysteria: speech disorders (aphasia followed by logorrhoea), blindness ('found herself in the dark'), hearing disorders ('the buzzing'), insentience, paralysis and the feeling of a dislocated body, powerfully materialised in the disembodied mouth that emerges out of the darkness.[15]

In rejecting the first person, Mouth insists on remaining dissociated from herself; she rejects the possibility of reuniting her fragmented self under a pronoun which would grant her a social identity,

[14] Salman Rushdie, *Shame* (London: Vintage, 1995).

[15] Pascale Sardin, *Samuel Beckett et la Passion Maternelle ou L'hystérie à L'œuvre* (Pessac: Presses Universitaires de Bordeaux, 2009), 75–96; Ravez, *Beckett et la psychanalyse*, 104.

the possibility of recreating affective links, and of speaking for herself (as in the distressing courtroom scene where she remains entirely dumb and passive). The soliloquy is oddly disaffected: emotions are not registered as such, but inferred only in terms of the physical effects they produce, as in the enigmatic episode set in Croker's Acre: 'dusk . . . sitting staring at her hand . . . there in her lap . . . palm upward . . . suddenly saw it wet . . . the palm . . . tears presumably . . . hers presumably . . . no one else for miles' (NI 380). The text retraces the steps of a logical reasoning (wet/tears/hers) which never makes it to the final stage, the emotional turmoil which must have produced the tears in the first place.

This disaffected character of the text is not sustained throughout, however. In the final moments of the play, one scene is associated unequivocally, and agonisingly, with the emotion of shame:

> practically speechless . . . even to herself . . . never out loud . . . but not completely . . . sometimes sudden urge . . . once or twice a year . . . always winter some strange reason . . . the long evenings . . . hours of darkness . . . sudden urge to . . . tell . . . then rush out stop the first she saw . . . nearest lavatory . . . start pouring it out . . . steady stream . . . mad stuff . . . half the vowels wrong . . . no one could follow . . . till she saw the stare she was getting . . . then die of shame . . . crawl back in. (NI 382)

The scene is horribly ambiguous: what starts out as an uncontrolled verbal outpour ends up 'in the nearest lavatory', and 'logorrhoea' veers into 'diarrhoea', performing the 'wordshit' that appeared in the earlier *Texts for Nothing*.[16] The ultimate horror of the scene lies in the fact that it happens in the public eye: 'till she saw the stare she was getting'. As Keir Elam has pointed out, '[t]he spasmodic movements of this disconcertingly disembodied organ suspended in the dark re-enact the elementary events referred to in Mouth's narration': in the moment of performance Mouth is on a stage, pouring out 'mad stuff' (NI 382), and getting odd stares from an 'uncomprehending' audience (NI 379). Mouth's mouth, then, is not just a mouth, but is reconfigured as a ubiquitous organ which serves multiple functions in the various episodes of the story, so that ironically, the invisible body reappears as the sum of its orifices. Elam comments: 'Thus the

[16] Keir Elam, 'Dead Heads: Damnation-Narration in the Dramaticules', in John Pilling, ed., *The Cambridge Companion to Samuel Beckett* (Cambridge: Cambridge University Press, 1994): 152; Samuel Beckett, *Texts for Nothing* (London: Calder, 1999), 46.

mouth, detached from its bodily context and so from its codified meaning (as 'mouth'), becomes a corporeal and semantic (black) hole onto and into which the spectator may project any number of literally organic senses: it takes on in turn the roles of vagina, anus, mouth proper, eye and ear.'[17]

The scene makes clear the way in which shame and theatricality are intimately linked. Shame, as Lacan argues after Sartre, always occurs under the gaze of the Other. In *Being and Nothingness*, Sartre famously conceptualised shame as an ontological experience in the sense that it awakens self-consciousness in the subject, through the experience, paradoxically, of being objectified by the Look of the Other – an experience which induces a painful form of self-knowledge:

> I have just made an awkward or vulgar gesture. This gesture clings to me; I neither judge it nor blame it. I simply live it. I realize it in the mode of for-itself. But now suddenly I raise my head. Somebody was there and has seen me. Suddenly I realize the vulgarity of my gesture, and I am ashamed. [. . . T]he Other is the indispensable mediator between myself and me. I am ashamed of myself as I *appear* to the Other.[18]

Picking up Sartre's reading of Jean Genet, Lacan argues that shame causes the subject to be 'turned inside-out like a glove', exposing what Lacan refers to as their shameful inner 'lining'.[19] For Lacan, this lining is woven out of the human, speaking subject's lack and excess, which concerns us all as subjects of both castration and jouissance. Shame turns us inside out, revealing the shameful lining of the powerful, controlled ego image we identify with and try to project outward. As such, there is an existential dimension to shame, which is an inherent condition of the human condition, though the stronger our ego image, the better we are likely to fend it off. Mouth's sheer vulnerability makes her intensely susceptible to shame, so that in her radical exposure, we are bound to recognise something of our own experience of existential shame. This is not to suggest that we can ever experience the kind of ego-shattering shame to which Mouth is subjected in her state of absolute abjection. Rather, I am suggesting

17 Elam, 'Dead Heads', 151.

18 Jean-Paul Sartre, *Being and Nothingness: A Phenomenological Essay on Ontology*, translated and with an introduction by Hazel E. Barnes (New York: Washington Square Press, 1992), 301.

19 Jean-Paul Sartre, *Saint Genet, Actor and Martyr*, translated by Bernard Frechtman (Minneapolis: University of Minnesota Press, 2012), 81. Lacan, 'The Subversion of the Subject', 693.

that Mouth's shame affects us beyond the radical unknowability of her experience because shame defines us ontologically.

The first aspect of existential shame according to Lacan is that it inevitably concerns us as speaking subjects, and thus as subjects of castration. In entering the symbolic realm, the subject becomes dependent on the constant play of signifiers that can never adequately represent them, and thus must relinquish the fantasy of supplementing the lack of the Other, thereby experiencing themselves, shamefully, as lacking. In the 'lavatory' scene, Mouth, who has suffered a lifetime of chronic aphasia, horribly discovers herself a speaking subject, and therefore a subject of lack: words seem to run through her, 'mad stuff' over which she has no control. Speech fails to insert her into an interpersonal process of communication, since 'no one could follow' – which is indeed very much the experience of the audience in the theatre. Later on, she adds that she herself had 'no idea what she was saying'. (NI 382) As we have seen, Mouth even fails to control the sounds she produces, and comes up with 'all the wrong vowels'. Facing the 'stare' of the audience (NI 379), she is mortified as a subaltern subject (a poor old Irish woman), but also as a speaking subject – a subject of lack.

However, this is only one half of what constitutes the experience of shame, which also reveals the subject as a desiring subject, pinning her down to her body. As Lacan points out after Freud, it is much more difficult for a neurotic patient to talk to her analyst about her fantasy than to confess to actually committing reprehensible acts. In *Desire and Its Interpretation*, Lacan mentions 'the state of being ill at ease . . . which often stops patients from revealing their fantasies for a long time. This ridiculous facet can only be explained by the relations we have already been able to perceive between the position of desire and the realm of comedy'.[20] Shame, for the neurotic subject, is first of all the shame of being a desiring subject, of being sustained by a fantasy, pinned down to a body which manifests itself as excess.[21] In the 'lavatory' episode, Mouth's soliloquy veers into a horribly shameful exhibitionist fantasy of defecation in public. In the extraordinarily terse syntax of the play's dramaturgy, this exhibitionist fantasy is being played out on the stage, before the audience's 'stare', just as it is being voiced. In Seminar 11, Lacan lists four partial drives, each of which corresponds to an excitable orifice: the oral, anal, scopic

[20] Jacques Lacan, *Desire and Its Interpretation: The Seminar of Jacques Lacan, Book VI*, edited by Jacques-Alain Miller, translated by Bruce Fink (Cambridge and Medford, MA: Polity, 2019), 438.

[21] Bernard, *Lacan et la Honte*, 60–2.

and invocative aural drives, which solicit respectively mouth, anus, eye and ear.[22] As we have seen, Mouth's mouth is a protean organ which morphs into the other organs of the drive as they are invoked in her speech. In other words, the play can be seen as the acting out of Mouth's shameful exhibitionist fantasy, as her body, metonymically reduced to its erogenous orifices, paradoxically returns as excess, in excess of what we are prepared to see on stage or screen.

Not I thus offers a condensed dramatic image of shame as the subject's experience and exposure of herself simultaneously as lack and excess. In Seminar 17, *The Other Side of Psychoanalysis* (1969–70), Lacan dwells on the notion of shame and proposes the concept of 'hontology' ('hontologie'), a portmanteau word which collapses the French words 'honte' (shame) and 'ontologie'. As David Bernard clarifies, psychoanalysis is not naturally amenable to ontology, which entails certainty, a belief in the possibility of a totalising knowledge about the subject or the world.[23] Hontology, however, by tying together shame and ontology, inscribes the very vacillation of the subject, as subject of lack and jouissance, at the heart of ontology. Hontology, then, is the ontological shame of being a subject; the discovery that the subject, as such, speaks and entangles herself in her jouissance. Here is Lacan:

> Dying of shame, then. Here, the degeneration of the signifier is certain – certain to be produced by the signifier's failure, namely, being toward death, insofar as it concerns the subject – and who else could it concern? Being toward death, that is, the visiting card by which a signifier represents a subject for another signifier . . .
>
> This visiting card never arrives at the right destination, the reason being that for it to bear the address of death, the card has to be torn up. 'It's a shame [*une honte*]', as they say, which should produce a (h)ontology [*hontologie*], spelled properly at last.[24]

As a speaking being, the subject is produced by a chain of signifiers which can only fail to represent her accurately. Her true habitus is the gap between signifiers, her being for death. Shame mortifies the subject (from the Latin *mortificare*, to make dead), makes her long to disappear from the stage; and yet, notes Lacan facetiously: 'It does

[22] Lacan, *Four Fundamental*, 180.

[23] Bernard, *Lacan et la Honte*, 116–18.

[24] Jacques Lacan, *The Other Side of Psychoanalysis: The Seminars of Jacques Lacan* 17, edited by Jacques-Alain Miller, translated with notes by Russell Grigg (New York and London: Norton, 2007), 180.

have to be said that it is unusual to die of shame'.[25] This paradox is forcefully dramatised in *Not I*, in which Mouth plays out both her wish to disappear from view (in her metonymic reduction to a lack, a hole) and her condition as a desiring being who inexorably reappears as a body in excess, a (literally) ob-scene collection of pleasurable orifices.

One possible effect of shame, Lacan observes, is that, in mortifying the subject, in unveiling her shameful inner lining, it may produce a push toward identification. Because shame reveals the subject as a hole, it invites her to cover it up again, to repair the mortified ego with the mantle of new identifications. Shame, Lacan offers, is itself 'the hole [in the subject] from which the master signifier arises'.[26] As Matthew Sharpe clarifies, master-signifiers are those that the subject 'most deeply identifies with, and which accordingly have a key role in the way s/he gives meaning to the world'. While they have no positive content, Lacan claims they are 'signifiers without a signified', they work to 'reorient the subject with respect to all of the other signifiers which structure his/her sense of herself and the world'.[27] The ego-ideal, then, weaves itself out of master-signifiers as a response to shame, the ontological primary affect of the living, speaking subject. In rejecting the use of the first person, however, Mouth refuses this dialectical counter-movement of re-identification. She has been literally defaced in shame, and she holds on to this state of defacement, speaking from the place of shame, resisting the lure of ontology, the appeal of recreating an 'I' which might be validated in the public (and her own) eye. Instead, as a hontological subject of lack and jouissance, she derails the psychoanalytic process of the talking cure, refuses the possible suturing of her wounded, gaping ego (yet another valence of the polymorphous hole on the stage) and in telling her story in the third person, opts instead for fiction. The poising of psychoanalysis versus creativity is not, of course, a valid alternative (quite the contrary in many cases), nor am I suggesting that Beckett embraces it uncritically. Yet in the light of Anzieu's reading of the Beckett/Bion relationship and its aftermath, it is possible to see in *Not I* an expression of Beckett's own reluctance to be cured of his shame, and perhaps to understand the excruciating experience of shame as essential to his creativity.

25 Lacan, *The Other Side*, 180.
26 Lacan, *The Other Side*, 189.
27 Matthew Sharpe, 'Jacques Lacan', *Internet Encyclopedia of Philosophy*, https://philpapers.org/rec/SHAJL

The relationship between shame and creativity is explored in a groundbreaking essay by Eve Kosofsky Sedgwick. She builds on psychologist Sylvan Tomkins's theory of shame to describe shame's ambivalence:

> As best described by Tomkins, shame effaces itself; shame points and projects; shame turns itself skin side out; shame and pride, shame and dignity, shame and self-display, shame and exhibitionism are different interlinings of the same glove. Shame, it might finally be said, transformational shame, is performance. Performance interlines shame as more than just its result or a way of warding it off, though importantly it is those things. Shame is the affect that mantles the threshold between introversion and extroversion, between absorption and theatricality, between performativity and – performativity.[28]

Although Sedgwick doesn't reference Sartre or Lacan, their image of the glove turned inside out returns here to signal the transformative power of shame, its unique way of resignifying self-effacement (induced by the performativity of the pointed finger or the stigmatising look that says, 'shame on you') as self-display (the performativity by which one produces oneself as subject by taking to the stage). The radical ambiguity of the theatrical image on which *Not I* rests – that of an absent body which is simultaneously a hypervisible body – superbly captures this paradox and makes the radically alienated Mouth one of the most poignant and powerful figures of the artist in Beckett's oeuvre.

In conclusion, let me return briefly to the question of the nature of Mouth's shame. If we read this shame as 'hontological' (the shame of living which, Lacan suggests, any speaking subject, as a subject of lack and jouissance, is bound to experience), then what do we make of who *she* is? – or rather of who the character in her story is, whom we can equate to her only by doing her a violence redoubled when we assume, as I have just done, that Beckett's characters are really versions of himself. If hers is the shame that we all experience, as speaking, desiring subjects, what do we make of the fact that she is Irish, old, poor, a woman, an orphan, and that hers is a history of multiple traumas that she can barely name?

If we recognise her as one of us, are we not in danger of overlooking the specificity of her disempowerment and radical otherness? And

[28] Eve Kosofsky Sedgwick, 'Shame, Theatricality and Queer Performativity: Henry James' *The Art of the* Novel', in *Touching Feeling. Affect, Pedagogy, Performativity* (Durham: Duke University Press, 2003), 38.

in recognising her shame as the paradoxical locus from which her voice as a storyteller springs, do we not run the risk of romanticising her disenfranchisement? If Mouth is partly, as I have suggested, an allegory of shame, then I would also insist that Beckett's theatrical practice in *Not I* never congeals Mouth into a conceptual figure of shame whom we might observe in a detached way (as Rushdie does, arguably, with Sufiya Zinobia in *Shame*). On the contrary, as I have observed over years of watching and discussing various performances of *Not I* with students, the striking visual and aural images conjured by the play in performance tend to elicit strong emotional, visceral responses: of compassion, disgust and sometimes utter boredom but also, very often, of intense embarrassment. It is as if Mouth's shame were spreading into the space of the classroom, referring each of us back to painful, intimate memories of shame while including us in an uncomfortable community of the shameful. This concurs with Sedgwick's observation that 'shame is both peculiarly contagious and peculiarly individuating'.[29] While Mouth's story remains beyond our reach, what we can know of her is the shame we share with her and experience anew in our bodies as we watch her excruciating performance of shame on stage or screen. Lacan's concept of hontology allows us to think that, while shame is always experienced in a specific moment, as the force that turns a particular subject inside out, revealing her shameful inner lining, and therefore marking her out, in the moment of shame, as different and lacking, as radically other, yet this experience of radical otherness, paradoxically, is one which can and must be experienced by all speaking subjects, provided they are willing to drop their mask of self-satisfaction, as Lacan asks his students to do, inviting them to return to the analyst's couch:

> You will say to me, 'What's the use of shame? If that is what the other side of psychoanalysis is, we don't want any'. My reply to you is, 'You've got enough to open a shop'. If you are not yet aware of this, then do a bit of psychoanalysis as they say. You will see this vapid air of yours run up against an outlandish shame of living.[30]

[29] Sedgwick, 'Shame, Theatricality', 36.
[30] Lacan, *The Other Side*, 182.

Part VI

Shame's Joyce

Chapter 12

Flirting with Shame: Performing Narration in *Ulysses*

Kezia Whiting

Freud introduces the concept of the superego in the *New Introductory Lectures* by describing patients who have delusions of being observed, informing his audience that 'they complain to us that perpetually, and down to their most intimate actions, they are being molested by the observation of unknown powers – presumably persons – and that in hallucinations they hear these persons reporting the outcome of their observation: now he's going to say this, now he's dressing to go out and so on'.[1] This intimate self-observation is disturbing and foreign to the patient's sense of self, even as it is right at the heart of them, knowing not only their past actions but also current and future ones. Freud implies that this interior monologue is capable of understanding the patient's actions and thoughts better than they do, since the voices 'report the *outcome* of their observation' as if they are able to synthesise and make sense of our intimate actions in ways we cannot. But what if, Freud goes on to hypothesise, the delusion of being observed in this most intimate and most detached way is not a delusion at all? He asks: 'How would it be if these insane people were right, if in each of us there is present in his ego an agency like this which observes and threatens to punish?'[2] This agency, with its power of observation and narration, Freud names the superego. In this chapter I argue that free indirect style, as reinvented by Joyce, exemplifies the strange dynamic of this foreign internal voice that watches, reports and judges the characters. Drawing this parallel between Freud's superego and free indirect style demonstrates the posturing at the heart of narrated

[1] Sigmund Freud, *New Introductory Lectures on Psychoanalysis* [1933], *The Penguin Freud Library* 2, translated by James Strachey (Harmondsworth: Penguin, 1973), 74.
[2] Freud, *New Introductory Lectures*, 74.

thought – Joyce's characters are aware of being seen, and of being seen being seen.

But free indirect style does not merely exemplify the observer characters feel bearing down on them: Joyce's free indirect style enfolds the representation of this awareness, so that it both produces and registers the self-awareness of the characters. For Freud, the subject is split into the self-observing and the self being observed, such that it becomes an object to itself: 'We wish to make the ego the matter of our enquiry, our very own ego. But is that possible? After all, the ego is in its very essence a subject; how can it be made into an object? Well, there is no doubt that it can be. The ego can take itself as an object, can treat itself like other objects, can observe itself, criticise itself, and do Heaven knows what with itself.'[3] And, in Joyce's use of free indirect style being seen facilitates the enmeshing of subject and object. The technique condenses and epitomises the characters' sense of being seen, just as Freud's superego organised and synthesised the patient's actions. Like Freud's perceptual apparatus which 'can in fact provide both an ever-ready receptive surface and permanent traces of the notes that have been made upon it', free indirect style as developed by Joyce is receptive to external and internal dynamics (such that they begin to bleed into one another) and retains permanent traces of that process of merging.[4]

Free indirect style is traditionally understood to be a scattering of subjective responses throughout objective reporting, with writers imperceptibly integrating mental reactions into the neutral-objective report of actions, scenes and spoken words.[5] But in modernist fiction, there are no 'mental reactions' that are not always already embedded in 'neutral-objective reports of actions, scenes, and spoken words', since, as Freud recognises, this apparently objective reporting voice is one that we all are capable of hearing describe what is most intimate to ourselves. Joyce produces character not interspersed with 'neutral-objective reports' but through these 'objective' reports, building on Freud to demonstrate the exteriority of thinking and subjectivity, and the evanescent borders of the subject. In his use of free indirect style, he depicts the repetitions, intrusions and gaps that structure thinking at all levels of consciousness. In merging exteriority with interiority,

[3] Freud, *New Introductory Lectures*, 73.

[4] Sigmund Freud, 'A Note Upon the Mystic Writing Pad' [1924], *The Standard Edition of the Complete Psychological Works of Sigmund Freud*, vol. XIX, translated by James Strachey (London: Vintage, 2001), 227–34, 228.

[5] Dorrit Cohn, *Transparent Minds: Narrative Modes for Presenting Consciousness in Fiction* (Princeton: Princeton University Press, 1978), 115.

Joyce's free indirect style inscribes the gaze of the other in the subject's self-understanding and functions itself as a representation of that gaze. The characters are constantly aware of how they might be seen by others, making the third person component of free indirect style as intimately bound to the subject as the first person.

This mode of narration flirts with shame, extending to others the fantasy of how the character would like to be seen and thus risking the puncture of that fantasy. Their awareness of being seen structures the character's anxiety throughout the story and often their excessive circumspection, even with themselves. From Bloom's self-monitoring to the obfuscation of Gerty's disability, this chapter charts the double movement of Joyce's free indirect style in producing the subject in the space between their self-fantasy and the shameful dissolution of that identity.

As Others See Us

A number of the stories of *Dubliners* culminate in the protagonist glimpsing themselves from an external vantage point and feeling ashamed. Perhaps most memorable is Gabriel's 'shameful consciousness of his own person' at the end of 'The Dead', but there is also the boy in 'Araby' who sees himself 'as a creature driven and derided by vanity; and my eyes burned with anguish and anger', and Little Chandler's cheeks 'suffused with shame' (65) in the final sentence of 'A Little Cloud'.[6] These moments, rather than a sudden realisation of how one might be seen by others after being blind to one's reception in the world, in fact reveal the characters' constant awareness of how they are seen by others throughout their stories, and their accompanying posturing. This moment of shame is more about the failure of their performance than an epiphany revealing their 'true' selves.

The characters' sense of being seen – even of their construction in narration – structures their anxiety throughout the story and often their excessive circumspection, even with themselves. Joyce's free indirect style writes itself across the split subject Freud describes, aligning itself with a character while producing an external vantage point from which they are seen, a spotlight they respond to throughout the story. Joyce's narration traces this apparent distance within characters' thoughts using the intricacies of an ironic free indirect style – ironic in the distance it effects hand in hand

[6] James Joyce, *Dubliners* [1914] (Oxford: Oxford University Press, 2000), 173; 24; 65.

with its proximity – to demonstrate the way the idea of being seen constitutes us as subjects.

In *Ulysses*, Bloom's conscious thoughts are often constructed as if to cover up the idea of Molly's infidelity from himself *and* others at once, deflecting shame through this defensive manoeuvre. Bloom's vigilance operates doubly. He wants to avoid not only the shame of being a cuckold, but, more than this, the shame of others knowing that he knows that he is being cuckolded. Bloom's thinking is itself a kind of performance (but a performance that constitutes, rather than hides, character), and its protective operation depends upon a certain reception. As Kimberly Devlin has argued, 'the self-conscious subject, the subject intensely aware of and sensitive to an other's eye', arises throughout Joyce's oeuvre.[7] Bloom first thinks of the line 'see ourselves as others see us' (from Robert Burns's 'To a Louse') when he is disgusted watching other men eating at the Burton Hotel, and again in 'Nausicaa' wondering about an unknown man walking by. Devlin claims that the Burns poem 'suggests that, much as we may try, we never do see ourselves as others see us'.[8] And indeed, the poem's final stanza, to which Joyce refers, exclaims: '*O wad some Pow'r the giftie gie us / To see oursels as ithers see us!*' clearly implying, as Devlin infers, that we cannot see ourselves from this external vantage point (and, if we could, we would see ourselves as ridiculous as the posh woman with the louse crawling throughout her finery).[9] For Devlin, Joyce's reference to this poem points to his 'interest in attempts to transcend the limits of self-perception by seeing the self through the eye of the other', but I want to suggest that, for Joyce, the eye of the other, rather differently than in Burns's poem, always infiltrates the way we see ourselves. We cannot not see ourselves as we *imagine* others see us.[10]

When Bloom sees toilets in a plumber's window in 'Lestrygonians', his thoughts turn to Röntgen rays, or X-rays, a topic he returns to throughout the day, and which develops the novel's own reflections on its ability to 'show' Bloom's thinking:

> Bare clean closestools waiting in the window of William Miller, plumber, turned back his thoughts. They could: and watch it all they way down,

[7] Kimberly Devlin, 'See Ourselves as Others See Us: Joyce's Look at the Eye of the Other', *PMLA* 104:5 (1989): 882–93, 882.

[8] Devlin, 'See Ourselves as Others See Us', 882.

[9] Robert Burns, *The Selected Poems of Robert Burns*, edited by David Daiches (London: Deutsch, 1979), 34; lines 43–4.

[10] Devlin, 'See Ourselves as Others See Us', 882.

> swallow a pin sometimes come out of the ribs years after, tour round the body changing biliary duct spleen squirting liver gastric juice coils of intestines like pipes. But the poor buffer would have to stand all the time with his insides entrails on show. Science.[11]

The poor buffer is of course a figure for Bloom himself, but the operations of narration are not as much like Röntgen rays as we might at first suspect – they reveal but also conceal him throughout the day and reveal him through the act of concealing him. 'Lestrygonians' takes full advantage of its time of day, and Bloom's hunger, to draw connections between thinking and eating, both of which, in this episode, follow a logic of recycling. All of the chewing and eating Bloom witnesses throughout 'Lestrygonians' is associated with the interior monologue that describes it, simultaneously describing both forms of rumination. On his way from the Burton Hotel, Bloom imagines using Röntgen rays to trace a green piece of food through the digestive system, 'Something green it would have to be: spinach, say. Then with those Röntgen rays searchlight you could', and then sees a ravenous terrier who chokes 'up a sick knuckly cud on the cobblestones and lapped it with new zest. Surfeit. Returned with thanks having fully digested the contents. First sweet then savoury. Mr Bloom coasted warily. Ruminants. His second course. Their upper jaw they move' (U 8.1029–34). The dog's regurgitation and remastication prompts Bloom to think of ruminants while also giving us a figure for the digestion of thoughts in this episode, just as his coasting warily (to avoid stepping in the dog's vomit), also describes the path of his thinking throughout 'Lestrygonians' – cautiously moving over the surface of ideas.

The episode ends with the word 'Safe!', acknowledging not just Bloom's avoidance of being seen by Boylan, but the operation of concealment, of safely getting to the end without being seen, that constitutes the entire episode. The task is not just to safely avoid being seen by Boylan at the end, but to conceal his thoughts about Molly and Boylan throughout the episode. And yet the interior monologue apparently sees Bloom's very thoughts, like Röntgen rays putting 'insides entrails on show'. So while his insides entrails might be on show, they are also hard at work to conceal through their performance of revelation.

[11] James Joyce, *Ulysses*, edited by Hans Walter Gabler, et al. (London: Vintage, 1986), 8; 1,045–50. Hereafter (U Chapter. Line).

Bloom tells himself to 'Think no more about that' when he begins to wonder if Boylan has a venereal disease:

> If he. . .?
> O!
> Eh?
> No. . . . . . No.
> No, no. I don't believe it.
> He wouldn't surely?
> No, no. (8.102–109)

Even before cautioning himself to think no more about that, what 'that' is is not explicitly stated. Instead, the interior monologue functions through a series of gaps, questions and negations. Later, Bloom even more telegraphically thinks: 'Today. Today. Not think', suggesting that perhaps what has been going on when he is successful in not allowing the imminent liaison between Molly and Boylan to rise to the surface is 'not thinking', despite there appearing to be an abundance of thoughts (U 8.1061–2). Bloom's thoughts are thoroughly self-conscious, almost as if he is listening to himself think, surveilling his thoughts just as we are. So, despite the almost excessive flow of thinking on display, the interior monologue reveals Bloom's thinking to us more in its gaps and obstructions: as Bloom discovers in using the tip of his little finger to blot out the sun's disk, something enormous can be concealed by something very small. When Bloom wonders if the blind stripling would 'feel it if something was removed. Feel a gap', he signals the logic of absence within Joyce's narration, which points us towards what is missing while also eliding it (U 8.1108–10).

But Bloom is not, of course, in complete control over the direction or associations of his thoughts, much as he tries to regulate them. Bloom's thoughts take on Molly's physical features just before he enters the Burton restaurant as a 'warm human plumpness' settles down on his brain (U 8.637). This phrase continues his thoughts about Molly, marking them as extimate – exterior, yet intimate – to him.[12] It is as if the thought of Molly comes to him and sits on his brain, taking control of it, so that he acquiesces to it: 'his brain yielded' (U 8.637–8). When Bloom thinks that Molly 'can be rude too', the surprising twist is that she will 'Blurt out' not what *she* is thinking, but 'what I was thinking', suggesting a conflation between

[12] Jacques Lacan, *The Ethics of Psychoanalysis: 1959–1960, The Seminar of Jacques Lacan, book VII*, translated by Dennis Porter (New York: Norton, 1986), 139.

himself and Molly that is continued in the 'warm human plumpness' settling down on his brain (U 8.116). In *Ulysses*, cognition is embodied not simply in the way the body shapes mental processes, but in the metaphors of the body to describe thoughts that accompany that embodiment.

Disgusted with the proximity of others eating in the Burton, Bloom describes one man as 'chewing the cud. Before and after', introducing the rumination theme that will be picked up later with the dog (U 8.674–5). His disgust centres on the comingling he imagines happening, that you 'Never know whose thoughts you're chewing', further unsettling our understanding of the thoughts we are reading as belonging to Bloom, and indeed, of thought itself as attributable to a single origin (U 8.717–18). This traversal of the boundaries of the self is repulsive to Bloom in general, at least partly because it encroaches on the representation of his intimacy with Molly, encapsulated in his memory of the day on Howth Head, when 'softly she gave me in my mouth the seedcake warm and chewed' (U 8.907). Bloom's memories of Molly are both protection and threat: making the comparison between himself then and now might bring his thoughts back to Boylan, but it also demonstrates the depth of his and Molly's relationship.

While Bloom is apparently sickened by the idea of comingling in the Burton Hotel, throughout 'Lestrygonians' he thinks his way into others. Although he always does this in terms of what it might be like *for him*, there is still an openness and generosity to this mode of his thinking. It is, however, and most importantly, another way for him to avoid thinking his own thoughts, by attempting to put into practice his speculation, 'If we were all suddenly somebody else' (U 6.836). Bloom tries the hardest with the blind man, but even this attempt to imagine what it is like to be someone else is eventually thwarted by his sense of himself.

Bloom thinks about what it might be like for the blind man to be 'with a woman, for instance. More shameless not seeing' (U 8.1125). The sentence break makes the referent of the adjective 'shameless' uncertain: does Bloom conclude that a woman would be 'more shameless' if she were not seen by her lover, or is it that the blind lover himself would be 'more shameless'? *More* shameless already oddly quantifies a *lack* of shame, as if being without shame only ever marks a certain threshold, rather than the complete absence of shame. Are we shameful *because* of what we see, or because we are seen? Bloom's phrasing, 'not seeing', leans towards because of what we see, implying that the blind man is shameless because he does not catch himself *in flagrante delicto*, does not see himself when his own self-conscious gaze would disrupt him. This track already begins to bring us back to Bloom, who is trying not to see himself too distinctly throughout this episode, warily blinkering himself from himself.

The narration repeatedly suggests that we do see ourselves as others see us, that we are always constructed and constructing ourselves by how we imagine we are seen and how we want to be seen. The poor buffer with his insides entrails on show constantly feels as if he is being seen, performing various furtive acts to mask his thoughts or desires, such as when he leaves the Burton and pretends to have been meeting someone. The formal pose of the narration keys us in to Bloom's own posturing: 'Mr Bloom raised two fingers doubtfully to his lips. His eyes said: – Not here. Don't see him', with the narration implicitly contrasting this performance with his actual reasons for leaving, revealed in the next line – 'I hate dirty eaters' (U 8.694–6).

At the end of the episode, Bloom performs similar diversionary manoeuvres:

> Afternoon she said.
>
> I am looking for that. Yes, that. Try all pockets. Handker. *Freeman.* Where did I? Ah, yes. Trousers. Potato. Purse. Where?
>
> Hurry. Walk quietly. Moment more. My heart.
>
> His hand looking for the where did I put found it his hip pocket soap lotion have to call tepid paper stuck. Ah soap there I yes. Gate. Safe! (U 8.1187–93).

The interior monologue displays Bloom's façade of thinking, conveying what Bloom wants to convey to whoever is seeing him, and not what he is actually thinking, though through their hesitations and gaps these anxieties are also suggested. Though less directly than outside the Burton Hotel, affectively loaded phrases slip through the performance here too, disrupting it. From 'Afternoon she said' (when Boylan will be visiting), Bloom manages to return to 'I am looking for that', narrating his actions as if this will give them authenticity. But what happens between the determined first person of 'I am looking for that' and the third person introduced after 'My heart'? Just as it did as he leaves the Burton, the third person points to the image Bloom would like to present, and hints at the gaze Bloom feels cornering him despite having reassured himself that Boylan did not see him. But the narration cannot maintain the third person over a single sentence, reverting to the flustered first person, which still valiantly presses on with the deception, jumping on any prompt to distract his thoughts as well as to perform preoccupation. The shifts between third person narration and interior monologue are a precursor for the novel's forays into free indirect style, with the ambiguity of just what these words mean – and the impossibility of teasing apart thought and performance – always apparent.

Even though we can see through Bloom's performance, it works: it helps Bloom 'not think'. The poor buffer with his insides on show is not quite as on display as the narration's style might suggest, with the recycling machinations producing an interior monologue unique in its presentation not of thinking, but of not thinking.

After such challenges of not thinking throughout the day, Bloom is finally presented in the narration just as he would choose. 'Eumaeus' is, as Hugh Kenner knows, 'the Uncle Charles Principle *in excelsis*, a stylistic homage in Bloom's style to Bloom': 'At last he feels like the hero of a novel, which for Joyce in fiction after fiction is the apotheosis to which fictional beings aspire. And he has his reward. He is treated to an episode written as he would have written it. The language is solemn, decorated, fulsome, periphrastic.'[13] We see this aspiration Kenner describes in many of the male characters of *Dubliners*, but it reaches its apotheosis in 'Eumaeus', where 'that consummation devoutly to be or not to be wished for' between narration and character is complete (U 16.1031). The narration is entirely taken over by Bloom's self-presentation, and with only rare risky moments when he has to not-think, there is little distinction, and much repetition, between dialogue and narration:

> it was just the wellknown case of hot passion, pure and simple, upsetting the applecart with a vengeance and just bore out the very thing he was saying as she also was Spanish or half so [. . .].
>
> — Just bears out what I was saying, he, with glowing bosom, said to Stephen, about blood and the sun. And, if I don't greatly mistake she was Spanish too. (U 16.1406–15)

The narration of 'Eumaeus' bears out what Bloom was saying, 'as if both their minds were travelling, so to speak, in the one train of thought' (U 16. 1580–1). Bloom presents himself spectacularly, gloriously, pleonastically, as he would love to be seen.

Flirting with Shame

So while Devlin is right that, Joyce, like Burns, suggests we never do see ourselves as others see us, Joyce also shows that it would be even more impossible to see ourselves without that externally posited gaze,

[13] Hugh Kenner, *Joyce's Voices* (Dublin: Dalkey Archive Press, 2007), 38; 35.

and that 'the self-conscious subject' forms their self-image through the eye of the other: we cannot help but see ourselves as some other might.[14] Joyce's free indirect style in particular – with its merging of interior and exterior topographies – demonstrates this intersubjective foundation of subjectivity.

In 'Nausicaa', Joyce demonstrates the role the gaze plays in enacting the enmeshment of subject and world ingrained in free indirect style. The digressive route of self-vision – through the gaze of an other – surfaces in Gerty and Bloom's exchanged glances, triangulated through free indirect style. Discussing Joyce's interpenetration of observer and observed, Tony Thwaites suggests that

> *oneself* is structurally taken out of itself in going through the detour of the other, *as seen by* the other[. . .] It is impossible to separate a Gerty who performs for herself, a Gerty who performs for Bloom, a Gerty who sees herself perform for Bloom, a Gerty whom Bloom sees performing, a Gerty who sees Bloom watching her perform, and so forth. With 'Nausicaa', narration and character, observer and observed, are abyssally internal to each other.[15]

Joyce's free indirect style perfectly illustrates 'the detour of the other' necessary for performing oneself, as the self-observation inherent in the narrational technique materialises in Bloom watching Gerty, and Gerty Bloom. Gazing at Bloom, Gerty smiles at the image of herself thus created, 'at the lovely reflection which the mirror gave back to her' (U 13.162).

Gerty's blush during the fireworks flirts with shame, marking the pleasure of being seen, and of putting oneself on display, of opening oneself to the possibility of what Bloom earlier calls 'lovely shame' (U 5.431): 'her face was suffused with a divine, an entrancing blush from straining back and he could see her other things too' (U 13.23–4). Referring to this moment in 'Circe', Bloom claims 'her artless blush unmanned me', which, in needing to qualify the blush as 'artless' in fact draws attention to the possibility of a blush not involuntary but deliberately manifested (U 15.1189–90). Gerty's glance moves from Bloom to the fireworks, with both Gerty and Bloom caught up in her performance of watching. And just as she performs watching the fireworks, so too does Bloom *perform* watching her:

[14] Devlin, 'See Ourselves as Others See Us', 882.
[15] Tony Thwaites, *Joycean Temporalities: Debts, Promises, and Countersignatures* (Gainesville: University Press of Florida, 2001), 107.

> she saw that he saw and then it went so high it went out of sight a moment and she was trembling in every limb from being bent so far back that he had a full view high up above her knee where no-one ever not even on the swing or wading and she wasn't ashamed and he wasn't either to look in that immodest way like that because he couldn't resist the sight of the wondrous revealment half offered. (U 13.726–32).

The 'wondrous revealment' here is only 'half offered', with Gerty's physical display also enacting a certain concealment. The narration 'half offers' the interaction between Gerty and Bloom, valorising it by painting over it in the language of romance and idolatry – she 'trembling', he unable to 'resist'. This continues in the next paragraph, where Bloom, in turn, blushes under her gaze, 'a pathetic little glance of piteous protest, of shy reproach under which he coloured like a girl' (U 13.7,442–3).

The episode showcases the enveloping technique of Joyce's free indirect style, folding 'the world in its mysterious embrace', encompassing styles from women's magazines, romance novels, even the 'oldtime chivalry' of courtly romance (U 13.1–2; 13.336).[16] As Karen Lawrence argues, 'the free indirect discourse, blending the resources of first and third-person narration, suggests that the troping of her mind comes from outside as well as inside, providing the space of a separate view'.[17] Only, I would suggest that this 'separate view', occupied by Bloom as he watches Gerty, does not provide space, since the awareness of being seen prompts Gerty's performance in the first place (in so far as she continually performs herself not necessarily specifically for Bloom, but for that 'observation of unknown powers' so aptly described by Freud). With everything that is folded in, there are clear variations in the texture of the narration. The glossy narration, with its 'womanly wise' tone, condescension and clichés derived from magazines, is punctuated by moments of anger, shame and embarrassment. We hear this tonal discrepancy early in the episode, even before Gerty herself is described: 'For Tommy and Jacky Caffrey were twins, scarce four years old and very noisy and spoiled twins sometimes but for all that darling little fellows with bright merry faces and endearing ways about them.'[18] The impatience with them that surfaces in 'very noisy and spoiled' is smothered by the tone of motherly affection as

[16] Thwaites, *Joycean Temporalities*, 97.

[17] Karen Lawrence, *Who's Afraid of James Joyce?* (Gainesville: University Press of Florida, 2010), 252.

[18] Joyce, *Ulysses*, 13.16–17.

the twins are morphed into props for the narration's performance of womanhood.

This performance develops in Gerty's blushing response to Cissy Caffrey's indelicacy:

> — On the beeoteetom, laughed Cissy merrily.
> Gerty MacDowell bent down her head and crimsoned at the idea of Cissy saying an unladylike thing like that out loud she'd be ashamed of her life to say, flushing a deep rosy red, and Edy Boardman said she was sure the gentleman opposite heard what she said. But not a pin cared Ciss. (U 13.262–7)

Edy's recognition of Bloom is incorporated into Gerty's free indirect style rather than set off as dialogue, suggesting Gerty's own awareness of his gaze, and its antecedent influence on her behaviour, while making explicit only Edy and Cissy's response to Bloom's presence. The blush epitomises the way performance constitutes the subject in Joyce – as Hugh Kenner affirms, 'if we ask whether costume is appropriate to wearer, we shall be reminded that the wearer's soul-stuff may be a void to which the costume lends a look of coherence'.[19] The blush is thus both deliberately called forth, performed, but it nonetheless reveals Gerty, and the ideologies permeating her. Shame is performed for others, demonstrating one's modesty or innocence even as it also necessitates comprehension of the situation and thus, to an extent, complicity in it. The sentence is hung up on Gerty's blush, with her both 'crimsoned' and 'flushing' apparently not enough, since it also adds that 'she'd be ashamed of her life to say' it, conveying Gerty's insistence upon her own decorousness. The sentence also emphasises the audibility of Cissy's comment: the free indirect style fixates on indices of speech with the idea of Cissy 'saying [it . . .] out loud', mortifying Gerty, who would be ashamed *to say* it. Even in Edy's reported speech the narration stalls on the spoken – 'Edy Boardman *said she* was sure [Bloom] heard what *she said*' – so that Edy and Cissy begin to blur together in their audibility while Gerty's silence singles her out. The the ladylike performance she aims for throughout 'Nausicaa' is achieved and maintained through her performance of shame here and elsewhere.

But like her less polished response to the Caffrey twins, Gerty's awareness of her disability punctures the performance. Her self-consciousness is evident when the ball Bloom throws back to Cissy rolls to Gerty and she 'drew back her foot but she wished the stupid

[19] Kenner, *Joyces Voices*, 52.

ball hadn't come rolling down to her and she gave a kick but she missed and Edy and Cissy laughed' (U 13.356–8). Her anger seems excessive until her disability is retrospectively taken into account.

The narration's hyper-awareness of Gerty's feet and ankle – having already drawn attention to the daintiness of her 'higharched instep' and 'wellturned ankle' with its 'perfect proportions' – suggests a pleasure in the aesthetics of the foot that, like Bloom's attempts not to think about Molly's infidelity, both covers over and fixates on her anxiety (U 13.168–9). Gerty's embarrassment signals her desire to present herself according to a certain image, with the free indirect style allowing Gerty to see herself as she would like to be seen, to turn her lame foot into an object of aesthetic appreciation.

After the ball incident, Gerty's attitude toward her friends shifts. Cissy, who moments earlier 'was sincerity itself, one of the bravest and truest hearts heaven ever made, not one of your twofaced things, too sweet to be wholesome', now, running in front of Bloom, becomes 'a forward piece whenever she thought she had a good opportunity to show off and just because she was a good runner she ran like that so that he could see all the end of her petticoat running and her skinny shanks up as far as possible. It would have served her just right if she had tripped up over something accidentally on purpose' (U13.278–80; 13.478–85). Gerty's aggression is directed towards Cissy's physical prowess, which is positioned in competition with Gerty's incapability. The descriptor 'piece' marks the transgression of these moments of frustration, intensifying what is already present in much of Gerty's section – a tone of sexual condescension and objectification that echoes Bloom's unsettling reflections on his daughter, Milly, as a 'pert little piece' and a 'wild piece of goods. Her slim legs running up the staircase' (U4.295; 4.429–30). As Thwaites notes when arguing that 'everything which at first appeared to be Gerty now also works as Bloom', the 'phrasing seems to be full of small Bloomian signature-effects'. For Thwaites, the narration of the first half of 'Nausicaa' is 'inhabited by at least two centers which are both incommensurate [. . .] and interpermeating', incorporating and merging Gerty's version of Gerty with Bloom's version of Gerty, and Gerty's version of Bloom with Bloom's version of Bloom, all coloured by the language of romance and popular culture to which both subscribe. But the 'one recurrent factor' which for Thwaites 'seems to point to Bloom rather than Gerty' – that 'neither Gerty nor the narrative appears to know, or register, that she is lame' – I think points to Gerty most emphatically.[20] The narration, and Gerty, are

[20] Thwaites, *Joycean Temporalities*, 104, 102, 105, 103.

always conscious of her lameness, just as Bloom is always conscious of Molly's looming adultery.

The bravura of the narration in exhibiting the aesthetics of Gerty's foot indicates the overlap between the possibility of shame and the necessity of being seen. In displaying her foot prominently, the narration risks puncturing the fantasy (both Gerty's and Bloom's), while sealing its successful sleight of hand. Backus and Valente demonstrate these same dynamics of risk and shame in terms of Gerty's commodification, arguing (with some irony, given her disability) that 'Gerty is walking a fine line, reorganising cultural signifiers so as to distinguish herself as a superior and hence marketable commodity, while at the same time risking our ridicule in calling attention to herself as commodity through her efforts at self-invention.' For Backus and Valente, the narration of the first half of 'Nausicaa' allows the reader to occupy both the position of shame and the position of critique that induces that shame: 'If we are at one level identified with the parodic consciousness that critiques Gerty's mode of being in the world, we are, at another level, inescapably immersed in that Being, and so we experience the shame of her parodic flagellation.'[21] Indeed, this oscillation is the calling card of free indirect style, positioning the reader as seeing through the narration in both senses of the phrase. We see with the character, experiencing their performance of themselves, even as we critique and see through it (just as they themselves do).

The revelation of Gerty's lameness straddles the divide between the change from the free indirect style of the first half of the episode and the interior monologue of the second half, which occurs as the focalisation moves from Gerty to Bloom. While the free indirect style already encompasses exteriority in its representation of Gerty, and her own self-consciousness, the switch to Bloom's interior monologue in this moment suggests the complete externality of the brusque summary of Gerty. The free indirect style points toward her disability, but cuts off before revealing it:

> She walked with a certain quiet dignity characteristic of her but with care and very slowly because – because Gerty MacDowell was . . .
>
> Tight boots? No. She's lame! O!
>
> Mr Bloom watched her as she limped away. Poor girl! (U 13.769–72)

[21] Margot Gayle Backus and Joseph Valente, 'An Encounter: James Joyce's Humiliation Nation', in Vicki Mahaffey, ed., *Collaborative Dubliners* (Syracuse: Syracuse University Press, 2012), 67.

Neither the stark limping nor the ennobling quiet dignity are intrinsically Gerty's understanding of her walk, with both discourses of disability seeing and defining her through the eye of an other. The moments just before this, in which the text highlights the difficulties of the terrain – its 'slippy seaweed', the growing darkness and the 'stones and bits of wood' come closer to Gerty's perspective, which evokes a problem not with her body but with the environment through which it has to manoeuvre. Yet the position of 'quiet dignity' on Gerty's side of the narrational split suggests its closer alignment with her self-vision, a way she has perhaps been taught to see her disabled body. But the narration is already itself moving 'with care and very slowly' towards Bloom, observing Gerty more and more from that external vantage until it will no longer wondrously reveal her, but give her up entirely to his gaze.

In the second half of 'Nausicaa', Bloom's thoughts keep veering towards Molly and Boylan's rendezvous, so that at times, as throughout *Ulysses*, Joyce exploits the indeterminateness of the pronoun to refer to more than one person. For instance, Gerty blurs into Molly when Bloom thinks 'wonder how she is feeling in that region. Shame all put on before third person' (U 13.997–8). Although he is thinking of Gerty after his masturbation, and how she might have responded to their exchanged glances, 'she' also refers to Molly, who he has just imagined behaving rather as he imagined Gerty was doing with him: 'Molly, he. Dress up and look and suggest and let you see and see more' (U 13.993–4). Bloom's phrase thus implicitly positions himself as the 'third person' origin of the gaze in Molly and Boylan's assignation, even as it also refers to Gerty's performance in the presence of her friends. Moreover, Bloom suggests that dressing up is an essential part of letting the other see and see more of yourself – that our costumes reveal us.

The phrase 'Shame all put on before third person' indicates the intersection of the concepts of shame, the social world and the gaze in the narration of Gerty. It claims simultaneously that: 1) it is a shame that Gerty's performance was all before others; 2) shame is introduced by a third person's presence, and that shame itself is a performance – 'all put on'; 3) the presence of the third person – at the least in the form of the idea of the social world or the reader – is necessary for this interaction to take place at all. The third person narrational perspective puts on shame, makes shame at once secondary and primary ('before' third person), intrinsic to us and yet external, or as Kenner says of the Uncle Charles Principle, 'as external as costume'.[22]

[22] Kenner, *Joyce's Voices*, 21.

Bibliography

Abrahamson, Lenny. *Prosperity* (2007), produced by Element Films: Ed Guiney, Andrew Lowe/RTÉ.

Acevedo Espinal, Sara M. '"Effective Schooling", The Age of Capital: Critical Insights from Advocacy Anthropology, Anthropology of Education, and Critical Disability Studies', *Canadian Journal of Disability Studies* 9:5 (2020): 265–301.

Aers, David. 'A Whisper in the Ear of Early Modernists; or, Reflections on Literary Critics Writing the History of the Subject', in David Aers, ed., *Culture and History, 1350–1600: Essays on English Communities, Identities, and Writings*, 177–202. New York: Harvester Wheatsheaf, 1992.

Ahmed, Sara. *The Cultural Politics of Emotion*. New York: Routledge, 2004.

Albert, Leonard. 'Gnomonology: Joyce's "The Sisters"', *James Joyce Quarterly* 27:2 (Winter 1990): 353–64.

Anderson, Hephzibah. '*Ruth and Pen* by Emilie Pine, Review: A World of Joy and Pain', *The Guardian*, 15 May 2022. https://www.theguardian.com/books/2022/may/15/ruth-pen-by-emilie-pine-review-a-world-of-joy-and-pain

Anzieu, Didier. *Beckett*. Paris: Gallimard, 1998.

Ash, Lamora. '*Ruth & Pen* by Emilie Pine – a Tale of Two Lives', *The Guardian*, 19 May 2022.

Ashburn, Meghan and Jules Edwards. *I Will Die on This Hill: Autistic Adults, Autism Parents, and the Children Who Deserve a Better World*. London: Jessica Kingsley Publishing, 2023.

AsIAm. Ireland's National Autism Charity. https://asiam.ie/statement-on-applied-behavioural-analysis-aba-therapy/

'Autism Spectrum Disorder: Diagnostic Criteria', Center for Disease Control and Prevention. https://www.cdc.gov/ncbddd/autism/hcp-dsm.html.

Backus, Margot Gayle and Joseph Valente. 'An Encounter: James Joyce's Humiliation Nation', in Vicki Mahaffey, ed., *Collaborative Dubliners*, 48–68. Syracuse: Syracuse University Press, 2012.

Balint, Peter. 'State Power and Breastfeeding promotion: A Critique', *Contemporary Political Theory* 17 (2018): 306–30. DOI:10.1057/s41296-017-0158-3

Ballou, Emily Paige, Sharon da Vanport, Morénike Giwa Onaiwu, eds. *Sincerely, Your Autistic Child.* New York: Beacon Press, 2021.

Banville, John. 'A Century of Looking the Other Way', *New York Times*, 22 May 2009. https://www.nytimes.com/2009/05/23/opinion/23banville.html.

Barbera, Mary. *Turn Autism Around: An Action Guide for Parents of Young Children with Early Signs of Autism.* London: Hay House, 2021.

Baron-Cohen, Simon. 'The extreme male brain theory of autism', *Trends in Cognitive Sciences* 6:6 (2002): 248–54. DOI: 10.1016/s1364-6613(02)01904-6

Bartky, Sandra. *Femininity and Domination: Studies in the Phenomenology of Oppression.* New York: Routledge, 1990.

Bauman, Zygmunt. *Wasted Lives: Modernity's Outcasts.* Cambridge: Polity, 2013.

Beckett, Samuel. *The Complete Dramatic Works.* London: Faber & Faber, 1986.

Beckett, Samuel. *Worstward Ho.* London: Calder, 1983.

Beckett, Samuel. *Texts for Nothing.* London: Calder, 1999.

Beiner, Guy. *Forgetful Remembrance: Social Forgetting and Vernacular Historiography of a Rebellion in Ulster.* Oxford: Oxford University Press, 2018.

Bender, Abby. 'Nursing the Revival: Patrick Pearse, Breastfeeding, and Sacrifice', in Joseph Valente and Marjorie Howes, eds, *The Irish Revival: A Complex Vision*, 277–91. Syracuse: Syracuse University Press, 2023.

Bergin, Osborn. *Irish Bardic Poetry*, edited by David Greene and Fergus Kelly. Foreword by D. A. Binchy. Dublin: Dublin Institute for Advanced Studies, 1984.

Bernard, David. *Lacan et la honte. De la Honte à l'Hontologie.* Paris: Champ Lacanien, 2011.

Bhuptani, Prachi H. and Terri L. Messman-Moore. 'Blame and Shame in Sexual Assault', in W. T. O'Donohue and P. A. Schewe, eds, *Handbook of Sexual Assault and Sexual Assault Prevention*, 309–22. New York: Springer, 2019.

Blassingame, John, ed. *The Frederick Douglass Papers Series One: Speeches, Debates, and Interviews Volume 1: 1841–46.* New Haven and London: Yale University Press, 1979.

Bochiccio, Sarah. 'The Female Painter whose Modern Art Shocked Ireland', *Artsy*, 18 April 2018, https://www.artsy.net/article/artsy-editorial-female-painter-modern-art-shocked-ireland.

Bogel, Fredric V. *The Difference Satire Makes: Rhetoric and Reading from Jonson to Byron.* Ithaca: Cornell University Press, 2001.

Bourdieu, Pierre. 'Belief and the Body', *The Logic of Practice*, 66–79. Stanford: Stanford University Press, 1990.

Bourdieu, Pierre. 'Structures, Habitus, Practices', *The Logic of Practice*, 52–65. Stanford: Stanford University Press, 1990.

Bourdieu, Pierre. *Masculine Domination,* translated by Richard Nice. Cambridge: Polity Press, 2001.

Braidotti, Rosi. *The Posthuman*. Cambridge: Polity, 2013.

Brandabur, Edward. 'The Sisters', in R. Scholes and A. Walton, eds, *Dubliners: Text, Criticism and Notes*, 340–3. New York: Norton, 1979.

Brandabur, Edward. *A Scrupulous Meanness*. Urbana: University of Illinois Press, 1971.

Breatnach, Liam. 'On Satire and the Poet's Circuit', in Cathal G. Ó Háinle and Donald Meek, eds, *Unity in diversity. Studies in Irish and Scottish Gaelic Language, Literature and History*, 25–35. *Trinity Irish studies / Léann na Tríonóide* 1 (2004): 25–35.

Brown, Julie. *Writers on the Spectrum: How Autism and Asperger Syndrome have Influenced Literary Writing*. London: Jessica Kingsley Publishers, 2009.

Brown, Terence. Introduction, *Dubliners*, vii–xlix. New York: Penguin, 2000.

Brown, Terence. 'Notes to *Dubliners*', 237–317. New York: Penguin, 2000.

Browne, Stephen. 'Like Gory Spectres': Representing Evil in Theodore Weld's *American Slavey As It Is*', *Quarterly Journal of Speech* 80 (August 1994): 277–92. doi.org/10.1080/00335639409384073

Budgen, Frank. *James Joyce and The Making of* Ulysses. New York: Harrison Smith and Robert Haas, 1934.

Burke, Mary. '"Disremembrance": Joyce and Irish Protestant Institutions', *Éire-Ireland* 55:1 (2020): 201–22. DOI: 10.1353/eir.2020.0008

Burns, Anna. *Milkman*. London: Faber & Faber, 2018.

Burns, Robert. *The Selected Poems of Robert Burns*, edited by David Daiches. London: Deutsch, 1979.

Burton, Joan. 'Magdalene Laundries. Our World', BBC News, https://www.youtube.com/watch?v=ChDRDrb7e-U, 27 September 2014.

Bush, Hilary, Lindsay Williams and Eva Mendes. 'Brief Report: Asexuality and Young Women on the Autism Spectrum', *Journal of Autism Developmental Disorders* 51:2 (2021): 725–33. DOI:10.1007/s10803-020-04565-6

Butler, Judith. *Gender Trouble: Feminism and the Subversion of Identity*. London: Routledge, 1996.

Byrne, Luke and Ryan Nugent. 'City Magdalene Site May Contain Human Remains, Expert Warned', *Irish Independent*, 6 March 2017.

Caball, Marc. *Poets and Politics: Reaction and Continuity in Irish Poetry, 1558–1625*. Cork: Cork University Press, 1998.

Caball, Marc. 'Dispossession and Reaction: the Gaelic Literati and the Plantation of Ulster', *History Ireland* 17:6 (November/December 2009): 24–7.

Cavar, [sarah]. 'The Queer Aut of Failure', *Lateral* 11:2 (Fall 2022). doi.org/10.25158/L11.2.14.

Chakrabarty, Dipesh. *Habitations of Modernity: Essays in the Wake of Subaltern Studies*. Chicago: University of Chicago Press, 2002.

Chapman Stacey, Robin. *Dark Speech: The Performance of Law in Early Ireland*. Philadelphia: University of Pennsylvania Press, 2007.

Clarke, Vivienne. 'New Vatican Document 'very disappointing', Says Campaigner', *Irish Times*, 2 June 2021. https://www.irishtimes.com/news/social-affairs/religion-and-beliefs/new-vatican-document-very-disappointing-says-campaigner-1.4582009.

Clear, Caitríona. *Women of the House: Women's Household Work in Ireland, 1926–1961: Discourses, Experiences, Memories*. Dublin: Irish Academic Press, 2000.

Cohen Shabot, Sara. 'Edible Mothers, Edible Others: On Breastfeeding as Ambiguity', in Sara Cohen Shabot and Christinia Landry, eds, *Rethinking Feminist Phenomenology: Theoretical and Applied Perspectives*, 155–70. London: Rowman and Littlefield, 2018.

Cohn, Dorrit. *Transparent Minds: Narrative Modes for Presenting Consciousness in Fiction*. Princeton: Princeton University Press, 1978.

Conrad, Kathryn. 'Women Troubles, Queer Troubles: Gender, Sexuality, and the Politics of Selfhood in the Construction of the Northern Irish State', in M. Cohen and N. Curtin, eds, *Reclaiming Gender*, 53–68. Basingstoke: Palgrave Macmillan, 1999.

Conrad, Kathryn. 'Queer Treasons: Homosexuality and Irish National Identity', *Cultural Studies* 15:1 (2001): 124–37. doi.org/10.1080/09502380010012630

Conrad, Kathryn. *Locked in the Family Cell*. Madison: University of Wisconsin Press, 2004.

Constable, Liz. 'Introduction: States of Shame', *L'Esprit Créateur* 39:4 (1999): 3–12.

Cook, Barb and Michelle Garnett, eds. *Spectrum Women: Walking to the Beat of Autism*. London; Jessica Kingsley, 2018.

Copjec, Joan. 'Vampires, Breast-Feeding, and Anxiety', *October* 58 (1991): 25–43. doi.org/10.2307/778796

Corless, Adrienne. 'Fussing About Low Breastfeeding Rates Reeks of Mother-Shaming', *The Journal*, 6 August 2018.

Corless, Catherine. *Belonging: A Memoir of Place*. Dublin: Hachette Books Ireland, 2021.

Corr, M, P. O'Mahony, J. Lovett and L. Kelly. 'Different Systems, Similar Outcomes? Tracking Attrition in Reported Rape Cases in Eleven Countries. Country briefing: Ireland, April 2009', https://cwasu.org/wp-content/uploads/2016/07/Ireland.pdf

Costello-Sullivan, Kathleen. *Trauma and Recovery in the Twenty-First-Century Irish Novel*. Syracuse, NY: Syracuse University Press, 2018.

Cox, Catherine. 'Institutional Space and the Geography of Confinement in Ireland,1750–2000', in Thomas Bartlett, ed., *The Cambridge History of Ireland, Vol. IV*, 673–707. Cambridge: Cambridge University Press, 2018.

Crowe, Catriona. 'The Commission and the Survivors', *Dublin Review* (Summer 2021). https://thedublinreview.com/article/the-commission-and-the-survivors/

Crowley, Una and Rob Kitchin. 'Producing Decent Girls: Governmentality and the Moral Geographies of Sexual Conduct in Ireland (1922–1937)', *Gender, Place and Culture* 15:4 (2008): 355–72. doi.org/10.1080/09663690802155553

Cullen, Damien. 'Sabina Higgins Calls Breastfeeding Drive "the most important thing in the world"'. *Irish Times*, 25 June 2018.

Curran, Barney. 'Magadelene Laundries. Our World', BBC News, 27 September 2014. https://www.youtube.com/watch?v=ChDRDrb7e-U

Davis, Thomas. *The Poems of Thomas Davis*. Dublin: James Duffy; London: Simpkin, Marshall and Co., 1846.

De Beauvoir, Simone. *The Second Sex*. London: Vintage, 1997.

Debord, Guy. *The Society of the Spectacle*. London: Rebus Press, 1967.

De Brún, Pádraig, Breandán Ó Buachalla and Tomás Ó Concheanainn, eds. *Nua-Dhuanaire*, vol. 1. Baile Átha Cliath: Institiúid Ardléinn Bhaile Átha Cliath, 1986.

Dee, Olivia. 'Three Families: Abortion is Now Legal in Northern Ireland But More Needs to be Done so Every Woman has Adequate Access', *The Conversation*, 20 May 2021.

Delahanty, Ian. 'A Noble Empire in the West': Young Ireland, the United States, and Slavery', *Britain and the World* 6:2 (2013): 171–91. doi.org/10.3366/brw.2013.0095

Delay, Cara. 'Women, Childbirth Customs and Authority in Ireland, 1850–1930', *Lilith 21* (2015): 6–18.

Devlin, Kimberly. 'See Ourselves as Others See Us: Joyce's Look at the Eye of the Other', *PMLA* 104:5 (1989): 882–93. doi:10.2307/462579

De Wispelaere, Jurgen and Judy Walsh. 'Disability Rights in Ireland: Chronicle of a Missed Opportunity', *Irish Political Studies* 22:4 (2007): 517–43. DOI: 10.1080/07907180701699265

Dickens, Charles. *American Notes for General Circulation*. London: Penguin, [1842] 2000.

Dickey, Susannah. *Tennis Lessons*. London: Penguin, 2020.

Doherty, Mary. 'Viewpoint: 'Weaponized Heterogeneity Only Harms the Most Vulnerable Autistic People', *Spectrum | Autism Research News*, 17 April 2023.

Duggan, Marian. *Queering Conflict: Examining Lesbian and Gay Experiences of Homophobia in Northern Ireland*. Farnham: Ashgate, 2012.

Dyas, Grace. *We Don't Know What's Buried Here*, unpublished MS.

Earley, Claire. 'Camera Club Profile – Mark Davis', accessed 24 June 2024. https://www.thetelegraphandargus.co.uk/news/17677545.camera-club-profile---mark-davis-i-love-capture-atmosphere-abandoned-buildings

Edwards, David. 'Political Change and Social Transformation, 1603–1641', in Jane Ohlmeyer, ed., *The Cambridge History of Ireland*, vol. 2, 48–71. Cambridge: Cambridge University Press, 2017.

Elam, Keir. 'Dead Heads: Damnation-Narration in the Dramaticules', in John Pilling, ed., *The Cambridge Companion to Samuel Beckett*, 145–66. Cambridge: Cambridge University Press, 1994.

Ellmann, Richard. *James Joyce*. New York: Oxford, 1959.

Ellmann, Richard. *James Joyce II*. New York: Oxford, 1980.

Ellmann, Richard, ed. *The Letters of James Joyce II*. New York: Viking, 1966.

Engel, Chris. 'From Malignant Shame to Resilience. From Addiction to Recovery', *Paces*, 27 June 2013. https://www.pacesconnection.com/blog/from-malignant-shame-to-resilience-from-addiction-to-recovery

Enloe, Cynthia. *Bananas, Beaches and Bases: Making Feminist Sense of International Politics*. Berkeley: University of California Press, 1989.

Enright, Anne. *The Gathering*. London: Jonathan Cape, 2007.

Enright, Anne. *Making Babies: Stumbling into Motherhood*. New York: Norton, 2013.

Enright, Mairead and Aoife O' Donoghue, eds. *Mother and Baby Homes Commission of Investigation Report, Draft Alternative Executive Summary (Alternative Report)*, 2021.

Evason, Eileen. *Hidden Violence: A Study of Battered Women in Northern Ireland*. Belfast: Farset Co-op Press, 1982.

Ferguson, Molly. 'The Changeling Legend and Queer Kinship in Caitriona Lally's Eggshells', *Irish University Review* 51:2 (Autumn/Winter 2021): 296–311. doi.org/10.3366/iur.2021.0520

Ferriter, Diarmaid. *The Transformation of Ireland 1900–2000*. London: Profile Books, 2005.

Fischer, Clara. 'Gender, Nation, and the Politics of Shame: Magdalen Laundries and the Institutionalization of Feminine Transgression in Modern Ireland', *Signs: Journal of Women in Culture and Society* 41:4 (2016): 821–43. DOI: 10.1086/685117

Fischer, Clara. 'Abortion and Reproduction in Ireland: Shame, Nation-building and the Affective Politics of Place', *Feminist Review* 122 (2019): 32–48. doi.org/10.1177/0141778919850003

Fitzpatrick, Lisa. 'Contemporary Feminist Protest in Ireland: #MeToo in Irish Theatre', *Irish University Review* 50:1 (2020): 82–93. doi.org/10.3366/iur.2020.0436

Fletcher, Alan J. *Drama and the Performing Arts in Pre-Cromwellian Ireland: Sources and Documents from the Earliest Times Until c.1642*. Cambridge: Brewer, 2001.

Fletcher, John and Martin Stanton, eds. *Jean Laplanche: Seduction, Translation, and the Drives*. London: ICA, 1993.

Floyd, Shawn. 'Aquinas: Moral Philosophy', https://iep.utm.edu/thomasaquinas-moral-philosophy/.

Forti, Simona. 'The Biopolitics of Souls: Nazism, Racism and Plato', *Political Theory* 34:1 (2006): 9–32. doi.org/10.1177/0090591705280526

Foucault, Michel. *The History of Sexuality*, Vol. 1. London: Penguin, 1976.
Foucault, Michel. *Society Must be Defended: Lectures at the College de France, 1975–1976*, translated by David Macey. London: Picador, 2002.
Freud, Sigmund. 'Dostoevsky and Parricide', *The Standard Edition of the Complete Psychological Works of Sigmund Freud: Volume XXI (1927–1931), The Future of an Illusion, Civilisation and its Discontents and Other Works*, translated and edited by James Strachey, 175–96. London: Hogarth Press, 1961.
Freud, Sigmund. *New Introductory Lectures on Psychoanalysis* [1933], *The Penguin Freud Library* 2, translated by James Strachey. Harmondsworth: Penguin, 1973.
Freud, Sigmund. 'Family Romances', *On Sexuality: The Penguin Freud Library* 7, translated by James Strachey, 221–5. Harmondsworth: Penguin, 1977.
Freud, Sigmund. 'A Note Upon the Mystic Writing Pad [1924]', *The Standard Edition of the Complete Psychological Works of Sigmund Freud*, vol. XIX, translated by James Strachey, 227–34. London: Vintage, 2001.
Freud, Sigmund. *The Interpretation of Dreams: The Penguin Freud Library* 4. Harmondsworth, Penguin, 1991.
Freud, Sigmund. 'Three Essays on the Theory of Sexuality', *The Standard Edition of the Complete Psychological Works of Sigmund Freud*, Vol. 7, 125–245. London: Vintage 2001.
Gaon, Stella. *The Lucid Vigil: Deconstruction, Desire and the Politics of Critique*. London: Routledge, 2019.
Garratt, Robert F. *Trauma and History in the Irish Novel: The Return of the Dead*. Basingstoke: Palgrave Macmillan, 2011.
George, Rita and Mark Stokes. 'Sexual Orientation in Autism Spectrum Disorder', *Autism Research* 11 (2008): 133–41. doi.org/10.1002/aur.1892
Gibbs, Sara. *Drama Queen: One Autistic Woman and a Life of Unhelpful Labels*. London: Headline Publishing Group, 2021.
Gifford, Don. *Joyce Annotated*. Berkeley: University of California Press, 1982.
Gillen, Sir John. 'Report Into the Law and Procedures In Serious Sexual Offences in Northern Ireland', 9 May 2019.
Gillies, William. 'A Poem on the Downfall of the Gaoidhil', *Éigse* 13:3 (1970): 203–10.
Gilmartin, Sarah. 'Review: *Eggshells,* by Caitriona Lally: Full of Action and Humor', *Irish Times*, 6 June 2015. https://www.irishtimes.com/culture/books/review-eggshells-by-caitriona-lally-full-of-action-and-humour-1.2238835.
Goring, Rosemary. 'Ruth and Pen, Emile Pine. Hamish Hamilton', *The Herald*, 31 May 2022, https://www.heraldscotland.com/news/20171907.ruth-pen-emilie-pine-hamish-hamilton/
Gott, Chloë K. *Experience, Identity & Epistemic Injustice within Ireland's Magdalene Laundries*. London: Bloomsbury Academic, 2022.

Goulding, June. *The Light in the Window.* London: Ebury Press, 2005.
Hale, Charles R. 'Giving Voice to the Magdalene Women A Review of 'Magdalen', a Play by Erin Layton', *Irish Central*, 4 September 2014.

Grissom, A, E. Fink and E. Zane. 'Verbal Fluency and Autism: Reframing Current Data Through the Lens of Monotropism', *Autism Research* 17:2 (2024): 24–337. DOI: 10.1002/aur.3071

Hamilton, Cynthia. 'Frederick Douglass and the Gender Politics of Reform', in Alan Rice and Martin Crawford, eds, *Liberating Sojourn: Frederick Douglass and Transatlantic Reform*, 201–40. Athens: Georgia University Press, 1999.

Hart, Michael F. 'The Sign of Contradiction: Joyce, Yeats and The Tables of the Law', *Colby Quarterly* 30:4 (1994): 237–43, https://digitalcommons.colby.edu/cq/vol30/iss4/3

Haughton, Miriam. 'From Laundries to Labour Camps: Staging Ireland's 'Rule of Silence' in Anu Productions' Laundry', *Modern Drama* 57:1 (21 January 2014): 65–93. DOI: 10.3138/md.0595R

Haughton, Miriam, Mary McAuliffe and Emilie Pine. 'Introduction: Commemoration, Gender, and the Postcolonial Carceral State', in *Legacies of the Magdalen Laundries*, 1–26. Manchester: Manchester University Press, 2021.

Herman, Judith Lewis. *Trauma and Recovery: The Aftermath of Violence – From Domestic Abuse to Political Terror*. New York: Basic Books, 1992.

Hogan, Caelainn. *Republic of Shame: Stories from Ireland's Institutions for 'Fallen Women'*. Harmondsworth: Penguin, 2020.

Hogan, Yvonne. 'What I Know About Feeding Babies', *Irish Independent*, 24 February 2020.

Inglis, Tom. 'Religion, Identity and Society', in Joe Cleary and Claire Connolly, *The Cambridge Companion to Modern Irish Culture*, 59–77. Cambridge: Cambridge University Press, 2005.

Jahn, Manfred. 'Second-Person Narration', in David Herman, Manfred Jahn and Marie-Laure Ryan, eds, *Routledge Encyclopaedia of Narrative Theory*, 522. London: Routledge, 2005.

Jellet, Mainie. 'An Approach to Painting', in Angela Bourke et al., eds, *The Field Day Anthology of Irish Writing, Vol. V, Irish Women's Writing and Traditions*, 1,085–6. Lawrence Hill, Derry, Northern Ireland: Field Day, 1991–2002.

Johnson, Louise H. 'The Source of the Chapter on Slavery in Dickens's *American Notes*', *American Literature* 14:4 (January 1943): 427–30.

Johnston, Elizabeth. 'Big Mother: Images of Breastfeeding in Popular Culture and Literature', in Ann Marie A. Short, Abigail L. Palko and Dionne Irving, eds, *Breastfeeding and Culture: Discourses and Representation*, 15–33. Bradford, ON: Demeter Press, 2018.

Joyce, James. *Dubliners*. New York: Penguin, 1967.

Joyce, James. *Dubliners*. Oxford: Oxford University Press, 2000.

Joyce, James. *Ulysses*. New York: Random House, 1986.

James Joyce, *Ulysses*, edited by Hans Walter Gabler et al., 8, 1,045–50. London: Vintage, 1986.

Joyce, James. *Stephen Hero*. London: Paladin, 1991.

Joyce, James. *Portrait of the Artist as a Young Man: A Norton Critical Edition*, edited by John Paul Riquelme. New York: Norton: 2007.

Joyce, James. *A Portrait of the Artist as a Young Man*. New York: Norton, 2022.

Kafer, Alison. *Feminist Queer Crip*. Bloomington: Indiana University Press, 2013.

Kant, Immanuel. *Grounding for the Metaphysics of Morals*. Indiana: Hackett Publishing, [1785] 1993.

Kelleher, Margaret. *The Feminization of Famine: Expressions of the Inexpressible?* Durham, NC: Duke University Press, 1997.

Kelly, Brendan. 'Ireland Must Tackle its Mental Health Services Deficit Disorder', *Irish Times*, 10 December 2019. https://www.irishtimes.com/opinion/ireland-must-tackle-its-mental-health-services-deficit-disorder-1.4109677

Kelly, Fergus. *A Guide to Early Irish Law*. Dublin: Dublin Institute for Advanced Studies [1988] 2005.

Kelly, John, ed. *The Spirit of the Nation*. Poole and Washington DC: Woodstock Books, 1998.

Kennedy, Seán. 'Here All Is Strange: Beckett Beyond the Normal', in Seán Kennedy, ed., *Beckett Beyond the Normal*, 1–15. Edinburgh: Edinburgh University Press, 2019.

Kennedy, Patricia and Jo Murphy-Lawless. 'The Maternity Care Needs of Refugee and Asylum-Seeking Women in Ireland', *Feminist Review* 73:1 (2003): 39–53. https://www.jstor.org/stable/1395990

Kennedy, Sinead. '"No Country for Young Women": (Re)producing the Irish State', in Oona Frawley, ed., *Women and the Decade of Commemorations*, 267–83. Bloomington: Indiana University Press, 2021.

Kenner, Hugh. 'Dubliners', in Peter Garrett, ed., *Twentieth Century Interpretations of Dubliners*, 41–3. Englewood Cliffs: Prentice-Hall, 1968.

Kenner, Hugh. *Joyce's Voices*. Dublin: Dalkey Archive Press, 2007.

Kenny, Enda. 'In Full: Enda Kenny's State Apology to the Magdalene Women', *The Journal*, 19 February 2013. https://www.thejournal.ie/full-text-enda-kenny-magdalene-apology-801132-Feb2013/

Killean, Rachel, Eithne Dowds and Anne-Marie McAlinden. 'Sexual Offence Trials in Northern Ireland: The Cultural and Legal Dimensions', in Rachel Killean, Eithne Dowds and Anne-Marie McAlinden, eds, *Sexual Violence on Trial: Local and Comparative Perspectives*, 3–12. London: Routledge, 2021.

Kilroy, Claire. '*Eggshells* by Caitriona Lally Review – a Daring Debut', *The Guardian*, 12 September 2015. https://www.theguardian.com/books/2015/sep/12/eggshells-caitriona-lally-review-novel-debut

Kinealy, Christine, ed. *Frederick Douglass and Ireland: In His Own Words*. New York: Routledge, 2018.

Kinsella, Carl. 'Mothers in Direct Provision Emergency Accommodation Refuse Food in Protest', *Joe*, 30 August 2019. https://www.joe.ie/news/families-in-direct-provision-food-679642

Kitchin, Rob and Karen Lysaght. 'Sexual Citizenship in Belfast, Northern Ireland', *Gender; Place and Culture* 11:1 (2004): 83–103. DOI: 10.1080/0966369042000188567

Knott, Eleanor. *The Bardic Poems of Tadhg Dall Ó hUiginn (1550–1591)*, 2 vols. London: Irish Texts Society, 1926.

Krautheimer, Richard. *The Pelican History of Art: Early Christian and Byzantine Architecture*. Harmondsworth: Penguin, 1965.

Krishnaswamy, Revathi. *Effeminism: The Economy of Colonial Desire*. Ann Arbor: University of Michigan Press, 1988.

Kristeva, Julia and John Lechte. 'Approaching Abjection', *Oxford Literary Review* 5:1/2 (1982): 125–49. https://www.jstor.org/stable/43973647

Lacan, Jacques. *The Ethics of Psychoanalysis: 1959–1960, The Seminar of Jacques Lacan, book VII*, translated by Dennis Porter. New York: Norton, 1986.

Lacan, Jacques. *The Four Fundamental Concepts of Psychoanalysis. The Seminar of Jacques Lacan, Book 11*, edited by Jacques-Alain Miller, translated by Alan Sheridan. New York and London: Norton, 1998.

Lacan, Jacques. 'The Function and Field of Speech and Language in Psychoanalysis, or Reason Since Freud', *Ecrits: The First Complete Edition in English*, translated by Bruce Fink, 197–268. New York: Norton, 2006.

Lacan, Jacques. 'The Subversion of the Subject and the Dialectic of Desire in the Freudian Unconscious', *Ecrits: The First Complete Edition in English*, translated by Bruce Fink, 671–702. New York: Norton, 2006.

Lacan, Jacques. *The Other Side of Psychoanalysis: The Seminar of Jacques Lacan 17 1969–1970*, translated by Russell Grigg. London: Norton, 2007.

Lacan, Jacques. *Desire and its Interpretation: The Seminar of Jacques Lacan, Book VI*, edited by Jacques-Alain Miller, translated by Bruce Fink. Cambridge and Medford, MA: Polity, 2019.

Lacan, Jacques. *The Object Relation: The Seminar of Jacques Lacan, Volume IV*. New York: Polity, 2021.

Lally, Caitriona. *Eggshells*. London: Borough Press, 2015.

Laplanche, Jean. *Après-Coup*. New York: The Unconscious in Translation, 2017.

Laplanche, Jean. 'The Drive and its Source-Object: its Fate in the Transference', *The Unfinished Copernican Revolution, Selected Works 1967–1992*, translated by Luke Thurston, 293–313. New York: Unconscious in Translation, 2020.

Laplanche, Jean and Jean-Bernard Pontalis. 'Projection', *The Language of Psychoanalysis,* translated by Donald Nicholson-Smith, introduction by Daniel Lagache, 349–56. New York: W. W. Norton, 1974.

Law, Jules. *The Social Life of Fluids: Blood, Milk, and Water in the Victorian Novel.* Ithaca: Cornell University Press, 2010.

Lawrence, Karen. *Who's Afraid of James Joyce?* Gainesville: University Press of Florida, 2010.

Layton, Erin. *Magdalen*. Unpublished manuscript.

Leach, Cristín. 'Book of the Week', RTÉ, 4 June 2022. https://www.rte.ie/culture/2022/0604/1302320-book-of-the-week-ruth-and-pen-by-emilie-pine/

Lentin, Ronit. 'Asylum seekers, Ireland, and the Return of the Repressed', *Irish Studies Review* 24:1 (2016): 21–34. doi.org/10.1080/09670882.2015.1113009

Limburg, Joanne. *Letters to My Weird Sisters*. London: Atlantic Books, 2021.

Lloyd, David. *Beckett's Thing: Painting and Theatre*. Edinburgh: Edinburgh University Press, 2016.

Long, Rebecca-Eli M. 'Security Blanket: Neuroqueer Knitting in Pandemic Times', *Lateral* 11:2 (2022). https://www.jstor.org/stable/48749186.

Luddy, Maria. *Prostitution and Irish Society, 1800–1940*. Cambridge: Cambridge University Press, 2007.

Mac Airt, Seán, ed. *Leabhar Branach: The Book of the O'Byrnes*. Dublin: Dublin Institute for Advanced Studies, [1933] 2002.

MacCraith, Mícheál. 'Creideamh agus athartha: idé-eolaíocht pholaitíochta agus aos léinn na Gaeilge i dtús an seachtú haois déag', in Máirín Ní Dhonnchadha, ed., *Nua-Léamha: Gnéithe de Chultúr, Stair agus Polaitíocht na hÉireann c.1600–c.1900*, 7–19. Baile Átha Cliath: An Clóchomhar, 1996.

MacKenzie, Alison. 'Why didn't you scream? Epistemic Injustices of Sexism, Misogyny and Rape Myths', *Journal of Philosophy of Education* 56 (2022): 787–801. doi.org/10.1111/1467-9752.12685

Maddox, Brenda. Introduction to *Dubliners*, vii–xxiii. New York: Bantam, 1990.

Magennis, Caroline. *Northern Irish Writing After the Troubles: Bodies, Intimacies, Pleasures*. London: Bloomsbury, 2021.

Mahaffey, Vicki. *Reauthorizing Joyce*. Cambridge: Cambridge University Press, 1988.

Mahaffey, Vicki. 'Silence and Fractals in "The Sisters"', in Vicki Mahaffy, ed., *Collaborative Dubliners: Joyce in Dialogue*, 23–47. Syracuse: Syracuse University Press, 2012.

Malone, Patricia. 'Measures of Obliviousness and Disarming Obliqueness in Anna Burns' *Milkman*', *Textual Practice* 36:7 (2022): 1,143–74. doi.org/10.1080/0950236X.2021.1900357

Manandhar, Mary. *Food, Nutrition and Poverty Among Asylum-Seekers in North-West Ireland*. Ireland Combat Poverty Agency, Poverty Research Initiative, 2006.

Mann, Bonnie. 'Femininity, Shame, and Redemption', *Hypatia* 33:3 (2018): 402–417. doi.org/10.1111/hypa.12432

Marvell, Andrew. *The Complete Poems*, edited by Elizabeth Story Donno. Harmondsworth: Penguin, 1985.

Matthews, Malcolm. 'Why Sheldon Cooper Can't Be Black: The Visual Rhetoric of Autism and Ethnicity', *Journal of Literary & Cultural Disability Studies* 13:1 (2019): 57–74. muse.jhu.edu/article/716936.

Maume, Patrick. 'Young Ireland, Arthur Griffith, and Republican Ideology: The Question of Continuity', *Éire-Ireland* 34:2 (Summer 1999): 155–74. 10.1353/eir.1999.0008

McAlinden, Anne-Marie and Clare Dwyer. *Criminal Justice in Transition: The Northern Ireland Context*. Oxford: Hart Publishing, 2015.

McAtackney, Laura. 'A Suitable Place to Remember? Derelict Magdalen Laundries as Possible Sites of Conscience in Contemporary Ireland', *Space and Culture* 25:2 (2022): 266–81. doi.org/10.1177/12063312211065560

McCormick, Leanne. 'One Yank and They're off: Interaction between U.S. Troops and Northern Irish Women 1942–1945', *Journal of the History of Sexuality* 15:2 (2006): 228–57. DOI:10.1353/sex.2007.0011

McGettrick, Claire, Katherine O'Donnell, Maeve O'Rourke, James M. Smith and Mari Steed. *Ireland and the Magdalene Laundries: A Campaign for Justice*. London: Bloomsbury, 2021.

McGill, Meredith. *American Literature and the Culture of Reprinting, 1834–1853*. Philadelphia: University of Pennsylvania Press, 2003.

McGlynn, Mary. '"Embodiment, Abstraction, and Hidden Reproductive History", Reproductive Justice and the Politics of Women's Health in Ireland', *Éire-Ireland: An Interdisciplinary Journal of Irish Studies* 56:3/4 (Fall/Winter 2021): 130–58. 10.1353/eir.2021.0018

McGlynn, Mary. *Broken Irelands: Literary Form in Post-Crash Irish Fiction*. New York: Syracuse University Press, 2022.

McInerney, Lisa. *The Glorious Heresies*. London: John Murray, 2015.

McKay, Susan. 'How the Rugby rape trial divided Ireland', *The Guardian*, 4 December 2018.

McKenna, Lambert, ed. *Dánta do chum Aonghus Fionn Ó Dálaigh*. Dublin: Maunsel, 1919.

McKibben, Sarah E. *Endangered Masculinities in Irish Poetry, 1540–1780*. Dublin: University College Dublin Press, 2010.

McKibben, Sarah E. 'Queering Early Modern Ireland', *Irish University Review* 43:1 (2013): 169–83. https://www.jstor.org/stable/24576819

McKibben, Sarah E. 'Guaranteeing What Cannot Be Guaranteed: Defending and Adapting Bardic Patronage in *Ag so an chomairce, a Chormaic* (*c*.1585) by Tadhg Dall Ó hUiginn', *North American Journal of Celtic Studies* 2:1 (2018): 1–36.

McLaughlin, Róisín. 'A Threat of Satire by Tadhg (Mac Dáire) Mac Bruaideadha', *Ériu* 55 (2005): 37–57. DOI: 10.3318/ERIU.2005.55.1.37

McNamara, Denise. 'Campaign to Recognise 800 Dead Tuam Babies', *Connacht Tribune*, 12 February 2014. http://connachttribune.ie/campaign-recognise-800-dead-tuam-babies/

McNamara, Robert. 'Good Shepherd Convent Taken Off the Market; Site Was Earmarked for 200 Homes', *Irish Echo*, 18 September 2019.

McManus, Damian. 'The Bardic Poet as Teacher, Student and Critic: A Context for the Grammatical Tracts', in Cathal G. Ó hÁinle and Donald E. Meek, eds, *Unity in Diversity. Studies in Irish and Scottish Gaelic Language, Literature and History*, 97–123. Dublin: School of Irish, Trinity College Dublin, 2004.

McManus, Damian and Eoghan Ó Raghallaigh, eds. *A Bardic Miscellany: Five Hundred Bardic Poems from Manuscripts in Irish and British Libraries*. Department of Irish: Trinity College Dublin, 2010.

Mildorf, Jarmila. 'Second-Person Narration in Literary and Conversational Storytelling', *Storyworlds: A Journal of Narrative Studies* 4 (2012): 75–98. DOI: 10.1353/stw.2012.0002

Milton, Damian. 'On the Ontological Status of Autism: The "Double Empathy Problem"', *Disability & Society* 27:6 (2012): 883–7. doi.org/10.1080/09687599.2012.710008

Miller, E. Ce. 'This Writer Works as a Janitor at the University that just Awarded her a Literary Prize', Bustle.com, 31 October 2018, https://www.bustle.com/p/eggshells-author-caitriona-lally-just-won-a-prestigious-award-from-the-university-where-she-works-as-a-janitor-13025835.

Miller, Jacques-Alain. 'On Shame', in Justin Clemens and Russell Grigg, eds, *SIC 6: Jacques Lacan and the Other Side of Psychoanalysis*, 11–28. Durham, NC: Duke University Press, 2006.

Mitchell, David T. and Sharon Snyder. *The Biopolitics of Disability: Neoliberalism, Ablenationalism, and Peripheral Embodiment*. Ann Arbor: University of Michigan Press, 2015.

Molony, John Neylon. *A Soul Came Into Ireland: Thomas Davis, 1814–1845: A Biography*. Dublin: Geography Publications, 1995.

Morgan, Hiram. 'Faith and Fatherland in Sixteenth-Century Ireland', *History Ireland* 3:2 (Summer 1995): 13–20.

Morrissy, Mary. 'Four Paintings and a Cloakroom', in Rhona Richman Kenneally and Lucy McDiarmid, eds, *The Vibrant House: Irish Writing and Domestic Space*, 47–57. Dublin: Four Courts Press, 2017.

Mull, Amanda. 'The Pandemic Has Erased Entire Categories of Friendship', *The Atlantic*, 27 January 2021. https://www.theatlantic.com/health/archive/2021/01/pandemic-goodbye-casual-friends/617839/

Mullen, Patrick R. *The Poor Bugger's Tool: Irish Modernism, Queer Labor, and Postcolonial History*. Oxford: Oxford University Press, 2012.

Mulvey, Helen F. *Thomas Davis and Ireland: A Biographical Study*. Washington: The Catholic University of America Press, 2003.

Munt, Sally. *Queer Attachments: The Cultural Politics of Shame*. Aldershot: Ashgate, 2007.

Murphy, Yvonne, William Duncan and Mary Daly. *Final Report of the Commission of Investigation into Mother and Baby Homes*. 12 January 2021. https://www.gov.ie/en/publication/316d8-commission-of-investigation/

Nerenberg, Jenara. *Divergent Mind: Thriving in a World That Wasn't Designed for You*. New York: Harper One, 2020.

Nic Eoin, Máirín. *B'ait Leo Bean: Gnéithe den Idé-eolaíocht Inscne i dTraidisiún Liteartha na Gaeilge*. Baile Átha Cliath: An Clóchomhar, 1998.

Nic Eoin, Máirín. 'Sovereignty and Politics, *c.*1300–1900', in Angela Bourke et al., eds, *The Field Day Anthology of Irish Writing*, 273–92. New York: New York University Press, 2002.

Ní Dhonnchadha, Máirín. 'Women in the Medieval Poetry Business', in Ailbhe Darcy and David Wheatley, eds, *Cambridge History of Irish Women's Poetry*, 40–56. Cambridge: Cambridge University Press: 2021.

Norris, David. 'The Unhappy Mania and Mr. Bloom's Cigar: Homosexuality in the Works of James Joyce', *James Joyce Quarterly* 31:3 (Spring 1994): 357–73.

Norris, Margot. *Suspicious Readings of Joyce's Dubliners*. Philadelphia: University of Pennsylvania Press, 2004.

Gabler, H. W. and W. Hettche, eds. James Joyce. *Dubliners*, 124–74. New York: Garland, 1993.

Howe, Stephen. 'Questioning the (bad) Question: Was Ireland a Colony?', *Irish Historical Studies* 36:142 (2008): 138–52.

Ó Buachalla, Breandán. *Aisling Ghear: Na Stiobhartaigh agus an tAos Léinn, 1603–1788*. Baile Átha Cliath: An Clochomhar, 1996.

Ó Corráin, Donnchadh. 'Cad d'imigh ar lámhscríbhinní na hÉireann?', in Ruairi Ó hUiginn, ed., *Oidhreacht na Lámhscríbhinní*, Léachtaí Cholm Chille, 34, 7–27. Maynooth: An Sagart, 2004.

Ó Corráin, Donnchadh. 'What happened Ireland's medieval manuscripts?', *Peritia* 22–3 (2011): 191–223.

Ó Cuív, Brian. 'Mo thruaighe mar tá Éire', *Éigse* 8:4 (1957): 302–8.

O Cuív, Brian. 'A Sixteenth-Century Political Poem', *Éigse* 15 (1974): 261–76.

Ó Fátharta, Conall. 'Special Report: Nuns Told Don't Co-operate as Bishop Tried to Thwart Probes into Bessborough Scandal', *Irish Examiner*, 23 November 2015.

O'Grady, Standish H. *Cat. Irish MSS in the British Museum*. London: Longman, 1926.

O'Keefe, Theresa. 'Menstrual Blood as a Weapon of Resistance', *International Feminist Journal of Politics* 8 (2006): 535–56. doi.org/10.1080/14616740600945123

O'Keefe, Theresa. 'Policing Unruly Women: The State and Sexual Violence During the Northern Irish Troubles', *Women's Studies International Forum* 62 (2017): 69–77. DOI:10.1016/j.wsif.2017.03.003

O' Neil, Cathy. *The Shame Machine: Who Profits in the New Age of Humiliation?* London: Allen Lane, 2022.

O'Neill, Jody. 'In the Arts, More and More People Are Presenting as Neurodivergent', *Irish Examiner*, 13 June 2002. https://www.irishexaminer.com/lifestyle/artsandculture/arid-40894646.html

O'Neill, Kevin and Rob McNamara. 'Anger as 200 Homes Approved for Good Shepherd Site', *Irish Echo*, 22 September 2018.

O'Neill, Peter. 'Frederick Douglass and the Irish', *Foilsiu* 5:1 (Spring 2006): 57–82.

Ó Raghallaigh, Tomás, ed. *Duanta Eoghain Ruaidh Mhic an Bhaird*. Gaillimh: O Gormain, 1930.

O'Riordan, Ellen. 'Findings of Mother and Baby Homes 'at odds' with Testimony, High Court Hears', *Irish Times*, 17 November 2021.

O'Riordan, Ellen. 'Rights of Eight Mother and Baby Home Survivors Breached Over Report, State Says', *Irish Times*, 19 December 2021.

O'Sullivan, Elizabeth J., Agnieszka O'Grady, Karolina Pawlak, and John M. Kearney. 'A Qualitative Exploration of the Attitudes and Experiences of Polish Breastfeeding Mothers in Ireland', *Journal of Human Lactation* 37:2 (2021): 370–379. DOI: 10.1177/0890334420959028

O'Toole, Fintan. Foreword to Valente and Backus, eds, *The Child Sex Scandal and Modern Irish Literature*, xi–xiv. xiii. http://www.nytimes.com/2009/05/23/opinion/23banville.html. Online.

Ó Tuama, Seán and Thomas Kinsella, eds. *An Duanaire 1600–1900: Poems of the Dispossessed*. Portlaoise: Dolmen Press, 1981.

Patterson, Lee. 'On the Margin: Postmodernism, Ironic History, and Medieval Studies', *Speculum* 65:1 (January 1990): 87–108. doi.org/10.2307/2864473

Patterson, Orlando. *Slavery and Social Death*. Cambridge: Harvard University Press, 2018.

Phillips, Adam. 'Just Rage', *The Beast in the Nursery: On Curiosity and Other Appetites*, 93–108. New York: Pantheon, 1998.

Pine, Emilie. *Notes to Self*. Dublin: Tramp Press, 2018.

Pine, Emilie. *Ruth & Pen*. Harmondsworth: Penguin, 2019.

Pittock, Murray. 'Slavery as a Political Metaphor in Scotland and Ireland in the Age of Burns', in Leith Davis, Holly Faith Nelson and Sharon Alker, eds, *Robert Burns and Transatlantic Culture*, 19–30. Farnham, Surrey; Burlington, VT: Ashgate, 2012.

Pollack, Tara, 'Calling to the Breast: Contradictions in Irish Breastfeeding Discourse', *Eye on Global Health*, 12 June 2019.

Pribek, James. 'Dubliner's Priests', in Oona Frawley, ed., *A New and Complex Sensation: New Essays on Joyce's Dubliners*, 133–42. Dublin: Lilliput, 2000.

Price, Devon. *Unmasking Autism: Discovering the New Faces of Neurodiversity*. Oxford: Blackwell, 2022.

Quigley, Michael. 'Grosse Ile: Canada's Famine Memorial', in Arthur Gribben, ed., *The Great Famine and the Irish Diaspora*, 133–54. Amherst: University of Massachusetts Press, 1999.

Raissian Kerri and Jessica Su. 'The Best of Intentions: Prenatal Breastfeeding Intentions and Infant Health', *SSM – Population Health* 5 (2018): 86–100. DOI: 10.1016/j.ssmph.2018.05.002

Ravez, Stéphanie. 'Beckett et la Psychanalyse', in Elisabeth Angel-Perez and Alexandra Poulain, eds, *Tombeau Pour Samuel Beckett*, 83–121. London: Aden, 2014.

Regan, Linda and Liz Kelly. 'Rape: Still a forgotten issue. Briefing Document For Strengthening the Linkages–Consolidating the European Network Project', September 2003. https://nokjoga.hu/wp-content/uploads/rape-still-a-forgotten-issue-2003.pdf

'Report of the Inter-Departmental Committee to establish the facts of State involvement with the Magdalen Laundries', updated 9 August 2021. https://www.gov.ie/en/collection/a69a14-report-of-the-inter-departmental-committee-to-establish-the-facts-of/

Rich, Adrienne. *Of Woman Born: Motherhood as Experience and Institution.* New York: Norton, 1995.

Rickard, Aoife. 'The Shame of Breast-Feeding? An Aspect of Irish Culture in Historical Perspective', *PaGes: Postgraduate Research in Progress* 4 (1997).

Ripley, C. Peter, ed. *The Black Abolitionist Papers Volume I the British Isles, 1830–1865.* Chapel Hill and London: University of North Carolina Press, 1985.

Rivière, Joan. 'Womanliness as Masquerade', in Russell Grigg, Dominique Hecq and Craig Smith, eds, *Female Sexuality: The Early Psychoanalytic Controversies*, 172–82. London: Routledge, 1999.

Rodgers, Nini. *Ireland, Slavery and Anti-Slavery: 1612–1865.* London: Palgrave Macmillan, 2007.

Rolston, Bill. 'Ireland of the Welcomes? Racism and Anti-Racism in Nineteenth Century Ireland', *Patterns of Prejudice* 38:4 (2004): 355–70. DOI: 10.1080/0031322042000298437

Roos, Bonnie. 'Spies in Joyce's 'The Sisters': Allegorical Histories, the Irish Rebellion, and *The Count of Monte Cristo*', *Joyce Studies Annual* (2018): 195–233. www.jstor.org/stable/26798632

Rose, Jacqueline. *On Not Being Able to Sleep: Psychoanalysis and the Modern World.* Princeton: Princeton University Press, 2003.

Rose, Martha Joy. 'Breastfeeding in the Public Arena: The Deployment of Mixed and Contradictory Racialized Messages', in Roksana Badruddoja and Maki Motapanyane, eds, *'New Maternalisms': Tales of Motherwork (Dislodging the Unthinkable)*, 149–67. Ontario: Demeter Press, 2016.

Rosquist, Hanna, Nick Chown and Anna Stenning, eds. *Neurodiversity Studies: A New Critical Paradigm.* London: Routledge, 2020.

Royal College of Surgeons of Ireland. 'Children in Direct Provision: A position paper by the Faculty of Paediatrics', December 2019. https://rcpi-live-cdn.s3.amazonaws.com/wp-content/uploads/2019/12/Direct-provision-position-paper-full-final-PDF.pdf

Rushdie, Salman. *Shame.* London: Vintage, 1995.

Russell, George. *Irish Statesman*, 27 October 1923.

Salecl, Renata. *Choice.* London: Profile Books, 2010.

Sardin, Pascale. *Samuel Beckett et la Passion Maternelle, ou l'Hystérie à l'Oeuvre.* Pessac: Presses Universitaires de Bordeaux, 2009.

Sartre, Jean-Paul. *Being and Nothingness: A Phenomenological Essay on Ontology*, translated and with an introduction by Hazel E. Barnes. New York: Washington Square Press, 1992.

Sartre, Jean-Paul. *Saint Genet: Actor and Martyr*, translated by Bernard Frechtman. Minneapolis: University of Minnesota Press, 2012.

Saunders, Emma. 'Emilie Pine: The Novelist Putting Autism Centre Stage', 4 May 2022. https://www.bbc.com/news/entertainment-arts-61227465

Scarry, Elaine. *The Body in Pain*. New York: Oxford University Press, 1985.

Schwartz, Regina and Valeria Finucci. *Desire in the Renaissance: Psychoanalysis and Literature*. Princeton: Princeton University Press, 1994.

Sedgwick, Eve Kosofsky. 'Shame, Theatricality and Queer Performativity: Henry James' *The Art of the Novel*', in *Touching Feeling: Affect, Pedagogy, Performativity*, 35–65. Durham: Duke University Press, 2003.

Senn, Fritz. 'He Was Too Scrupulous Always: Joyce's "The Sisters"', *James Joyce Quarterly* 2 (Winter 1965): 192–5. www.jstor.org/stable/25486483

Sharpe, Matthew. 'Jacques Lacan', *Internet Encyclopedia of Philosophy*. https://philpapers.org/rec/SHAJL

Sheffer, Edith. *Asperger's Children: The Origins of Autism in Nazi Vienna*. New York: W. W. Norton and Company, 2018.

Sibonokuhle, Ndlovu. 'Humanness and Ableism: Construction and Deconstruction of Disability', in Melissa Steyn, ed., *Decolonising the Human: Reflections from Africa on Difference and Oppression*, 65–85. William Mpofu: Wits University Press, 2021.

Silverman, Kaja. *Male Subjectivity at the Margins*. New York: Routledge, 1992.

Silvertint, Eva. 'Embrace Autism', https://embrace-autism.com/autism-and-camouflaging/

Simms, Katharine. 'Bardic Poems of Apology and Reconciliation', in Liam Mac Amhlaigh and Brian Ó Curnáin, eds, *Ilteangach, Ilseiftiúil: féilscríbhinn in ómós do Nicholas Williams = A Festschrift in Honour of Nicholas Williams*, 175–91. Dublin: Arlen House, 2012.

Simms, Katharine. 'Poems to the Medieval O'Donnell Chiefs and their Historical Context', *North American Journal of Celtic Studies* 1:1 (May 2017): 45–60 10.2307/nortamerceltstud.1.1.0045

Singer, Julie. *Neurodiversity: The Birth of an Idea*. Kentucky: Singer, 2017.

'S.I. No. 57/2015 – Commission of Investigation (Mother and Baby Homes and certain related Matters) Order 2015', https://www.irishstatutebook.ie/eli/2015/si/57/made/en/

Smith, James M. 'The Politics of Sexual Knowledge: The Origins of Ireland's Containment Culture and the Carrigan Report (1931)', *Journal of the History of Sexuality* 13:2 (2004): 208–33. www.jstor.org/stable/3704856

Smith, James M. *Ireland's Magdalen Laundries and the Nation's Architecture of Containment*. Manchester: Manchester University Press, 2008.

Smith, James M. 'Knowing and Unknowing Tuam: State Practice, the Archive and Transitional Justice', in Katherine O'Donnell, Maeve O'

Rourke and James Smith, eds, *Redress: Ireland's Institutions and Transitional Justice*, 356–82. Dublin: University College Dublin Press, 2022.

Smyth, Lisa. *Abortion and Nation: The Politics of Reproduction in Contemporary Ireland*. Aldershot: Ashgate, 2005.

Smyth, Lisa. 'The Cultural Politics of Sexuality and Reproduction in Northern Ireland', *Sociology* 40:4 (2006): 663–80. doi.org/10.1177/0038038506065

'Social Welfare', https://www.gov.ie/en/category/social-welfare/.

Stenning, A. C. 'Misfits and Ecological Saints: strategies for Non-Normative Living in Autistic Life Writing', *Disability Studies Quarterly* 42:1 (2022). https://dsq-sds.org/index.php/dsq/article/view/7715

Stenning, Anna. 'Autism and Cognitive Embodiment: Steps Towards a Non-ableist Walking Literature', in David Borthwick, Pippa Maryland and Anna Stenning, eds, *Walking, Landscape and Environment*, 149–67. London: Routledge, 2019.

Sylwiakrupa, 'Good Sheperd Magdalene Convent, Cork', youtube.com/watch?v=4OZ5j73P5Yk

Tan, Catherine. *Spaces on the Spectrum: How Autism Movements Resist Experts and Create Knowledge*. New York: Columbia University Press, 2024.

Tarrant, Roslyn C. 'Factors Associated With Duration of Breastfeeding in Ireland: Potential Areas for Improvement', *Journal of Human Lactation* 27:3 (2011): 262–71. DOI: 10.1177/0890334411413097

thebettyfordclinic. 'Abandoned Magdalene Laundry in Donnybrook, Dublin, Ireland'. https://www.youtube.com/watch?v=YETH7W0yCBg

Thwaites, Tony. *Joycean Temporalities: Debts, Promises, and Countersignatures*. Gainesville: University Press of Florida, 2001.

Timins, Michael. '"The Sisters": Their Disease', *James Joyce Quarterly* 49:3/4 (Spring–Summer 2012): 441–54.

Trigg, Dylan. 'The Psychoanalysis of Ruins', *3AM Magazine* (December 2012).

Trigg, Stephanie. '"Shamed be . . .": Historicizing Shame in Medieval and Early Modern Courtly Ritual', *Exemplaria* 19:1 (2007): 67–89. DOI:10.1179/175330707X203228

Valente, Joseph. 'There's a Girl Inside', *Journal for Cultural and Religious Theory* 15:2 (Spring 2016): 116–21.

Valente, Joseph. 'Modernism and Cognitive Disability: A Genealogy', in Jean-Michel Rabaté, ed., *A Handbook of Modernism Studies*, 379–98. New York: Wiley, 2016.

Valente, Joseph. 'All Better? Recovery Anxiety in the Writing of Autism', *Journal of Literary & Cultural Disability Studies* 12:4 (2018): 477–94. muse.jhu.edu/article/709541.

Valente, Joseph. 'This Disability Which Is Not One: Autistic Intermittency in Mark Haddon's *The Curious Incident of the Dog in the Night-Time*', *Contemporary Literature* 62:1 (Spring 2021): 35–66. muse.jhu.edu/article/849039

Valente, Joseph. 'Mamafesta: Joyceance and the Law of the Mother', in Eve Watson, ed., *James Joyce's Writing and Psychoanalysis*. London: Routledge, forthcoming.

Valente, Joseph and Margot Gayle Backus. *The Child Sex Scandal in Modern Irish Literature: Writing the Unspeakable*. Bloomington: Indiana University Press, 2020.

Van der Kolk, Bessel. *The Body Keeps the Score: Brain, Mind, and Body in the Healing of Trauma*. New York: Penguin Books, 2014.

Van Esterik, Penny. 'Foreword: What Flows Through Us: Rethinking Breastfeeding as Product and Process', in Tanya Cassidy and Abdullahi El Tom, eds, *Ethnographies of Breastfeeding: Cultural Contexts and Confrontations*, xv–xxiii. London: Bloomsbury, 2015.

Van Vliet, K. J. 'Shame and Resilience in Adulthood: A Grounded Theory Study', *Journal of Counseling Psychology* 55:2 (April 2008): 233–45. https://doi.org/10.1037/0022-0167.55.2.233.

Veale, Angela, Bryan Fanning and Dawn Connor. *Beyond the Pale: Asylum-Seeking Children and Social Exclusion in Ireland*. Dublin: Irish Refugee Council, 2001.

Waisbren, Burton A. and Florence L. Walzl. 'Paresis and the Priest: James Joyce's Symbolic Use of Syphilis in "The Sisters"', *Annals of Internal Medicine* 80 (June 1974): 758–62. DOI: 10.7326/0003-4819-80-6-758

Walker, Nick. *Neuroqueer Heresies: Notes on the Neurodiversity Paradigm, Autistic Empowerment, and Postnormal Possibilities*. Fort Worth: Autonomous Press, 2021.

Wall, Glenda. 'Moral Constructions of Motherhood in Breastfeeding Discourse', *Gender & Society* 15:4 (2001): 590–608.

Walsh, Paul. *Beatha Aodha Ruaidh Uí Dhomhnaill*. 2 vols, vol. 2, 118–23. Dublin: Irish Texts Society, 1948–57.

Walzl, Florence L. 'Joyce's 'The Sisters': A Development', *James Joyce Quarterly* (Fall 2012–Winter 2013): 73–118. www.jstor.org/stable/24598774

Weiss, Karen G. 'Too Ashamed to Report: Deconstructing the Shame of Sexual Victimization', *Feminist Criminology* 5:3 (2010): 286–310. DOI:10.1177/1557085110376343

'What is Hoarding Disorder?', https://www.psychiatry.org/patients-families/hoarding-disorder/what-is-hoarding-disorder.

Whelehan, Seamus. 'Bessborough the Secret Penitentiary', *Cork Views & News*, 21 October 2014.

White, Sîan. 'A Hair–Trigger Society and the Woman Who Felt Something in Anna Burns' *Milkman*', *Genre* 54:1 (2021): 11–137. doi.org/10.1215/00166928-8911537

Whitehead, Anne. *Trauma Fiction*. Edinburgh: Edinburgh University Press, 2004.

Willey, Angela, Banu Subramaniam, Jennifer A. Hamilton, and Jane Couperus. 'The Mating Life of Geeks: Love, Neuroscience, and the New Autistic Subject', *Signs* 40:2 (Winter 2015): 369–91. DOI: 10.1086/678146

Wills, Clair. 'Family Secrets', *New York Review of Books*, 16 August 2018. https://www.nybooks.com/articles/2018/08/16/family-secrets/

Wills, Clair. 'Coda: Edna O'Brien and Eimear McBride', in Eric Falci and Paige Reynolds, eds, *Irish Literature in Transition: 1980–2020, vol. 6*, 295–304. Cambridge: Cambridge University Press, 2020.

Wills, Clair. 'Architectures of Containment: Ireland's Lost Children', *London Review of Books* 43:10 (2021). https://www.lrb.co.uk/the-paper/v43/n10/clair-wills/architectures-of-containment

Williams, Bernard. *Shame and Necessity*. Berkeley: University of California Press, 2008.

Wolf, Joan. *Is Breast Best? Taking on the Breastfeeding Experts and the New High Stakes of Motherhood*. New York: NYU Press, 2011.

Wong, Denise. 'Gazing Beyond the Fourth Wall: Shame and Second-person Narration in *Fleabag*', *Textual Practice* (2021): 1–23. doi.org/10.1080/0950236X.2021.1971751

Wood, Marcus. *Blind Memory: Visual Representations of Slavery in England and America*. New York: Routledge, 2000.

Yeats, W. B. *Autobiographies*. New York: Scribner, 1999.

Yeats, W. B. 'The Tables of the Law', https://www.gutenberg.org/files/43611/43611-h/43611-h.html

Yergeau, Melanie Remi. *Authoring Autism: On Rhetoric and Neurological Queerness*. Durham: Duke University Press, 2017.

Index

EU Authorised Representative:
Easy Access System Europe Mustamäe tee 50, 10621 Tallinn, Estonia
gpsr.requests@easproject.com

Printed and bound by CPI Group (UK) Ltd, Croydon, CR0 4YY
29/09/2026
02224986-0008